£25
with
pamphlet

THE COMMON SPRING

Essays on Latin and English Poetry

THE COMMON SPRING

Essays on Latin and English Poetry

Niall Rudd

BRISTOL
PHOENIX
PRESS

First published in 2005 by
Bristol Phoenix Press
an imprint of The Exeter Press
Reed Hall, Streatham Drive,
Exeter, Devon, EX4 4QR
UK

www.exeterpress.co.uk

The right of Niall Rudd to be identified
as author of this work has been asserted by him
in accordance with the Copyright, Designs and
Patents Act 1988

British Library Cataloguing in Publication Data
A catalogue record for this book is available
from the British Library

ISBN 1-904675-48-4

Printed in Great Britain by
Antony Rowe Ltd, Chippenham

Contents

Preface

All these papers appeared originally in periodicals, except for **2**, **3**, **7** and **12**, which are published here for the first time. The longer Latin chapters of the first half were written for presentation to university students or members of the Classical Association; but I hope that such readers may also find something of interest in the second half, where the emphasis is mainly on English poets. Conversely, students of English may find something in the earlier chapters which they can relate to their normal reading.

The selection has been made with a view to variety. Two shorter pieces (**4** and **10**) argue that on a specific question one view is right and the other wrong. Two longer papers (**11** and **16**) criticise opinions which have been held by important figures and have, I believe, had an undue influence. Two (**5** and **6**) attempt to illustrate how imagery can contribute to a poem's structure and meaning. Four (**1**, **12**, **13** and **15**) examine how an earlier writer's material has been transformed by a poet in a later age; in one case (**14**) only the context has been changed. Two papers (**8** and **9**) are concerned with Shakespeare's use of his Latin reading. One (**2**) is a traditional survey of the *Aeneid*, except for the contention that, while Aeneas represents the course of history as decided by Jupiter (with some important contributions from Juno), he is not inherently superior to the other main characters; the *Aeneid*, like the *Iliad*, recounts heroic struggles without celebrating the victory of good over evil. Three (**3**, **7**, and **17**) are designed to show that, while our opinions on certain matters are necessarily subjective or tentative, there is still a vital place in literary criticism for precision and objective truth; the degree of certainty must depend on what question is being asked. If there is any philosophy behind the selection as a whole, it can best be described as 'progressive conservatism' – a concept drawn from Canadian politics.

It remains to thank my friend and former colleague John Betts

vii

for offering to publish these papers, and to acknowledge, with gratitude, the work done by both him and Jean Scott in preparing them for the press. Since there is very little overlap between one chapter and another, no index has been provided.

Niall Rudd, Liverpool,
April 2005

Acknowledgements

Numbers **2**, **3**, **7** and **12** are here published for the first time. For permission to republish the remaining pieces, thanks are due to the original editors who have kindly given permission, as follows: **1** from *Proceedings of the Virgil Society* 22 (1996) 53-77; **4** from *Classical Philology* 75 (1980) 68-9 (by permission of Chicago University Press); **5** from *Classical Quarterly* 32 (1982) 152-5 (by permission of Oxford University Press); **6** from *Classical Views* 30 (1986) 43-8; **8** from *Shakespeare Survey* 55 (2002) 199-208 (by permission of Cambridge University Press); **9** and **10** from *Hermathena* 129 (1980) 23-8, and 158 (1995) 9-15 respectively; **11** from *University of Toronto Quarterly* 32 (1963) 155-9 (by permission of University of Toronto Press); **13** from *Essays in Criticism* 34 (1984) 216-28 (by permission of Oxford University Press); **14** from *Notes & Queries* 231.1 (March 1986) 99; **15** from *Hermathena* 158 (1991) 5-17; **16** from *Ramus* 10 (1981) 140-58; and **17** from *Classical Views* 40 (1996) 283-303.

Acknowledgements

1 Virgil's Contribution to Pastoral

[From *Proceedings of the Virgil Society* 22 (1996) 53-77.][1]

As pastoral poetry is about shepherds (*pastores*), we expect it to present an age-old peaceful existence, quite different from that of warriors, hunters – or even farmers. In Theocritus' bucolic idylls this expectation is largely fulfilled. The occasional references to hunting (e.g. 5.106-7 and 8.58) are entirely incidental; in *Idyll* 10, which is about harvesters, one character has ceased to be an effective workman since he has fallen in love; *Idyll* 21, about fishing, is not by Theocritus. It seems that strenuous work is only accepted when it has been stylised and frozen into a work of art. Thus, in *Idyll* 1.39-43, a carved bowl shows an old fisherman and a rough rock on which the old fellow energetically gathers up a big net for a cast, with every sign of intense effort: 'you would say he was fishing with every ounce of his strength from the way the sinews stand out all around his neck'.[2] The pastoral life itself is idealised. Wolves and drought rarely obtrude; we hear nothing of endless walking over rough terrain, the discomforts of a shepherd's hut, the strain of tending sick animals in bad weather. The main factor disturbing the shepherd's tranquillity, whether for pleasure or pain, is love.

Hard work belonged to a different tradition, that of Hesiod's *Works and Days* and Virgil's *Georgics*. The distinction is observed in the story of Cain and Abel (*Genesis* 4). Cain offered agricultural produce as a gift to the Lord; Abel offered the first-born of his flock. And the Lord rejected the first gift but accepted the second. Why? It is not made clear how Cain is supposed to have been at fault. One wonders whether the story reflects the notion that agriculture was imposed on man by the primal curse: 'Cursed is the ground for thy sake; in sorrow shalt thou eat of it all the days of thy life ... in the sweat of thy face shalt thou eat bread, till thou return unto the ground' (*Genesis* 3.17 and 19); whereas the shepherd's life was closer to our pre-lapsarian state. Certainly Hesiod's description

1

of the golden age points in that direction: 'They lived like gods, without sorrow of heart, remote and free from toil and grief ... the fruitful earth unforced bare them fruit abundantly and without stint. They dwelt in ease and peace upon their lands with many good things, rich in flocks and loved by the blessed gods' *(Works and Days* 112-20 [Loeb edn]). There the spontaneously growing crops are pure fantasy; the flocks are not.

When compared with those early conditions, the squalor of the present suggests that we have abused nature, broken God's laws and fallen into sin, as in Hesiod's story of Prometheus and Pandora *(WD* 47-82), the serpent and the tree (Genesis 3), or the evil Lycaon (Ovid, *Met.* 1.211-43). Hence the restoration of the golden age or paradise would appear as a kind of redemption. This allowed pastoral motifs to flow readily into Christian channels. One thinks of the shepherds abiding in the fields, the good shepherd, the lamb of God and so on. Similarly the sentimental love of the Greek herdsmen was transmuted into the spiritual love of Christ. Such developments are, of course, illustrated in art as well as literature.[3]

So far we have spoken of the pastoral life as earlier and easier, more healthy and spontaneous, more 'natural' than life in the city. But 'natural' is a notoriously ambiguous word. As well as meaning 'unspoilt', it can also mean 'raw', even 'savage'. Except for a few passing hints, such defects are not ascribed to the herdsmen of pastoral poetry. In spite of their simple life, they are not normally portrayed as uncouth, though an ironic awareness that they are so sometimes lurks behind the genre. This was what William Empson had in mind when he said, 'Whereas most fairy stories and ballads are written by and for [the people], but not about them, pastoral is (ostensibly) about the people, but not written by them or for them'.[4] Hence the convention that herdsmen speak an educated literary language and have sensitive feelings about love. This polite convention is already operating in Theocritus, whose Greek is a mixture from different periods and places.[5]

In Theocritus' bucolic idylls we encounter a pattern in which a disconsolate herdsman sings by himself *(Idylls* 3 and 11); or two herdsmen hold a conversation (4), which may lead to a song (1), an exchange of songs (7, 9 and 10), or an actual singing contest

(5, 6 and 8). From the last type we can abstract a scene in which, on a sunny day in late spring or summer, when sheep are grazing on the hillside, two herdsmen meet and exchange banter. This leads to an invitation, or challenge, to a singing match. Stakes are agreed and an umpire is found. The trio then withdraws into suitably pleasant surroundings (*locus amoenus*), a cave or the shade of a tree, and the contest begins. After singing in turn about topics of love, music and country life, the contestants finish; and a decision is announced. This brings us to the first of the five bases on which Virgil constructs his innovations:

1. *Theocritean and bucolic*

Even in his earliest pieces Virgil departs significantly from his 'model'. But this category is still valid, in that his changes are mainly stylistic changes from within the genre. This could be illustrated from the competition piece *Ecl.* 3 (or from 7, which is somewhat later); but here I will use the formally simpler *Ecl.* 2, which draws on Theocritus' *Idylls* 3, 6, 10 and 11.[6] It is a solo, sung from the shelter of the woods during the heat of the day by the lovelorn Corydon. He begins: 'O cruel Alexis, do you care nothing for my songs? Do you not pity me at all? Are you forcing me in the end to die?' This is an adaptation of Theocritus 3.6-9: 'O graceful Amaryllis, why do you peep no more from this cave of yours and call me in – me, your sweetheart? Do you hate me, then? ... You will make me hang myself'. Whereas Theocritus' shepherd delivers a serenade to the cave-dwelling Amaryllis, Corydon is by himself: everything that follows presents what is going on in his mind. The Greek shepherd speaks only as a lover; Corydon is aware of himself as a poet. Again, hatred is stronger than indifference; and hanging more graphically precise than death. Finally, in the first line, Virgil puns on Alexis' name, connecting it ironically with ἀλέγω ('I care'; cf. line 6). So on this very small piece of evidence Corydon is gentler, more introspective, more clever and less specific than his prototype. In view of σιμός ('snub-nosed') in line 8, he may also be less grotesque; but this comes out much more clearly when he is compared with the Cyclops in poem 6. There, and in poem 11, Polyphemus is no longer the monster of the *Odyssey*; he is young,

tame and sentimental; but he is still monocular. In *Idyll* 6, then, a
shepherd adopting the role of Polyphemus sings:

> I am not as ugly as they say. Not long ago on a calm day I
> stared into the sea, and my beard looked very handsome,
> and so did my one eye, to my way of thinking; and the
> reflection of my teeth was whiter than Parian marble. But,
> to avoid the evil eye, I spat three times on my chest as the
> hag Cotyttaris taught me.   (*Idyll* 6.34-9)

Virgil's Corydon says:

> And I am not so ugly. The other day I saw myself on the
> shore when the wind was still and the sea calm. If a reflection
> never lies, I would not be afraid to let you judge between me
> and Daphnis.   (*Ecl.* 2.25-7)

Here Theocritus' grotesqueness and his touch of superstition have
gone; but so has his vividness. The presence of Daphnis in *Ecl.* 2
is explained by the fact that in *Idyll* 6 the singer is in competition
with Daphnis – but in music, not in beauty. 'A reflection never
lies' sounds like a proverb; but, as Clausen points out, Virgil
will also have learned from his Epicurean studies that deception
arises, not from the reflection as such, but from false inference.

At the end of *Idyll* 11 Polyphemus, who has been hoping to
entice Galatea out of the water, gives up:

> Ah Cyclops, Cyclops, where have your wits wandered?
> You'd have more sense if you went and wove cheese-
> baskets and gathered greenery for your young lambs. Milk
> the ewe that's by; why chase the one who flees? Perhaps
> you'll find another prettier Galatea.   (*Idyll* 11.72-6)

Corydon says:

> Ah Corydon, Corydon, what madness has seized you? The
> vine on your leafy elm is only half pruned. Why not go and
> weave something useful from twigs and soft rushes? You'll
> find another Alexis if this one rejects you.   (*Ecl.* 2.69-73)

The rustic maxim 'milk the ewe that's by' is not in Virgil; and the cheese-baskets have become just 'something useful'. So too, earlier in the eclogue (43), Thestylis takes the place of 'the dark-skinned woman servant of Memnon' (*Idyll* 3.35). Such changes involve a loss of earthiness and colour. As for the conclusion of the two passages, the effect is much the same; for in neither case is the relief permanent – see *Idyll* 11.12 (πολλάκι, 'often') and *Ecl.* 2.4 (*assidue*, 'repeatedly').

In yet another idyll a singer says: 'Goat goes after clover; wolf after goat; crane after plough; and I am crazy for you' (10.30-1). In *Ecl.* 2 Corydon says: 'The fierce lioness follows the wolf; the wolf in his turn the goat; the wanton goat follows the flowering clover; and Corydon you, o Alexis. Each is drawn by his delight' (63-5). In each case a series leads up to the singer's desire for his beloved. Theocritus' series is uneven: A-B, C-A, D-E. Virgil's goes A-B, B-C, C-D; and he rounds it off with a *sententia* of Epicurean colouring: *trahit sua quemque voluptas*. So Virgil is tidier and more logical; but his conventional adjectives do little work; his fanciful lioness does not belong to the realistic series;[7] and he has toned down the frenzy of Theocritus' singer (ἐγὼ δ' ἐπὶ τὶν μεμάνημαι, 'and I am crazy for you'). Toning down of another kind takes place in *Ecl.* 3.8, where the bawdiness is conveyed by an ellipse; contrast *Idyll* 5.41-3 and 116-17.

Reverting to *Idyll* 11, we notice the poem is addressed to Nicias, Theocritus' friend, who is a doctor. It reminds him that there is no cure for love, except music. Virgil omits the epistolary framework and the humorous preamble, producing a miniature internal drama. Not being a Cyclops, Corydon is a less broadly comic figure. When Polyphemus boasts he has cattle, milk and cheese, he adds: 'And I can pipe as no other Cyclops here' (11.38). Corydon also refers grandly to his cattle, milk and lambs; but, as he must then add something different, he says (24), 'And I sing as Dircaean Amphion used to sing on Attic Aracynthus' (*Amphion Dircaeus in Actaeo Aracyntho*). Greek mythological and geographical names, alliteration and assonance, weak caesura in the third foot and hiatus in the fifth, the polysyllabic ending – all combine to produce a learned and self-consciously beautiful effect. The line may even come from a Callimachean poet (Clausen suggests Parthenius).

Now while Corydon's claims about his livestock can be overlooked as a lover's hyperbole, this sophisticated verse is quite beyond him. The slyly amusing device, whereby poet speaks to reader above the head of his character, is not unknown in Theocritus. The herdsman in *Idyll* 3 is surprisingly adept at citing mythological parallels (40-51), while the simple Cyclops in 11 unwittingly conforms to the requirements of a formal serenade. Here, however, Virgil plays the trick more often: we are told in line 4 that the eclogue's polished verses are *incondita* ('unformed, crude'); and we have already noted the pun on Alexis (6 and 56) along with the Epicurean associations of *imago* and *voluptas* (27 and 65). Another example is *rusticus es, Corydon* (56), where *rusticus* can have both a neutral and a pejorative meaning ('countryman' / 'bumpkin').

Other, more serious, touches also point beyond the bucolic convention. Whereas in *Idyll* 6 Damoetas gives Daphnis a Pan-pipe and receives a straight pipe in exchange (43), in Virgil we hear that Damoetas was on his death-bed when he bequeathed the syrinx to Corydon, that the gift symbolised the handing on of an art as a kind of sacred trust (37-8).[8] The contrast between the cooling of the day as the sun goes down and the persistence of Corydon's passion may have been prompted by Meleager's epigram addressed to another Alexis (*Anth.Pal.*12.127). Finally, the woods are already beginning to assume (3-5, 31, 60, 62) a greater importance than they had possessed in Theocritus. In the course of the *Eclogues* the woods come to have a special connection with pastoral verse. The key passages are: 'If I sing of woods, let them be woods worthy of a consul' (4.2); 'My Thalia did not blush to live in the woods' (6.2); and 'You are playing woodland music on a slender pipe' (1.2). This explains why Milton ended *Lycidas* with the much-misquoted line 'Tomorrow to fresh woods and pastures new'.

2. *Theocritean but not bucolic*

Apart from his pastoral idylls, Theocritus composed in several other forms. Gow prints 24 epigrams, of which 4 are of the type 'I have dedicated (or X has dedicated) this object to that deity' (nos. 2, 10, 12 and 13). *Epigram 2* reads:

> Daphnis of the white skin, who plays pastoral melodies
> on his lovely pipe, has dedicated these gifts to Pan: his
> pierced reeds, his throwing stick, a sharp javelin, a fawn-
> skin, and the wallet in which he carried his apples.

Though the content is pastoral, the poem itself is a dedicatory epigram, not a bucolic idyll. Taking a hint, perhaps, from *Idyll* 5.53-4 and 58-9, where two herdsmen *promise* gifts to nymphs and Pan, Virgil has in *Ecl.* 7 composed two such epigrams, the second answering the first. The first reads:

> To thee, Delia, little Micon[9] offers this head of a bristling
> boar and the branching antlers of a long-lived stag. If this
> luck remains, then thou shalt stand full length in polished
> marble, thy ankles bound high with crimson buskins.
>
> <div align="right">(<i>Ecl.</i> 7.29-32)</div>

So here, and in 33-6, Virgil has presented an independent dedicatory epigram, using it as a quatrain in a shepherds' singing-match. Another, shorter, example is in *Ecl.* 5.42-4, where Virgil has expanded Daphnis' dying words from *Idyll* 1.120-1 into an instruction for a tomb and a sepulchral epigram.

Theocritus also wrote an imaginary wedding-song for Helen of Troy, sung by a choir of Spartan girls (*Idyll* 18). It celebrates the good fortune of the worthy Menelaus and the beauty and skills of Helen; then, after asking a blessing for the happy pair, it ends 'Hymen o Hymenaeus, rejoice in this wedding'. Other epithalamia were available to Virgil: from Greek poetry both early (Alcman and Sappho) and more recent (Parthenius); and from the Latin neoterics (Catullus, Calvus and Ticida).[10] Certain features of the Roman ritual were mentioned by Catullus, notably torches (61.15), the arrival of the bride (61.77) and the throwing of nuts (61.121). Catullus also, drawing on the Greek poetic tradition, referred to the evening star shining from Mt. Oeta (62.7). In *Eclogue* 8 we find a very different situation. In a song, sung by Damon, a jilted shepherd reveals that his former sweetheart Nysa is marrying another man. With bitter sarcasm he says: 'Mopsus, cut fresh torches, your wife is being escorted to you. Scatter nuts, bridegroom; for you the evening Star is leaving Oeta' (8.29-30). The jilted shepherd hates Mopsus, who apparently deserves the treacherous wife he is getting: *o digno coniuncta viro* (32). So Virgil has put these normally happy epithalamic features into a poem of angry complaint and incorporated the whole piece in a pastoral song.

Another epithalamic motif occurs in *Ecl.* 4, where the Fates sing *talia saecla currite* to their spindles ('Run on, you happy ages'; 46-7). This recalls the refrain of the Fates at the wedding of Peleus and Thetis in Catullus 64.327. Moreover, the famous line *incipe, parve puer, risu cognoscere matrem* ('Begin, small boy, to recognise your mother with a smile'; *Ecl.* 4.60) was surely prompted by the baby in Catullus 61, who is supposed to smile at his father: *dulce rideat ad patrem* ('Let him sweetly smile at his father'; 212). The anticipation of a child's birth, naturally appropriate to a wedding-poem, is implied in Theocritus, *Idyll* 18: 'Surely she will bear a wonderful child if it be like its mother' (21). As in the case of the epigrams, I am not arguing that Virgil drew on Theocritus' words. My point is simply that, whereas Theocritus' epithalamium is quite separate from his bucolic idylls and has no pastoral features, Virgil embodied elements of an epithalamium in two of his eclogues.[11]

The most striking instance in this category, however, is the song of Alphesiboeus in the second part of *Ecl.* 8. To appreciate what Virgil has done here, we have to remind ourselves of Theocritus' *Idyll* 2. There Simaetha, an unmarried woman, is living alone except for her servant. In desperation she resorts to magic in order to win back her lover, Delphis. The first part of this powerful poem consists of a sixteen-line introduction explaining Simaetha's fears and setting out her intentions. Then comes a series of nine incantatory stanzas interspersed with a refrain: 'O magic wheel, draw that man to my home'. In the second part Simaetha recalls how Delphis became her lover; and this narrative section is punctuated by another refrain: 'Tell, lady moon, whence came my love'. In a final section Simaetha reveals that she suspects Delphis of being unfaithful; that she is resolved to win him back or consign him to Hades. How then did Virgil adapt this wholly unpastoral poem to his purpose? Except for a few details, he ignored the introduction and the narrative; but he took over the incantations and turned them into a song which is sung by the shepherd Alphesiboeus.

This was a crucial decision; for it broke the identity of singer and sufferer. Like Damon in the first part of the eclogue, Alphesiboeus is *not* miserable; nor is he performing magic. He is enjoying himself in the countryside on a fine clear morning. His song also implies a change of setting. Whereas Simaetha lives in a town, Virgil's woman has her house in the country – *ducite ab urbe domum* ('lead him home from the city') is the refrain. And what is the lover called? Not Delphis, but the familiar pastoral name, Daphnis. As for the song itself, Virgil has reduced Theocritus' pathetic intensity. He has nothing corresponding to *Idyll* 2.38-41: 'Look, the sea is still, and still are the breezes. But not still is the torment within my breast. I am all on fire for him who has made me not, alas, a wife, but a miserable girl, no longer a virgin'. The point is clearer still when we compare:

> The man who betrayed me once left these articles behind
> as pledges of his love. Now in the very doorway I entrust
> them to you, o Earth. These pledges guarantee Daphnis to
> me.   (*Ecl.* 8.91-3)

with:

> Delphis lost this fringe belonging to his cloak, which I now
> shred and cast into the cruel flames. Ah torturing Love, why
> have you clung to me like some leech of the fen, sucking all
> the dark blood from my body?'   (*Idyll* 2.53-6)

The weird supernatural element has also been played down. Simaetha's magic wheel has given way to *carmina* – a clever choice, since the word can mean both songs and spells. In lines 95-9 of the eclogue we hear of werewolves, necromancy and the charming of crops – all highly melodramatic examples of witchcraft. But they are not supposed to be taking place within the poem. 'I have seen such things happen,' says the speaker; but they are not going on now. Likewise, in line 69 spells are said to be *capable* of drawing down the moon. In Theocritus' mime that in a sense is what happens. Simaetha invokes Hecate (the infernal aspect of the moon goddess); and the dogs of the town begin to howl on her approach (35-6). Virgil's woman, however, does not invoke Hecate. Her dog

is called Yapper (*Hylax*) and, when he barks, it may be a sign that
Daphnis has returned (107). So the eclogue has the possibility
of a happy ending, whereas the idyll retains a wistful sadness as
Simaetha bids farewell to the moon:

> Farewell, o Queen, and turn your steeds towards the ocean.
> I will bear my longing as I have endured it until now. O
> moon, on your gleaming throne, farewell; and farewell, you
> other stars that follow the chariot of quiet Night.
>
> (*Idyll* 2.163-6)

3. *Roman public events in Theocritean dress*

Ecl. 5 is generally thought to be early because of the reference to
Eclogues 2 and 3 in 85-7. If that is true, one would expect it to
exhibit prominent Theocritean features; and in fact it does. The
shepherds Menalcas and Mopsus meet and exchange pleasantries.
At Menalcas' request Mopsus next sings a lament for Daphnis. This
is based on *Idyll* 1 but there are some important differences. First,
Virgil has added a few touches reminiscent of post-Theocritean
pastoral; e.g., the animals without food (25-6) recall the *Lament for
Bion*, 23-4. A non-bucolic feature already noted is the sepulchral
epigram (43-4). More significant, Virgil has shifted one's attention
from the dying Daphnis and his bitter recriminations to the
blighting effects of his death on the countryside. With this shift, the
role of Aphrodite disappears. In Theocritus Daphnis had in some
way fallen foul of the goddess and she was, directly or indirectly,
responsible for his death. Virgil says only that his death was cruel
(20) and was brought about by the Fates (34).

After a polite interchange, Menalcas then celebrates the resur-
rection and apotheosis of Daphnis. The text implies that this song
was actually composed some time before the first: compare *iam
pridem* ('in the past' ; 55) with *nuper* ('recently'; 13). But when
the two were put together they formed a natural sequence, which
Klingner compared to Good Friday followed by Easter Monday.
Another notable feature of the songs is their identical length –
twenty-five lines. Formal symmetry was becoming more important
for Virgil than it had been for Theocritus.

In addition to all this, *Ecl.* 5 adumbrates another development. In 49 BC, as Caesar was preparing to face Pompey, a kite is said to have dropped a branch of laurel on the forum.[12] In 45, after the battle of Munda, it was decreed that Caesar should always wear a laurel wreath; that his lictors should have laurel in their *fasces*; and that his messenger should carry laurel on his spear.[13] In 42 BC everyone was obliged to wear or carry laurel at the birthday ceremonies.[14] Numerous divine honours were voted to Caesar before March 44.[15] Then in July of that year a comet which appeared for seven days was seen as a sign that Caesar's soul had been received in heaven. In January 42 BC, at the instance of the triumvirs, those honours were officially confirmed and others were added. Caesar's birthday (13 July) was to be observed on the 12th to avoid conflict with the most important day of Apollo's games; but, as the month had already been named after Julius, and as Caesar's games lasted from July 20 to 30, whereas Apollo's lasted only from the 6th to the 13th, 'the month now belonged more to Caesar than to Apollo'.[16] In addition, various attractive things, not normally attributed to a successful general, were attached to Caesar's cult, e.g. *pax, concordia, clementia* (peace, harmony and clemency), *pietas* (the affection felt for the great man by his people) and *salus* (the security and prosperity they enjoyed thanks to his achievements). These blessings must surely have been stressed by Antony in what Cicero calls *tua illa pulchra laudatio, tua miseratio, tua cohortatio* ('Yours was that fine laudation, yours the commiseration, yours the exhortation'; *Philippics* 2.91). This assumption is supported by the great set piece in Dio 44.36-49, especially 45-9, which adverts again and again to Caesar's kindness and humanity. The same is true of Appian's account in *Bellum Civile* 2.144-6. At the end of 145 he has Antony say, 'Let us conduct this sacred man to the blessed ones, chanting for him the customary hymn and lamentation'. Dio's Antony incorporates elements of a dirge in his peroration: 'Of what avail, Caesar, was your humanity? Of what avail your inviolability? Of what avail your laws? ... Woe for your grey hairs spattered with blood! Alas for your torn robe ...!' (49). Suetonius speaks of the lamentations uttered by crowds of foreigners (*Divus Julius* 84).

In view of all this, it was surely inevitable that in the late 40s BC a poem lamenting the cruel death of a superhuman benefactor, rehearsing his services, describing the grief of his people and affirming his divinity, should have been associated with the death and apotheosis of Caesar, the more so since Daphnis received his name from the laurel[17] and his cult was juxtaposed in Virgil's text with that of Apollo (*Ecl.* 5.65 ff.). A negative point may be added: as we saw, Virgil removed all reference to the circumstances of Daphnis' death. Had he taken over the erotic background outlined by Theocritus, that would have impeded the association with Caesar; for Venus would never have caused the death of her own descendant.

None of this means that Daphnis *is* Caesar in the *Eclogues*. Such an equivalence is not apposite in 3, 7 or 8, and is ruled out for 9 by line 47, where Daphnis is separate from Caesar's star. Nor can we even say that Daphnis *is* Caesar throughout *Ecl.* 5. There he is in the first instance the legendary Sicilian shepherd; he is also, in spite of his youth (54), a master and teacher of music (46-9); and he is also a vegetation-spirit like Bacchus and Ceres (79). Such a fluid situation is not uncommon in the *Eclogues*. Thus 'Menalcas' in *Ecl.* 5.86 reveals that he composed *Eclogues* 2 and 3; but it does not follow that Menalcas *is* Virgil in *Eclogue* 3 or in 10, or even that Menalcas is consistently Virgil in 9. The terminology of identity, equivalence or even continuous allegory is too crude and rigid for the *Eclogues*. To appreciate those poems, the empiric has to relax his usual criteria and try to catch the hints and echos, the glimpses and half-lights, that Virgil has provided.

'The Messianic Eclogue' (or 'The Pollio', as it was sometimes called) represents a further stage in Virgil's transformation of pastoral. This can be seen in three areas. First, the pattern is more complex than in *Ecl.* 5, the material being arranged in groups of seven lines, divided as follows:

$$3 \qquad\qquad\qquad\qquad 2+2$$
$$4+3 \qquad\qquad\qquad 7$$
$$3+4 \qquad\qquad 2+5$$
$$28$$

Secondly, the poem is an unusual example of pastoral. True, the Sicilian Muses are invoked; the golden age is described in pastoral terms (the goats will come of their own accord, the herds will be safe, and flowers will burst from the little boy's cradle); and Virgil imagines himself singing the young man's achievements in the guise of an Arcadian shepherd. Yet the opening line proclaims that this is an extension of the genre: *paulo maiora canamus* ('let's sing something a bit loftier'); these woods must be worthy of a consul. So the poem is, in part, a tribute to the consul Asinius Pollio. Now Theocritus had written two elaborate encomia, one to Hiero of Syracuse (*Idyll* 16), the other to Ptolemy Philadelphus of Alexandria (*Idyll* 17). Both were over one hundred lines long and each contained an adroit but unmistakable appeal for patronage. In spite of a hint in *Idyll* 7.93, such praises were not characteristic of the bucolic idylls. But here again Virgil takes a more expansive view of the genre. In *Ecl.* 3.84-9 Pollio is both a practising poet and a powerful statesman; he also (according to most scholars) appears in *Ecl.* 8.6-13.[18]. In the latter we cannot be sure that the praises formed part of the original poem. In *Ecl.* 4, however, the tribute is clearly integral. The same may be said of the compliment to Varus in *Ecl.* 6.6-12.

Yet Pollio's function in the poem is limited to the fact that he is consul at the time of the marvellous child's conception. The child himself is altogether more important; and here we reach our third point – that in *Ecl.* 4 the bucolic convention is being used in an unprecedented way as the vehicle of a political prophecy. As the fifth eclogue spoke of a divine man, the fourth heralds the birth of a divine child, who will bring a new era of peace. Speculation about the child's identity is inevitable. Recent discussions conclude, without qualification, that Virgil was referring to the hypothetical son of Antony and Octavia, who married in the autumn of 40 BC.[19] It is argued that after Philippi Antony was the strongest of the triumvirs; that in a poem addressed to Pollio, an adherent of Antony, Virgil would naturally be referring to the latter; that the marriage of Octavian to Scribonia, contracted a few months earlier, would now be irrelevant. If we ask why Virgil has been so vague, we are told that precision was needless, since everyone who mattered knew the truth; or that to have specified Antony would have diminished the glory of Pollio; or that Virgil was writing in an oracular style which made explicit information inappropriate.

Most of this is convincing enough; but it needs, I think, to be blurred a bit at the edges. First, in the winter of 41 BC Antony was considerably embarrassed by the actions of his wife and brother which led to the débâcle at Perusia. As his relations with Octavian deteriorated, it was he who went to see Octavian, not *vice versa*; and, as a result of the Peace of Brundisium, Octavian's gains reduced the gap between the two warlords. Again, the position of Octavian vis-à-vis the poem cannot be so easily dismissed. After the spring of 40 BC, Virgil would have had dealings with him either directly or indirectly through his officers *(Eclogues* 1 and 9 are relevant to this period), whereas he had no dealings with Antony. So Virgil may well have thought it impolitic to celebrate the latter in unambiguous terms. 'Everyone who mattered knew' – well, perhaps; but did they tell the rest? In antiquity a claim to be the child was made by Asinius Gallus, Pollio's son;[20] other claims were made on behalf of Augustus, Marcellus, and Jesus Christ. But neither of the two modern candidates was ever mentioned. What would have happened, one wonders, had Octavian and Scribonia hit it off and she had borne a son instead of a daughter? Virgil might have preserved a sphinx-like inscrutability. As for the oracular style, that was probably an effect rather than a cause. In other words, when he came to praise Pollio and to celebrate the Peace of Brundisium, Virgil reflected first on the complexities of the situation. A son of Antony's might indeed supply a focus of loyalty; but Octavian was a potent presence and might not welcome the secondary role of maternal uncle. Moreover, there might in the end be no son, or even no child. So better not be too precise.[21] An utterance modelled on that of the Cumaean Sibyl would be more prudent; it would be more appropriate to the proclamation of a new epoch in history, with all the portentous religious associations attending such a change; and it would make a more impressive and intriguing poem.

In Theocritus' *Idyll* 7 three friends walk out from town to a harvest festival. They fall in with a goatherd (Lycidas) who is a well-known poet. The narrator and he agree to perform turn about, and each sings a love-song. Then Lycidas branches off, while the others continue to the scene of the festival, which is described in joyful and sumptuous language. In *Ecl.* 9 Virgil omits the narrative, presenting a dialogue between two countrymen. One is called Lycidas; but, unlike Theocritus' character, he is a *young* poet who has not yet become famous. Also, he and Moeris are walking *into* town. But these minor inversions do not prepare us for the extraordinary conversation which follows and totally inverts the mood of Theocritus' poem. In answer to Lycidas' cheerful greeting, Moeris reveals that he has been evicted from his farm and now has to work for the new owner. His broken phrases mirror his distress:

> *o Lycida, vivi pervenimus, advena nostri*
> *(quod numquam veriti sumus) ut possessor agelli*
> *diceret: 'haec mea sunt; veteres migrate coloni'.*

> O Lycidas, we have lived to see the day – something we
> never feared – when an interloper – as occupier of our
> little farm – should say, 'This is mine; you former tenents,
> shift.   (*Ecl.* 9.2-4)

Here, then, is a theme of violence and misery, drawn from the all-too-real experience of Virgil's contemporaries. We may safely assume that such material had never before been included in a pastoral dialogue; that now, for the first time, the genre was being used as a vehicle for complaint.

At line 30 the second theme takes over – that of poetry or song. In principle it is quite unconnected with the tragedy of eviction, though the two themes are woven together by the figure of Menalcas. Thus we hear that Menalcas tried to avert the evictions by his songs, that he was lucky, like Moeris, to escape with his life. What a loss he and his poetry would have been! Three of Menalcas' lines, based on *Idyll* 3.3-5 but also recalling *Ecl.* 3.96-7, are sung by Lycidas (23-5). Three more of them are sung by Moeris (27-9); they conclude the theme of eviction. After that, the attention shifts to Moeris. He sings five lines about Polyphemus and Galatea (recalling *Idyll* 11). He is followed by Lycidas, who sings five more lines about the benign effects of Caesar's star (cf. the phenomenon described in *Ecl.* 5.58-64). So the singers, in chiastic order, have equal numbers of lines. At 53-4 Moeris declines to sing any more; Menalcas will supply all that Lycidas desires. In 64-6 Lycidas tries to persuade Moeris to continue; but again he says, 'No, let's wait until Menalcas comes'. So the structure and movement of the poem are dominated by the figure of the absent Menalcas. Furthermore, while Lycidas (as he acknowledges) has not yet made the front rank, and Moeris is too old to remember the songs he used to sing, Menalcas is at the peak of his career. So in the characterisation, too, Menalcas is the central figure.

Whereas less than half of *Ecl.* 9 deals with the evictions, *Ecl.* 1 deals with nothing else. Here the dispossessed farmer has not been re-employed; he has become a homeless and hopeless wanderer. His protests are correspondingly more strident: 'A godless soldier will possess these well-cultivated acres of fallow-land; an uncouth outsider will possess these crops' (70-1). Conversely, the other speaker is not someone returning on a visit, as Lycidas seems to be, but a local resident who has appealed against eviction and won his case. His feelings are those of heart-felt relief and gratitude. As a result, *Ecl.* 1 is both a more happy and a more melancholy poem than *Ecl.* 9 – an amalgam of weal and woe which foreshadows the ambivalence of the *Georgics* and the *Aeneid.* More specifically, it projects an interestingly balanced attitude to the young Caesar; for, as the benefactor who saved Tityrus from ruin is surely Octavian, so the *impius miles* who expelled Meliboeus should probably be thought of as one of Octavian's soldiers, whose commander was ultimately responsible for the tragedy.

Both characters have Greek names. Tityrus formerly had a partner called Galataea and now lives with Amaryllis. Meliboeus describes two beautiful visions of the pastoral world which he is leaving (51-8 and 75-8).[22] So outwardly they are still Theocritean shepherds; but the dress is wearing thin. Meliboeus is saying farewell to his homeland (*patria*; 3-4); he will join the other exiles who are wandering to Africa, Scythia, the Oxus and Britain – all on the frontiers of the Roman empire. The hills of Sicily and Cos have been left behind. Tityrus has been to the city of Rome, where freedom (*libertas*) has smiled upon him. In his previous servitude (*servitium*) he took no thought for his personal property (*peculium*); but now, thanks to a young man (*iuvenis*), he has been allowed to retain his land.[23] When he speaks of the Parthian drinking from the

Saône and the German from the Tigris, he too is referring to the Roman empire, but only in a rhetorical figure. If the poem extends in space to the edges of empire, it reaches forward in time to the renaissance and after; for the note of complaint and indignation sounded by Virgil is heard again in *Lycidas* and *The Shepheardes Calender.*

4. *Greek but not Theocritean*

The presence of such material has already been noted in *Ecl.* 2 (Meleager's epigram on Alexis) and in *Ecl.* 5.25-6 (the *Lament for Bion*). *Ecl.* 7.45-60 may owe something to the discussion of the seasons in Bion, fragment 2 (Gow); *Ecl.* 9.51-2 certainly recalls Callimachus' famous epigram on Heraclitus (*Anth. Pal.* 7.80). Other passages are cited by editors of the *Eclogues*; but by far the most striking instance in this category is *Ecl.* 6. Virgil has given the poem a pastoral framework, which makes it (just) suitable for inclusion in his collection. In lines 1-12 we are told that the poet's early verse was Syracusan, meaning Theocritean. When he attempted something grander to honour the military feats of Varus, he was checked by Apollo, who said, 'A shepherd should make his sheep fat, but sing a fine-spun song'. In 13-22 Silenus is caught napping by two shepherds and a nymph, and is induced to tell stories. The longest (that of Pasiphae) takes place in what might be called, in a general sense, a pastoral setting. In 67-73 Linus, 'shepherd of divine song', welcomes the Roman poet Gallus, and urges him to accept the pipes of Hesiod (who really *was* a shepherd) from the Muses. At the end evening comes: the flocks have to be rounded up.

Yet the framework is somewhat factitious. Apollo, in spite of his cult title Nomios, had no special interest in pastoral poetry. His injunction to Virgil is adapted from the *Aetia* of Callimachus, where he says, 'Poet, make your victim as fat as possible, but keep your Muse slender' (1.22-4 [Loeb edn]). Similarly the songs which he is supposed to have sung by the Eurotas (82-3) were not pastoral idylls. Old Silenus was said to be knowledgeable (he was, after all, tutor to the young Dionysus); he took an interest in music and dancing; and his reputation as a story-teller is illustrated by the marvellous anthropological tales which he told to King Midas.[24]

However, as far as we know, he was not associated with pastoral poetry; and certainly the tale of Pasiphae could not be mistaken for bucolic idyll. As for Linus, the son of Apollo, the story of how he was brought up among lambs was told by Callimachus (*Aetia* 1.26-8), not by Theocritus. Even in Virgil he points Gallus towards aetiological poetry (72-3).

In the songs of Silenus, which make up the body of *Ecl.* 6, we meet first an account of the creation of the world, followed by the creation of human beings (Pyrrha) and the Golden Age of Saturn's rule (*Saturnia regna*). In spite of the very compressed treatment (what happened to the flood?) we are bound to think of the beginning of Ovid's *Metamorphoses*. This impression is confirmed as Silenus goes on to sing of Pasiphae, the Proetides, Atalanta, Phaethon's sisters, and Tereus and Philomela, all of whom are mentioned by Ovid. Now for all its elaborate sophistication the *Metamorphoses* recalls its earliest ancestors, the *Catalogues* and the *Eoiai* of Hesiod. Even a glance at the fragments of those poems reveals the names of Deucalion and Pyrrha, Atalanta, the Proetides, Europa, Peleus, Ariadne and the Calydonian boar. Long before Ovid, Hesiod was admired by the Alexandrians, because of his traditional learning and because he offered a respectable alternative to Homer: one thinks, for instance, of Callimachus' dream *(Aetia* 1.2 and 4.112) which was prompted by Hesiod's own account of his consecration as a poet; of Aratus' debt to Hesiod as expressed in Callimachus' epigram 29; and of the scholar-poet Euphorion's *Hesiod,* mentioned in the *Suda.* The tradition of mythological poetry was carried on by Parthenius of Nicaea, who was linked with Callimachus and Euphorion by Lucian and Pollianus.[25] One of Parthenius' works was entitled *Metamorphoses*; it included the story of Scylla, daughter of Nisus (fragment 20) – a tale already referred to by Callimachus (*Hecale* 288) and later retold by Ovid *(Met.* 8.1 ff.). This story, conflated with that of Homer's monster, appears among the songs of Silenus (*Ecl.* 6.74 ff.). At some stage, probably in the mid 60s BC,[26] Parthenius had been brought by Cinna to Rome, where he became a major influence on the neoterics and reputedly taught Virgil Greek (Macrobius, *Sat.* 5.17.18). His poetry has gone but we do have his prose summaries of tragic love-stories, which he drew from various sources, including Philitas, Nicander,

Hermesianax, Apollonius and Euphorion. These he presented to Cornelius Gallus for use in his hexameter poems and his elegies (preface to *Tragic Love Stories*). Among the stories we find those of Apollo and Daphne (no.15) and Byblis and Caunus (no.11), familiar to us from Ovid, *Met.* 1.452 ff. and 9.453 ff.; also three tales from Euphorion (nos 13, 26, and 28).

This brings us to Gallus. Since Silenus' story of his consecration comes in a list of mythological poems, one assumes that, whatever else he may have written, Gallus is being consecrated as a mythological poet. This is supported by the fact that he receives as a gift from the Muses the pipes of Hesiod (69 ff.). With the aid of these he is to tell of the origin of the Grynaean Grove. Grynium, on the coast of Asia Minor south of Lesbos, was a cult-centre of Apollo. According to Servius on *Ecl.* 6.72, the grove was the scene of a contest in prophecy between Mopsus and Chalcas: Mopsus won; and Chalcas died of shame. Significant for our purpose are the following points: (1) some such competition already figured in the works of Hesiod;[27] (2) Parthenius in his *Delos*, a poem about another cult-centre of Apollo, used the words 'Grynaean Apollo' (Γρύνειος Ἀπόλλων, fragment 6); (3) Servius says that the contest in the Grynaean Grove was in 'the poem of Euphorion which Gallus rendered into Latin'.[28]

From this network of connections one infers that the songs of Silenus represent the mythological poetry of Hesiod, as revived and elaborated by the Alexandrians, Parthenius and Gallus – not the bucolic idylls of Theocritus.

5. *Roman poetry in Theocritean dress*

In *Idyll* 7, the freest of Theocritus' bucolic poems, the narrator disclaims the title of best poet; he is, he says, as yet no match for Sicelidas or Philitas (39-41). His travelling companion apparently shares his admiration; certainly he has similar views about the proper scope and style of modern poetry: those who try to vie with Homer are wasting their time. In *Ecl.* 9.35-6 Lycidas says he has not yet reached the eminence of Varius and Cinna.[29] He does not, however, enlarge on the poetic creed of the moderns – a creed which was to be made explicit in the opening of *Ecl.* 6. Later in *Ecl.* 6, as

we have just seen, Virgil describes how Gallus was consecrated
by Linus as a mythological poet. (It was a scene which Gallus
may well have described already.) Now, in *Ecl.* 10, an entire poem
is devoted to that same fellow-poet. Arethusa, invoked in the first
line, is the nymph of the spring which emerged at Syracuse. As
she had already figured in Theocritus' lament for Daphnis (*Idyll*
1.117) and in the *Lament for Bion* (10 and 77), it was appropriate
for Virgil to address her in his lament for Gallus.

Although this is the latest eclogue, the music is still perceptibly
Greek and Theocritean:

> πᾷ ποκ᾿ ἄρ᾿ ἦσθ᾿, ὅκα Δάφνις ἐτάκετο, πᾷ ποκα, Νύμφαι;
> ἦ κατὰ Πηνειῶ καλὰ τέμπεα, ἦ κατὰ Πίνδω;
> οὐ γὰρ δὴ ποταμοῖο μέγαν ῥόον εἴχετ᾿ Ἀνάπω,
> οὐδ᾿ Αἴτνας σκοπιάν, οὐδ᾿ Ἄκιδος ἱερὸν ὕδωρ.

> Where were ye, Nymphs, where were ye, when Daphnis
> was wasting away? In the lovely valleys of Peneus or of
> Pindus? For surely ye did not haunt the mighty stream of
> Anapus, or the peak of Etna, or the sacred waters of Acis.
>   (*Idyll* 1.66-9)

Equally mellifluous are the lines of Virgil:

> *quae nemora aut qui vos saltus habuere, puellae*
> *Naïdes, indigno cum Gallus amore peribat?*
> *nam neque Parnasi vobis iuga, nam neque Pindi*
> *ulla moram fecere, neque Aonie Aganippe.*

> What groves or glades kept ye, ye Naiad maids, when
> Gallus was wasting away with a humiliating love? For
> the heights of Parnassus caused no delay, no, nor those of
> Pindus, nor Aonian Aganippe.'
>   (*Ecl.* 10.9-12)

There we recognise a motif of the pastoral lament, one which
recurs in Milton's *Lvcidas*: 'Where were ye, Nymphs, when the
remorseless deep / Closed o'er the head of your loved Lycidas?';
and again, astonishingly, in O'Casey's *Juno and the Paycock,*
where Juno cries (at the end of Act 3): 'Blessed Virgin, where
were you, when me darlin' son was riddled with bullets?'

Before we attempt to summarise the content of *Ecl*.10, it may be well to examine the status of Arcadia in pastoral (and some cognate poetry) *before* this piece was written. In Theocritus Arcadia is called εὔμηλος ('rich in sheep') in *Idyll* 22.157.[30] It is also 'mother of flocks' in the *Homeric Hymn to Pan* (30) and birth-place of Pan (35-7). He is associated with Mt. Maenalus and Mt. Lycaeus in *Idyll* 1.123-4, and with Arcadia in general in *Idyll* 7.106-7. As the god of Arcadia he is offered a steer by Glaucon and Corydon in Erucius' epigram (*Anth. Pal.* 6.96); and he, along with the nymphs, receives a gift from a shepherd in an epigram by Anyte (*Anth. Plan.* 16.291). He is promised a sacrifice by a herdsman in *Idyll* 5.58. Pan is also associated, naturally, with pipes and pipe-music, as in *Idyll* 1.3, in *Epigram* 2 of Theocritus, and in Bion's fragment 10.7. An epigram of Anyte describes a statue of Pan playing a pipe (*Anth. Plan.* 16.231). In the *Homeric Hymn*, Pan delights in music and dancing (19.1-37). A connection with Theocritus is indicated in *Idyll* 1.124-5, where the dying Daphnis urges Pan to leave Arcadia and come to Sicily.

Similar references occur in the *Eclogues*. Pan protects flocks and herdsmen (2.33); he is the inventor of Pan-pipes (2.32-3 and 8.24); a music contest between him and Virgil is imagined, with Arcadia as judge (4.58-9; cf. *Lament for Bion*, 55-6). *Ecl.* 8 has the refrain *incipe Maenalios ... versus* ('begin on verses of Maenalus'); in 7 Thyrsis and Corydon are two Arcadians (*Arcades ambo*), ready to sing antiphonal song (4-5); at line 25 Thyrsis calls on the shepherds of Arcadia to recognise his rising talent.

So pastoral poetry does have clear links with that old and mysterious country. However, two negative points need to be made.[31] First, Arcadia is not presented as a place with a glorious climate, where shepherds enjoy a life of gaiety and ease, dallying with their loves in shady nooks. On the contrary, according to Polybius (4.20-1), Arcadia's musical tradition developed as a way of relieving the harshness of life in a rough, forbidding, land. Second, in none of the poetry examined so far is Arcadia used as a setting for a bucolic idyll.

In *Ecl.* 10 Gallus appears not only as a friend of Virgil but also as a poet, a lover, and an army commander. It is the combination of these various roles that makes the poem so complicated. The following scheme, along the lines of that provided by Gordon Williams,[32] suggests what is happening.

1-8 (8 lines): Address to Arethusa.[33] Gallus has requested a poem from Virgil. It will be a poem about Gallus' troubled love; the woods will echo in sympathy.

9-30: Arcadia mourns for Gallus, who is pining away in unrequited love. (Since, as we have seen, neither Theocritus nor Virgil employed Arcadia as a setting, it is a reasonable inference that Gallus had done so in his *Amores*.) Figures human and divine come and reason with him. 'Why this madness?' says Apollo. 'Your beloved Lycoris has gone away with another man to the snowy north.' Pan tells him his tears are futile; Amor is indifferent to his sufferings.

31-69: Gallus' monologue.

31-4: I shall die happy if you Arcadians (Arcadia being the land of song) tell of my love in bucolic verse (which is what Virgil is doing in response to Gallus' request).

35-43: I wish I had been one of your number – a shepherd or a vineyard-worker. Then I would be lying with my love among the willows, beneath the vine. Here are cool springs, soft meadows, and woods, Lycoris. Here I would live out my life with you. (This glimpse of a sentimentalised Arcadia came, one suspects, from one of Gallus' own love-poems.)

44-9: As it is, I am a soldier on active service, while Lycoris is far away among the snows of the Rhine. May that cruel climate do her no harm! (This again sounds like a situation which Gallus the soldier had described in his verse.)

50-61: I shall take up pastoral poetry and live in the woods and mountains, hunting wild animals (an escapist fantasy of a very different kind). Yet this arduous life will not provide a cure for my passion. The god of love has no sympathy for human woes.

62-9: So farewell to the woods. Yes, and farewell to song. The god of love is deaf to poetry, whatever pains we submit to, Amor conquers all; let us accept his dominion.

70-7 (8 lines): Address to the Muses. May this poem please Gallus. Now evening is coming; it is time for the herdsman to drive his goats home.[34]

Certain points remain obscure. How far, for instance, were

Gallus' love-elegies or *Amores* related to his real experience? Or again, when Gallus says, 'I will go and play on the Sicilian shepherd's pipe the poems which I composed in Chalcidic verse' (50-1), what does he mean?[35] And do lines 62-3 indicate that Gallus deliberately abandoned poetry? Such problems lie outside our present scope. The above scheme is intended only to suggest how Virgil's tribute to Gallus and his poetry is conveyed within the form of a Theocritean pastoral.

It remains to discuss, briefly, how far we have been talking about a progressive development in Virgil's *Eclogues*. 'Development' implies an assumption about chronology; and here three questions have to be distinguished: (1) to what time does a poem refer? (2) when was it written? (3) when was it published in its final form as part of the collection? The only question relevant to this inquiry is (2). What we know about the composition of the *Eclogues* is that 2 and 3 (at least) came before 5; that 4 belongs to the autumn of 40 BC; and that 10 is the last. The changes described in this paper are all compatible with that sequence. Many scholars would go further and argue that while 2, 3 and 5 belong to the first half of the book, 1, 6 and 10 belong to the second. That scheme, which is slightly more precise, can also accommodate the procedure followed here.[36]

In the end, however, I am concerned here not so much with stages of development as with various modes of innovation. It is not important to determine whether, say, *Ecl.* 9 is a more radical departure from the Theocritean model (and therefore theoretically later) than *Ecl.* 4. After all, *Ecl.* 10, which proclaims itself the latest, is in some respects more Theocritean than *Ecl.* 6. If we want to think of the *Eclogues* as a whole, it is best to think of them, not as 'one of the few perfect books'[37] (there are too many difficulties for that), but rather as a series of experiments which could have taken place in several different sequences within the limits mentioned in the last paragraph. These daring and memorable experiments are the work of a still youthful poet, between the ages of, say, 28 and 31, already aware of his powers. His procedure was to abstract and take over a kind of formal framework from Theocritus and to transform it by incorporating more and more new and unexpected material until the framework ceased to be of further use. He then took over from Hesiod a different form – that of the agricultural didactic poem – and changed that until he needed it no more. Finally, he took over the largest and grandest form of all from Homer himself and, by filling it with Italian and Hellenistic content, transformed it into the *Aeneid*. Such are the lines on which Rome's greatest poet may be seen to have developed.

Related Material:

'Architecture: Theories about Virgil's *Eclogues*' in *Lines of Enquiry* (Cambridge, 1976; repr. 2004) 119-44.

2 Necessity and Invention in the *Aeneid*

[Previously unpublished]

The sort of necessity I have in mind is that imposed by history or legend. Imagine a historian writing about eleventh-century England. On reaching the battle of Hastings he may contend, in the traditional way, that King Harold was killed by an arrow entering his eye. Or he may reject that piece of tradition as a misconception arising from a misreading of the Bayeux Tapestry. What he cannot do is to maintain that William never reached England; or that, having done so, he and the Normans were defeated.

According to Servius,[1] Augustus proposed to Virgil that he should write an epic about Aeneas and the foundation of Rome. Since the Julian family claimed descent from Aeneas, Augustus presumably expected a poem which would glorify him as the culmination of the Aeneas legend. In the event, of course, Virgil delivered something much more than a piece of propaganda; but, as he had accepted the emperor's commission, he had to bring Aeneas to Italy. That, in turn, meant that he had to get him out of Troy. He did not have to bring him to Carthage; but, having done so, he had to contrive his departure. Again, when Virgil, on one of his visits to Rome, looked out of the window, he observed people wearing the toga and conversing in Latin – not wearing bonnets and jabbering in Phrygian. So his epic had to point to a Latin future, which meant that the Trojan immigrants would have to merge into the Latin population. Before that happened, there were to be awful wars (*bella, horrida bella*; 6.86). So the Trojans needed to acquire substantial numbers of troops. Evander could provide only a small detachment; but he was able to point out that Mezentius had fled to Turnus, leaving the Etruscan army ready to accept Aeneas' leadership (8.475-96). This treatment of Mezentius, which was quite contrary to earlier accounts,[2] shows how daring Virgil was prepared to be in modifying details

25

of the story to meet his larger requirements. This over-arching necessity is so obvious that it is usually forgotten. And yet it takes precedence over more sophisticated speculation about Virgil's commitment to Stoic theories of fate.

In working on the traditional material, Virgil first played a kind of confidence trick on his readers by persuading them that his poem was not based on the Aeneas legend (as at several points it was) but rather that the hugely important events described in the poem gave rise to the legend. As a result of this subtle process, which is everywhere at work, Virgil's became the standard version of the legend for future ages.

Secondly, Virgil presents necessity in theological terms. The Trojans' actions take place in response to a progressive revelation of Jupiter's will. Naevius in the third century may already have shown the way, describing how the Trojans were directed at various points by Venus or Jupiter.[3] However, we may fairly surmise that Virgil gave a new and dramatic emphasis to the way in which the will of heaven was fulfilled by a series of decisions taken by agents who firmly believed in their own freedom. This point becomes clear at the very beginning of the story. In Homer's *Iliad* (20.302 ff.) Poseidon says that Aeneas is destined to survive the Trojan War and to save the house of Dardanus from extinction. From this germ grew a number of versions of Aeneas' escape:[4] when Troy fell he was elsewhere; he was miraculously guided out of the city by Venus; he was allowed to leave by the Greeks because of an earlier friendship with Odysseus; or he actually betrayed the city, because of his hatred of Priam, and was therefore given safe conduct. These explanations were at best unheroic, at the worst disreputable. So something else had to be devised – something which would enable Aeneas to retain his stature as a hero and yet to escape in safety.

In Book 2, unlike Laocoon, Aeneas did not oppose the admission of the horse. Along with the rest he was duped by the plausible Sinon into accepting it. Now he lies asleep. Suddenly the dead Hector appears in a dream. 'All is lost,' he says. 'You must leave Troy and found a city overseas' (2.294-5). Aeneas pays no attention whatever. He seizes a weapon and makes for the citadel: 'How glorious it is to die in battle!' (317). He then meets Panthus, the priest of Apollo. 'Troy is finished,' says Panthus. 'Such is Jupiter's will' (324). So what does the pious Aeneas do? He calls on his comrades to join him in a suicidal charge: 'Let us die' (353). They cut down some of the enemy and don their armour. (The Greek Sinon is not the only trickster in the story.) Eventually the ruse is discovered and many of the Trojans are slain. Aeneas now calls Troy to witness that he has done everything in his power to get himself killed (431-4). Later Venus intervenes: Heaven, she says, has resolved on the destruction of Troy; 'be quick, my son, and escape' (619). She leads Aeneas back to his family in the palace. Anchises refuses to leave but urges Aeneas to make good his escape (638-42, cf. 733). Instead of obeying, Aeneas prepares to dash back into battle (670). Eventually Anchises is persuaded by an omen to give way (701 ff.); and the family makes for the city gate. Anchises again urges Aeneas to flee (733) but in the darkness and confusion Creusa, Aeneas' wife, is lost. Once more Aeneas charges back into the burning city (749-51). He desists only when the ghost of Creusa says that the gods are destroying Troy and warns him to escape (777-8). So before Aeneas finally leaves he has been told four times, and on supernatural authority, that Troy is doomed; he has been urged to flee on five occasions.

What is gained by all this? First, on the most obvious level, Aeneas' stubbornness provides a centre round which Virgil has built the most vividly exciting of all the books of the *Aeneid*. Without that stubbornness or heedlessness no dramatic narrative would have been possible. Secondly, by stressing Aeneas' eagerness to fight to the last, Virgil has demonstrated his hero's commitment to the old ideal: 'It is a fine thing for a good man to fall dead in the front line, fighting for his country'.[5] He has also demonstrated his gullibility (the horse), his cunning (the change of armour), his rashness ('let us die'), as well as his ultimate acquiescence. We have to accept that it was through these facets of Aeneas' character that destiny was fulfilled. He is not a puppet. His behaviour is far too credibly perverse for that.

Book 2 offers many other examples of Virgil's invention: only a few can be mentioned here. In 192-4 Sinon, the Greek infiltrator, reports an alleged prophecy of Chalcas: 'If the horse is admitted, Asia will some day advance to the walls of Pelops in a great war'. The Trojan listeners assume that the Asian army will advance from

Troy to Mycenae. That is the interpretation intended by Sinon
but it is incorrect. The reader, however, knows that hundreds of
years later the prediction will turn out to be true when the Trojans
(now Romans) conquer Greece. That kind of irony has often been
associated with Sophocles.

Another type of invention, also encountered in Greek tragedy,
has been revealed by the study of Virgil's imagery. The horse, we
are told, is made of wood, with ribs and a hollow interior (16-
20). One strand of imagery sees it as a living creature pregnant
with armed men – for instance *uterum* ('womb'; 20, 38, 243 and
258); *feta armis* ('pregnant with weapons'; 238); *armatos ...
fundit* ('pours out [or bears] armed men'; 328-9). Another strand
suggests comparison with a ship: *alvus*, *caverna* and *uterus* could
all be used of a ship's hold; the contraption is mounted on wheels
and dragged along by hawsers (235-6).[6] This in turn points to a
connection with the Greek fleet, one reinforced by three instances
of juxtaposition. After describing the building of the horse (15-
20), Virgil begins the next line with the words *est in conspectu
Tenedos* ('in sight is Tenedos'), the island where the fleet is
hiding. Later, when Sinon has given a false account of the horse's
purpose, we read: *ecce autem gemini a Tenedo tranquilla per alta
/ ... angues / incumbunt pelago pariterque ad litora tendunt* ('But
lo from Tenedos across the calm deep ... twin serpents are leaning
on the sea and making side by side for the shore'; 203-5). The
serpents, as we shall see, prefigure the Greek fleet. Finally, when
the horse has been pulled in and the Trojans are sleeping, the fleet
is on its way: *et iam Argiva phalanx instructis navibus ibat / a
Tenedo* ('And now the Argive host with its ships in formation was
moving from Tenedos'; 254-5). Yet a third strand of imagery links
the horse with the serpents. Both are said to glide: the serpents
lapsu effugiunt ('glide in flight'; 225-6); the horse *illabitur urbi*
('glides into the city'; 280).

In view of Bernard Knox's classic article on serpent and flame
in Book 2, little need be said on that topic.[7] The article, which
contained much that was new and perceptive, made a strong
impression when it first appeared in 1950, though it is fair to point
out that it would not have been possible without the discoveries
of the new critics, some of whom (notably Cleanth Brooks) were

Knox's colleagues in Yale. Moreover, glancing back over the editorial tradition, one comes across occasional remarks which look like germs of the same way of thinking and serve to endorse it. Why, for instance, do the snakes come from Tenedos? 'Because,' says the fourth-century Servius a little obviously, 'they indicate that the ships are going to come from there'. Why are there only two? Three, after all, was a magic number and three snakes would have accounted neatly for Laocoon and his two sons. Donatus (late 4th century) says in effect, 'The two snakes prefigure the two Atridae'. This can hardly be proved; but it plausibly answers the question and receives negative support from the fact that Virgil's snakes are unnamed. If he had given them names, as some Greek writers did, the connection with Agamemnon and Menelaus would have been that much harder.

Henry's edition (1873-92) elaborated the parallel between the serpents and the army in considerable detail. Not all of his note is convincing but at several points he anticipated the conclusions of Knox: the serpents carry fire in their eyes; they kill Trojans; and they end up on the citadel (Henry's note on 2.193-200). Finally, a general linguistic point from the same passage. The serpents are said to make for Laocoon *agmine certo* (212). *OLD* includes the phrase under *agmen*, sense 1 b, which denotes 'the movement of flowing or gliding objects'; but in senses 4-8 *agmen* has military associations. T.E. Page, in his edition (1894 on), is aware of both meanings, which cannot be embraced in a single English word. Yet, if a translator chooses to expand, he is being false to Virgil's compactness – a familiar dilemma.

A special case of ambivalence occurs when a poet's words are given a different sense when detached from their context. As Aeneas contemplates scenes from the Trojan War painted in Dido's temple, he says to Achates: *sunt hic etiam sua praemia laudi, / sunt lacrimae rerum et mentem mortalia tangunt* (1.461-2). Jackson Knight expands: 'Even in this far land honour gets its due, and they can weep at human tragedy; the world has tears as a constituent part of it, and so have our lives, hopeless and weary; and the thought how things always have their own death in them breaks our hearts and wills, and clouds our vision'.[8] Deryck Williams is more laconic: *sunt lacrimae rerum* becomes 'people are sympathetic', not 'the

world is full of sorrows'. Williams is clearly right. The last two
thirds of Jackson Knight's note, however true, do not represent
what Virgil actually says.[9]

After Aeneas' departure from Troy the next necessity was to
get him to Italy. What route was he to follow? There were some
seventeen stopping-places in the Aeneas legend as noted by Dio-
nysius of Halicarnassus and others. The American scholar, R.B.
Lloyd, drawing on the large work of Jacques Perret, showed how
Virgil made what might be called a creative selection, removing
some places because of conflicting versions of the story, omitting
or combining others to avoid monotony or for the sake of
economy. The plague in Crete, the encounter with the Harpies and
the discovery of the Greek Achaemenides – all these, it seems,
were taken by Virgil himself from Apollonius and Homer. Such
episodes, apart from their poetic associations, provided tests for
the courage and ingenuity of the refugees.[10]

In addition to the route there had to be some principle of guid-
ance. No doubt Venus (or Creusa) could have conveyed precise
instructions. Then Anchises and Aeneas would have known exactly
what to do and where to go. And what a disaster that would have
been! The first half of the epic would have lacked all suspense.
Instead, Virgil contrived a series of gradual revelations. To be
sure, we learn in Book 1 that Jupiter has promised to produce from
Trojan stock a new imperial race – *Romanos, rerum dominos* ('the
Romans, lords of creation'; 1.282). Yet Aeneas and his followers
know nothing of this.[11] The stages in their enlightenment are: (1)
'You will found a great city across the sea' (Hector in 2.294 f.); (2)
'You will reach a western land where the Lydian Tiber flows; there
you will enjoy happy days with a royal wife' (Creusa in 2.780).
Both predictions are vague; and the first, in so far as it implies that
Aeneas himself will found Rome, is inaccurate.[12] They initially
sail north by northwest to Thrace but are forced to abandon their
site because of religious pollution. They then go south to make
enquiries at Delos, where they are told (3) 'Seek the land of your
forebears' (Apollo in 3.95 f.). However, thanks to a human and
fallible Anchises, the oracle is interpreted as meaning Crete. There
Apollo reveals through the Trojan gods that (4) the western land
is called Italia (3.163-6), a name repeated by the harpy Celaeno

in the Strophades (3.253-4). At Buthrotum in Epirus (the modern Albania) the prophet Helenus, inspired by Apollo, (5) warns the Trojans to sail round Sicily and land at Cumae near Naples; the Sibyl, Apollo's priestess, will then reveal more (3.441 ff.). So, whereas in Book 2 destiny was disclosed at the outset and then, in spite of being repeated, was disregarded and postponed, here it is revealed step by step and is gradually and painfully fulfilled through human error as well as through determination and obedience.

While these glimpses move the Trojans forward towards the future, a different force pulls them in the other direction. At the first landfall in Thrace Aeneas sacrifices to Venus and the other gods, makes ready to found a settlement and assigns a name to the people – *Aeneadae* (3.17-21). In Crete he begins to build walls and construct a citadel, calling the place *Pergamum* (3.132-4). On Leucas the Trojans sacrifice to Jupiter and hold *Ilian* games (3.279-81). These episodes show a greater variety of ritual than is given by Dionysius, who regularly records the foundation of a temple to Venus.[13] More important is the recurrence of Trojan names. This becomes even more striking at Buthrotum, where a Trojan settlement has already been established, complete with Ilian citadel (336), a Chaonian harbour (293), a Scaean Gate (351), a river Simois (302) and a river Xanthus (350 and 497). Aeneas looks on the community with envy: *vobis parta quies* ('*your rest is won*'; 495). For the inhabitants have done just what he yearns to do: they have built a replica of the old Troy. As we read this powerfully nostalgic section, we realise that it is the fullest development of a theme sounded at the beginning of the book: *litora cum patriae lacrimans portusque relinquo / et campos ubi Troia fuit. feror exul in altum ...* ('Weeping I leave the shore and harbour of my native land and the plains where Troy once stood; I am carried out to sea, an exile'; 10-11). That theme, indeed, was stated, at the very opening of the poem: Aeneas is *fato profugus* ('an exile by fate's decree'; 1.2); and it has not yet been concluded. To be sure, when the Penates urge Aeneas into the future, they explain that Italy is their proper home, because Dardanus originally came from there (3.167) – a point later recalled by King Latinus (7.206). Yet, although the Trojans' journey may, in the light of history, be conceived as a *nostos* or return, they themselves, unlike Odysseus, do not feel that they are going home. The best they can hope for, like many an emigrant since, is to give an old name to the town they build in the new world. Psychologically, as Brooks Otis has pointed out,[14] this orientation to the past will have to be unlearned when they reach Italy; meanwhile a resurgent Troy is the only dream strong enough to sustain them.

It has already been remarked that Virgil did not have to take Aeneas to Carthage. However, he saw that if, like Naevius, he did so, he could invent something new and impressive on the basis of the Calypso episode in the *Odyssey* and the story of Jason and Medea in Apollonius. He knew it would have to be a *tragic* love-affair; for tradition demanded that Aeneas should eventually leave. So, once again, everything depended on Virgil's inventiveness. Oddly enough, another Latin poet had shown him what not to do. One of the intractable problems in Catullus 64 is the contrast between the courageous and self-sacrificing Theseus who tackles the Minotaur and the apparently callous and ungrateful Theseus who suddenly deserts Ariadne. I say 'apparently'; for it is conceivable that Catullus intended us to imagine that Theseus was robbed of his memory by Bacchus, who wanted Ariadne for himself. Neither solution, however, suited Virgil. For if Theseus left Ariadne voluntarily, then such a wretch was no model for Aeneas; if, however, he was under a spell, he could not be used either, because (as we have seen before) Virgil was determined that such crucial acts should come as the result, not of magic, but of conscious moral choice.

Everyone acknowledges that Book 4 is Dido's book. She holds the centre of the stage and the emotional weight of the action is mostly carried by her. Nevertheless, if Aeneas' choice was to have any artistic significance, it had to be preceded by a moral struggle; and that, clearly, is what Virgil intended. In 4.266 Hermes, Jupiter's emissary, sneeringly accuses him of acting like a husband (*uxorius*). Why? In 281, recalled to obedience, Aeneas is anxious to leave the sweet land (*dulcis relinquere terras*). Why *dulcis*? One recalls the famous line in Book 6: *invitus, regina, tuo de litore cessi* ('It was against my will, o queen, that I left your shore'; 6.460). After Dido's first appeal, Aeneas *obnixus curam sub corde premebat* ('with a struggle suppressed the woe which he felt in his heart'; 4.332). After Dido's second appeal, Aeneas is described as *multa gemens, magnoque animum labefactus amore* ('with many a groan, his heart tottering under great love'; 4.395) – *his* groans, *his* heart, so surely, though it has been contested, *his* love. At line 440 Dido's sister, Anna, tries to persuade him to change his mind but the divinity blocks the man's 'indulgent ears' (*placidas aures*). In other words, had it not been for the god's intervention, Aeneas was likely to succumb. In 441 ff. comes the famous oak simile: the tree is buffeted by the winds but, though its leaves fall, it stands firm. So Aeneas is buffeted by the appeals of Dido and Anna but, though his tears fall, he stands firm. The women, to be sure, are weeping too; but to deny tears to Aeneas does violence to the simile. Finally, when he met Dido in the underworld, he 'burst into tears' (*demisit lacrimas*) – unequivocally *his* tears – 'and addressed her with tender love' (*dulcique adfatus amore est*; 6.455).[15]

So Aeneas left Carthage with bitter regrets. Yet once again Virgil invented a factor that made his decision psychologically convincing. It has often been remarked that, as soon as Aeneas was deprived of Anchises' presence, he failed. Now, to bring Aeneas back into line, that presence has to be reasserted. Granted, the final stroke comes from Jupiter through Mercury; but Mercury appears only once, whereas every night Anchises has been appearing in Aeneas' dreams, admonishing him and shattering his peace of mind (4.353). In our Freudian parlance we speak of a 'father figure'. The term is modern but the insight which it has given us only increases our respect for the ancient poet. Anchises, who had led the Trojans across the Aegean, could not have condoned his son's behaviour in Carthage (which was a strong reason for having him die in Sicily).[16] Though he speaks from the grave, his influence is still all-important; for he represents Aeneas' past life – all the love and loyalty he felt for his family and city. Virgil supplied an unforgettable symbol of this at the end of Book 2: *cessi, et sublato montis genitore petivi* ('I gave in, and taking up my father, I headed for the hills'; 2.804). In taking up Anchises, Aeneas shoulders his past, just as at the end of Book 8, in taking up his shield, he shoulders the future: *attollens umero famamque et fata nepotum* ('raising on his shoulder the glory and the destinies of his descendants'; 8.731).

Yet, ever since the flame descended on Ascanius / Iulus' head and the comet pointed towards Mount Ida (2.680-700), Anchises had recognised that the Trojans were being directed elsewhere. He was in charge of the voyage in Book 3; he recalled Aeneas to his duty in Book 4. So in spite of being a figure of the past he moves the refugees forward. This double role is seen again in Book 5. The sacrifice to him by Aeneas revives his memory, reinforcing the Trojans' sense of identity and strengthening their resolution; and the games which take up most of the book are held in *his* honour. Towards the end he again plays a decisive part in the action. The women, we are told, are still mourning for Anchises. Without him they cannot go on; they have had enough of the sea; they want and beg for a city (*urbem orant*; 5.617) – a city like the old Troy, with a Xanthus and a Simois (633-4). This is the nostalgia which we have already encountered in Book 3. Here, at the instigation of Juno's agent, it is fanned into violent action: the ships are set on fire. Eventually, in answer to Aeneas' prayer, Jupiter sends a rainstorm to extinguish the flames.

> *at pater Aeneas, casu concussus acerbo,*
> *nunc huc ingentis, nunc illuc pectore curas*
> *mutabat versans, Siculisne resideret arvis*
> *oblitus fatorum, Italasne capesseret oras.*

> But father Aeneas, stunned by this bitter blow, turned his thoughts this way and that within his heavy heart, pondering whether he should forget about his destiny and settle in the fields of Sicily, or aim to reach the shores of Italy.
>
> (*Aen.* 5.700-3)

So even at this late stage Aeneas seriously considers calling off the whole enterprise. It is quite clear that, although it is necessary for him to reach Italy, he himself believes he is free to do otherwise. In the end he is persuaded to continue, first by Nautes, who suggests that the old and unfit should be left with the Trojan Acestes in Sicily, and finally by Anchises himself, who summons him to a meeting in Elysium.

One of the great pieces of Virgilian invention is Aeneas' visit to the underworld. Homer's *Nekuia in Odyssey* 11 provided, of course, the point of departure; but once Virgil decided to include a *katabasis* or descent, he was faced with the challenge of making it relevant to his plan. This involved several changes. One notes initially, perhaps, certain changes of gender: the male seer Tiresias gives way to the female Sibyl; Odysseus' mother is replaced by Aeneas' father; and instead of Greek heroines there is a parade of Roman heroes. Beneath these apparently superficial changes lie certain fundamental differences of approach and outlook. Odysseus asks his mother about home – how goes it with his father, son, and wife? So what she has to tell him is news of a private and domestic kind. Anchises, on the other hand, tells of a nation – a great imperial nation, which will come into being long after Aeneas' death, but which depends on him for its inception. In the same way, the heroines seen by Odysseus are mythological figures from a timeless past; but the pageant witnessed by Aeneas is a view of the future, and those who march in it are destined to be major figures in Roman history.

How, then, can Aeneas, four hundred years before the foundation of Rome, see the people who are going to play these famous roles? This is where the Pythagorean section comes in. To moderns Pythagoras is known mainly for his geometric theorem; in antiquity he was also renowned for his ideas about the transmigration of souls. Here these ideas are expounded by Anchises in fifty lines of great beauty, beginning:

> *animae quibus altera fato*
> *corpora debentur Lethaei ad fluminis undam*
> *securos latices et longa oblivia potant*

> Souls which are due to receive other bodies by fate drink at
> the streams of Lethe which banish trouble and bring ever-
> lasting forgetfulness.   (*Aen.* 6.713-15)

The function of the passage is to prepare Aeneas for the parade of heroes. There is nothing in Homer about the pre-existence of the soul; and there is no evidence that Virgil himself believed it, any more than Ovid believed in the splendid Pythagorean passage

which he included in *Met.* 15.60-478. However, we are asked to
accept the doctrine within the framework of the epic. The doctrine,
moreover, is combined with the idea that the course of history has
been preordained by heaven. Thus it is supposedly possible to see
not only the people of the future but also what they do and suffer
in their new bodies. The film, as it were, has already been made.
As a privileged person Aeneas is admitted to a preview.

I now want to go back to a point nearer the beginning of Book 6
and to recall who it is Aeneas meets as he walks through Hades
with the Sibyl: first is the helmsman Palinurus, who was lost
overboard on the voyage from Sicily (Book 5); then comes the
famous encounter with Dido, who belongs to Book 4; finally Dei-
phobus appears, telling how he was killed at Troy, thus relating
him to Book 2. One could make the formal point that Virgil was
partial to chiastic patterns: the opening of the *Eclogues* is a case
in point.[17] That is a perfectly legitimate observation; but is there
any more to be said? Brooks Otis believes that Aeneas has to
face certain traumatic episodes from his past and free himself of
their burden before proceeding with his mission (p. 297). This is
going a bit further into Freudian theory than the conception of
Anchises as 'a father figure'; for the traditional Roman family
head or *paterfamilias*, was just that. Some words from a sane and
sensitive critic may help to focus our thoughts:

> The modern reader may invest Aeneas with a greater
> range of insight and choice than he could have possessed
> for his creator, and may also create an implied author,
> with access to value-systems which lie in fact beyond the
> limits of the poem and of the pagan world. Yet the reader,
> importing these, is not, save in the narrowest and most
> scholastic sense 'misinterpreting' the *Aeneid*. Indeed he
> may be uncovering a more significant text, one that may
> be related to a greater range of insights into history and
> humanity.[18]

Returning to *Aeneid* 6, it is clear that Aeneas is taken into his
past, that he does revive some deeply disturbing memories, and
that, having been shown by Anchises, in the culmination of his

prophetic role, a vision of the future, he never looks back.[19] He is confidently aware of his mission. So, in following Otis, we are not importing anything alien into the context. We are using the findings of Freud (and, if we like, his terminology) to bring out the implications of what Virgil is doing. That is an extension – surely a legitimate extension – of the original passages. Whether we can *always* venture as far as Gransden suggests without parting company with Virgil, is another matter. There must he some control over the reader's caprice; and the obvious control is the text.

When the Trojans steer into the Tiber in Book 7, Virgil utters a new invocation, aware that he is embarking on a greater task (*maius opus moveo*; 7.45). This shows that notionally the epic falls into two parts. Servius (on 7.1) tried to do better than this, talking of an 'Odyssean' and an 'Iliadic' half. However, a moment's thought shows that Book 2 is not Odyssean; Book 8 is not Iliadic; and the games in Book 5 are out of place. In this century several scholars have tried to discern the 'structure' of the *Aeneid*, using the books as building-units;[20] these 'structures' are not Virgil's invention but that of his critics. To take one example, in all the proposed blue-prints Book 6 is linked with Book 8 because of the vision of Rome's future in the underworld and the designs on Aeneas' shield. But the vision represents only about one seventh of Book 6 and the shield only about one seventh of Book 8. Moreover, if pictures of the future are a vital structural feature, then the prophecy of Jupiter in Book 1 has to be included; and why not the prophecy of Helenus in Book 3? Or consider the exploits and death of Pallas in Book 10. This has to be connected not only with his funeral in Book 11 but also with his appearance in Book 8 and his posthumous role at the end of Book 12. In other words we are dealing with themes or motifs as in a symphony or a great tapestry. Such themes can be expanded and linked to others. Thus Pallas is naturally connected with Evander, while they, in turn, can be linked to Lausus and Mezentius – and to other fathers and sons.[21] The books as units are unimportant.

As an example of how such themes can bind the two parts of the work together we may start with the foot-race in Book 5 (291-361); its most striking competitors are Nisus and Euryalus. The latter is a beautiful boy of about fifteen; Nisus (about seventeen) is his lover. After Aeneas has set out some highly desirable prizes, the race begins. Nisus leads for most of the way but near the finishing line he slips on a patch of muck and blood. Salius, who is lying second, is about to take first place when he is brought down by Nisus; Euryalus runs on to win. Naturally Salius protests but Euryalus retains the prize by resorting to tears.[22] Youth, beauty and love, along with an eager desire for prizes and glory and an adolescent impulsiveness – these are the characteristics we remember from the sports-meeting, an occasion when Aeneas actually laughs (5.358).

Those same characteristics recur in Book 9, where, in a serious military operation, they prove disastrous (176-449). The Trojan camp is under siege. Nisus and Euryalus get permission to slip through the enemy lines and obtain help from Aeneas. Instead of hurrying on to Pallanteum, they begin to kill the sleeping soldiers. As they break off, the vain Euryalus takes a fancy to a dead man's helmet and puts it on. The glitter gives him away and they are both killed. Instead of censuring this reckless and unmilitary behaviour, Virgil abandons epic anonymity to record his personal tribute: *fortunati ambo! si quid mea carmina possunt, / nulla dies umquam memori vos eximet aevo* ('Blessed pair! If my song has any power, no day shall ever erase you from the memory of time'; 9.446-7). This tribute and the subsequent lament of Euryalus' mother (473-502) are striking illustrations of Virgil's tender sensibility.

In the chapters on Gigantomachy in his impressive book on the *Aeneid* Philip Hardie suggests that at certain points the forces which oppose Aeneas are analogous to those Hesiodic figures which opposed Zeus.[23] Hardie calls them 'demonic' – a term heavily loaded with evil, which is appropriate enough in Hesiod's context but, as several of Hardie's passages show, is not applicable to the *Aeneid*. For his description of the cave in 1.50-63, Virgil may owe something to Theogony 729ff., as Hardie (pp. 91-2), following Buchheit, maintains. However, the Hesiodic passage is about Titans; Virgil's is about winds – winds which, however wild, can be commanded, first (indirectly) by Juno, then by Neptune. Later the gigantic Pandarus and Bitias are compared to pines and oaks, and Bitias to a pile of masonry (9.674, 681 and 711); but they are on the Trojan side. The Giants are said to fight with rocks; but so does Hercules (8.250). At the battle of Actium the ships of both sides are mountainous (8.692); and both fleets use fire (8.694). Another huge, monstrous, shape is Fama, sister of Coeus and Enceladus (4.179). She is certainly an evil (174) and a filthy goddess (195). Yet she acts against Dido, furthering the plans of Jupiter. Then there is the terrible Aegaeon with his hundred arms and hands and his fifty fire-breathing mouths. Here, if anywhere, is a figure with demonic qualities; but the warrior compared to him is Aeneas himself (10.565-70). So it seems fair to conclude that, while certain forces and phenomena are elemental, they are essentially expressions of raw power, capable of acting for or against the Trojans.

Fire calls for some additional comment. In Book 2 flames burn Troy and play benignly about Ascanius / Iulus' head (680-84). Later Lavinia's fire foretells both glory and disaster (7.76-80). So when we read that Turnus has a fire-breathing Chimaera on his helmet (7.785-6) and that his sword was made by Vulcan (12.90-91), we should not be so impressed as to forget that Aeneas' sword was also made by Vulcan (8.612-13 and 621) and that the crest on his helmet also flashes fire (8.620 and 10.270-1). In view of these parallels, it cannot be right to imagine that Turnus' fire-breathing Chimaera puts him, by analogy, into the same category as the monstrous Cacus.[24] After all, no one maintains that, because Turnus sends forth glittering flashes (*micantia fulmina*; 9.733) from his shield and offers frequent sacrifice to Jupiter (10.619-20), he must be a human analogue of the king of the gods.

As for the Chimaera, what about the ship of that name with its gigantically named skipper, Gyas? Surely that must be a sinister combination? But no; this *Chimaera* is part of the Trojan fleet (5.223).

All this has large implications. There has been – and still is – a widespread assumption that anyone who opposes, or even delays, the chief hero must have some moral defect – a defect which accounts for his or her death.[25] Why this assumption should be made so often about the *Aeneid* and not about the *Iliad* is something of a mystery. Perhaps it has to do with the conception of Virgil as

a 'naturally Christian soul' (*anima naturaliter Christiana*). Or
is it because anyone who opposes the pious (*pius*) Aeneas must
ipso facto be impious? Or does it result from a misapplication (or
misunderstanding?) of Aristotle's concept of *hamartia* or fatal
flaw? I do not pretend to know. However, the idea is, in any case,
surely wrong; for in spite of all the scholastic ingenuity expended
in the search for a moral explanation, it is not to be found in the
text. Virgil never claims to sing of the victory of good over evil, or
of light over darkness. Dido acts with fury only after she has been
betrayed and humiliated.[26] Turnus, with good reason, sees Aeneas
as an interloper who intends to rob him of his promised bride
(7.365-6). So his rage, too, is perfectly understandable. Although,
like Dido, he has the misfortune not to be part of Jupiter's plan
(i.e. the rise of Rome), he has all the qualities of an epic hero,
being handsome, aristocratic and brave. He is also not without
piety (7.438-9 and 471; 9.18 ff.; and 10.619-20).

His ferocity, of course, is undeniable. (Has not Apollo warned
Aeneas through the Sibyl [6.89] that he must encounter another
Achilles?) A good example comes at 12.101 ff., where Turnus is
driven by *furiae*.[27] Meanwhile, what of Aeneas? The answer comes
at once: *nec minus interea maternis saevus in armis / Aeneas acuit
Martem et se suscitat ira* ('Meanwhile Aeneas is *no less savage* in his
mother's armour, sharpening his warlike spirit and working himself
into a rage'; 12.107 f.). Later, like forest fires or raging torrents,
both Aeneas *and* Turnus rush over the battlefield with anger boiling
inside them (12.521-8). As with Aeneas in Troy, Turnus' ferocity
occasionally leads to rashness (9.756-61). But those who deplore
Turnus' *violentia* seem to forget the insensate fury of Aeneas in
10.545-605 – a fury which continues off the battlefield, when he
offers up eight young prisoners as a human sacrifice for the death
of Pallas.[28] Here is a blind test: *terribilis saevam nullo discrimine
caedem / suscitat irarumque omnis effundit habenas* ('a figure of
terror, he awakens cruel, indiscriminate slaughter, giving free rein
to his fury'). And who is the character described? For the answer,
see 12.498-9.

Why, then, does Turnus die? The answer is quite clear. Turnus
dies because he is in the way; and being a man of heroic temper (in
every sense) and the protégé of a major deity, he is not prepared to

stand aside. Had he done so, there would have been no *Aeneid*.

This brings us to the death of Turnus, the episode which represents the final instance of necessity. The gentle and much-lamented Deryck Williams used to say, 'There should have been a better way'. But within the iron frame of a Homeric poem, where Aeneas and Turnus were re-enacting the final clash of Achilles and Hector, no other way was possible. To raise up Turnus and give him a sporting handshake would have been an unthinkable piece of bathos. So all Virgil could do was to make the killing intelligible. One must approach this controversial scene free from the assumption that Aeneas has evolved into a model of Stoic patience and self-control. (We have adduced ample evidence to the contrary.) The second thing is to ask what triggered his last act of violence, when he was on the point of responding to Turnus' plea for mercy.[29] It was, of course, the sight of the belt which Turnus had stripped from Pallas. That sends us back to Book 10, where, after Pallas' death, 'Pallas, Evander, everything stands before Aeneas' eyes, the table he had approached as a stranger, the promise sealed with a handshake' (10.515-17). That in turn sends us back to the whole splendid episode of Aeneas' visit to Evander, where the king provided troops including his son: 'I hand over to you Pallas, my hope and consolation. Under your tutelage may he grow used to enduring war and the grim business of Mars, and to watching your exploits. And may he admire you from his earliest years' (8.514-17).

All that is important. For it means that when Aeneas notices the belt he is overwhelmed, not just by vengeful fury but also by remorse. At the very moment of his final triumph he is reminded of his failure – failure to discharge his debt to his host and ally, failure to protect Evander's son. Given, then, that the killing of Turnus was necessary, it had to be carried out, not in cold blood but in a blaze of anger. To fuel Aeneas' anger in this way, which had no precedent in Homer's equivalent scene, was surely Virgil's last great inventive achievement; for it showed that Aeneas' *furor* was the natural outcome of his *pietas*.

The general view of the *Aeneid* indicated here (and argued at greater length elsewhere)[30] is that, while Virgil glorified Roman power and presented it as a great historical development presided over by Jupiter and Fate, he could not pretend that this often terrible process had any regard for the deserts of individual people. Even those who belonged to the chosen nation had no guarantee of survival. As in the *Iliad*, where 'Patroclus also died',[31] there was no reliable link between good character and good fortune. So when Ripheus is killed – 'the most just of all the Trojans and the staunchest champion of fairness' – all Virgil can do is to resign himself to incomprehension: *dis aliter visum* ('the gods decided otherwise'; 2.428).

There is, however, one qualification which should be stated more clearly than it was in the article just referred to. Long ago Conington said, 'It is only of the events preceding the settlement that the poet really treats' (vol. 2, p. 29); or, as Philip Hardie puts it, 'The central theme of the poem ... is the struggle necessary before home can be founded: *tantae molis erat Romanam condere gentem*'[32]. We should therefore be prepared to distinguish figures like Cacus or the Harpies or the mythical sinners in Hades from the human characters who take part in the action proper. Moreover, after Rome has been founded, 'history' begins; and that occasionally includes villains like Mettus (8.642), Tarquinius Superbus (6.817) and Catiline (8.668). In very recent times, while Augustus, with his victories and temple-building, represents the culmination of Aeneas' heroism, his foes are presented as hateful, like Antony with his barbaric forces and Egyptian wife (8.685-8); or as monstrous, like the barking Anubis (8.698); or as somewhat outlandish, like the conquered peoples (8.722 ff.). In those scenes at Actium and before the temple of Apollo (8.678-728) the deafening sound of Augustan propaganda drowns Virgil's Homeric music. True, we meet occasional triumphalism in the Iliad but here the trumpet of a Homeric warrior has been replaced with the massed brass bands of imperial Rome. Perhaps, in view of people's all too vivid memories, that was unavoidable. After such protracted civil war, the relief of the 20s BC must have been enormous. And one readily concedes that, if Actium had gone the other way, the result would have been very different from the Augustan Age. Nevertheless, the tone of those verses (8.671-728), for all its grandeur, does not produce quite the same effect as Jupiter's prophecy in 1.257-96 or Anchises' famous words in 6.851-3; for in both those passages Roman power is combined

with peace and good government and no specific enemies are
named. So, while the patriotic impact must have been immense
at the time, in a post-imperial age the reader may not be sorry to
find that those fifty-odd lines can be read in about three minutes
– less time than it takes to bellow *Land of Hope and Glory* on the
last night of the Proms.

Related Material:

'Dido's *Culpa*' in *Lines of Enquiry* (Cambridge, 1976; repr. 2004)
    32-53.
'The Idea of Empire in the *Aeneid*' in R.A. Dardwell and J.
    Hamilton (eds), *Virgil in a Classical Tradition* (Nottingham,
    1986) 28-42.
'Towers and Citadels in the *Aeneid*' in M. Stokes and T.L. Burton
    (eds), *Mediaeval Literature and Antiquities*: Studies in Honour
    of Basil Cottle (Cambridge, 1987) 3-12.
'Chaucer and Virgil' in *The Classical Tradition in Operation*
    (Toronto, 1994) 3-31.

3 Horace's *Odes*: a Defence of Criticism

[Previously unpublished; lecture to a Dublin audience]

The traditional but now rather unfashionable thesis of this paper is that, in interpreting a Horatian ode, there is a scale of probability above which is truth and below which is either falsehood or ignorance; and that such a scale should form the basis of our emotional and aesthetic response. I am talking of truth in specific cases, not about 'Truth' with a capital T, which may safely be left to metaphysicians. The activity in question involves judgment, (the Greek *krinein* – root of our 'criticism'). If an academic rejects every assertion about a poem or if he accepts every assertion as of equal value, he has renounced the business of criticism and is no longer true to his calling.

Let us start with form. In *Odes* 1.4, without translating, we can see that *nunc decet* (11) answers *nunc decet* (9); that *pulsat pede* (13) answers *quatiunt pede* (7); that *iam* (16) answers *iam* (5); and that *nec ... nec* (18-19) answers *neque ... nec* (3-4). So syntactically the ode is in the form of a chiasmus balanced about the centre. That discovery, I would suggest, is as certain as anything in the natural sciences. I do not know who first made it[1] but, once it had appeared in print, everyone could verify it for himself. The pattern was not invented by a critic and then projected onto the ode; it was a feature of the ode itself.

In mood a rather different division is evident. In line 13 joy at the return of life suddenly turns to sombre reflection on the coming of death. That coming is described: *pallida mors aequo pulsat pede pauperum tabernas* – six plosives in one line ('pale death beats with impartial foot the poor man's cottage ...'). That sequence is objective and audible. Need we doubt that it enacts the knocking of Death described in the words? (You kicked at the door with the heel of your sandal, which of course had no toe.) The joyful and sombre parts of the ode contain certain antithetical images – especially of

45

loosening and bondage, coldness and warmth. Interestingly, they are not limited to their expected places. Cold, for example, appears in the spring section as well as in the death section. Again, I was probably not the first to notice this criss-crossing of images; but when I did, it was the result of testing a hypothesis – that there are other correspondences in addition to *solvitur* (1) and *solutae* (10).[2] Again, as in science, anyone can check the point for himself. I admit, however, that images are not always as clear as these.

One other small observation: in the phrase *domus exilis Plutonia* (17) *exilis* means 'without substance', not just in the sense of 'ghostly' but, more importantly, in the sense of 'without assets'. It thus supplies an ironic antithesis to *Plutonia*, which means 'rich' (Pluto being Ploutos, a god of substance). What evidence is there for this contention? In *Epistles* 1.6.45 a house where there are not many superfluous luxuries is regarded by the rich man as *exilis: exilis domus est ubi non ... multa supersunt* ('a meagre house is one where there are not many superfluous objects').

Consider now the famous opening of *Odes* 2.14: *eheu, fugaces, Postume, Postume, / labuntur anni* ('alas! Postumus, Postumus, the years glide swiftly by'). Why the repetition? Surely it must convey emphasis or urgency, as in *Epode* 7.1: *quo, quo scelesti ruitis?* ('where, where are you rushing, you wicked people?'). However, the name Postumus implies 'born after the death of the father' (*OLD* b), a meaning appropriate to an ode about the transience of human generations –think of the heir in the final stanza.

Then there is metre. Paying tribute to Pindar in *Odes* 4.2 Horace writes:

> *fervet immensusque ruit profundo* (7)
> *laurea donandus Apollinari* (9)
> *seu deos regesve canit deorum* (13)
> *sive quos Elea domum reducit* (17)
> *plorat et viris animumque moresque* (22)
> *aureos educit in astra nigroque* (23)
>   *invidet Orco* (24).

All those lines belong to a single periodic sentence reaching from 5 to 24. So the syntax flows across five stanza-divisions. In five of the lines the usual caesura after the fifth syllable is obliterated. The norm is represented by line 22: *plorat et viris //*; but that line ends with a potentially extra syllable (*-que*), which is elided into the first syllable of the next line. Similarly the *-que* of *nigroque* in line 23 is elided into *invidet*. So the poetry flows across stanza-divisions, across caesurae and across line-endings. That is an objective fact; but what is the explanation of these extraordinary effects? The answer, again, is given by the sense: Horace is mirroring the flow of Pindar's verse, which in stanza 2 is compared to a river in spate rushing down a mountainside.

Chiastic patterns, sound effects, corresponding images, ironical juxtapositions, rhetorical repetitions, significant names, metrical surprises – these are just some of the constituents of poetry; when pointed out, they are usually seen to be obvious.

Specific investigations of this kind, of course, assume a correct text. What is probably the earliest printed edition of the *Odes* (Venice, 1471) may be consulted in the British Library. Though a historic document, it contains numerous errors, some of a very superficial kind. In *Diffugere nives* (4.7), for example, it has *genibusque sororibus* (5), *frigora nitescunt* (9) and *praeter Aeneas* (15). Such blunders are understandable in the infancy of printing. They are easily detectable (for they make nonsense) and they are readily corrected. Other corruptions are deeper and a few have persisted up to our own time. In 3.1.41-4 four luxuries are enumerated: (1) marble, (2) purple, (3) wine, (4) ointment. Local adjectives are supplied in three cases: (1) *Phrygian* marble, (3) *Falernian* wine, and (4) *Persian* ointment. So the 'star-like purple' (*sidere clarior*) of (2) is an awkward anomaly. For *sidere* Nisbet recently conjectured *Sidone*, Sidon being a city commonly associated with the production of purple-dyed garments.[3] This convincing conjecture is accepted in the latest Teubner text and in David West's translation.[4]

In *Odes* 4.4.33-4 we have *doctrina sed vim promovet insitam / rectique cultus pectora roborant*. This is translated by Bennett (Loeb edn) as 'Yet training increases inborn worth'. So far, so good; but he then continues, 'and righteous ways make strong the heart'. Horace is talking about the effects of nurture on nature. 'Ways' is not a good parallel to 'training'. The ancient scholiast, Porphyrion, says *recti* is a genitive singular. This means that *recti cultus* means 'the study (or pursuit) of what is right'. That requires a singular verb; so Shackleton Bailey (see n. 4) was surely right to make the very slight correction *rectique cultus pectora roborat* ('the study of what is right strengthens the heart'). One concludes, then, that in a diminishing number of places progress is still possible; but a text that satisfies everyone will never be achieved, and there remain points where there must always be doubt. One such case is *Odes* 3.4.10, where as a toddler Horace got lost and was, he tells us, covered with leaves by the wood-pigeons. This miracle happened *Vulture in Apulo / nutricis extra limen Apuliae* ('on mount Vultur in Apulia outside the threshold of my nurse Apulia'). Since Apuliae is merely a senseless and unmetrical repetition of *Apulo* directly above it, the original word can never be certainly restored. Nevertheless, after 2,000 years Horace's text is relatively sound – sounder than, say, that of Propertius, and much sounder than that of Shakespeare.

We return now to interpretation, this time to the study of an entire ode, 1.14. A few years ago Robin Nisbet asked a well-known Cambridge Hellenist the following question: 'Some people think that Horace's ship is a real ship, some think it's a political ship, some think it's a woman, some think it's a poetry-book ... now what do you think?' The critic replied that Horace meant the poem to be open-ended; in other words it meant all or any of these things – though he eventually conceded that it was not about a football match. A real ship could hardly have changed from 'an object of anxious disgust' (*sollicitum taedium*) to 'an object of love and serious concern' (*desiderium curaque non levis*); these terms would suit a woman, though the battered ship was a common metaphor for a decrepit whore[5] and would therefore be quite wrong for a fashionable mistress. If the ship were a poetry-book, it should come near the end of the collection; for the ship, we are told, is nearing harbour (cf., for instance, the end of Ovid, *Ars Amatoria* 1 and *Remedia Amoris*). In favour of the ship of *state* are the following points: (1) Quintilian in the late 1st century AD explicitly gives this explanation (8.6.44); (2) a poem by Alcaeus described a ship in distress and Heraclitus (1st century AD?) says the storm represents the danger to the city coming from the tyrant Myrsilus; (3) a papyrus from the second century AD, which preserves a fragment from a commentary on Alcaeus' poem, mentions the return of Myrsilus;[6] less directly, (4) *Odes* 1.37 opens with a translation of Alcaeus 332, which celebrated the death of Myrsilus. So a political background is indicated. In their note on 1.14.18 Nisbet-Hubbard say that in expressing his *desiderium* Horace is like an ἐραστὴς τῆς πόλεως. True, but to establish the allegory with the state we need a Latin parallel to show that *desiderium* could be used for something other than a person; one is provided by the elder Pliny (*NH* 8.44) when he uses *medium desiderium* of Alexander's 'central interest', natural science. Similarly we need an example of *cura* as a non-personal love-object. Again the elder Pliny obliges: in *NH* 5.88 he describes the city of Palmyra as a serious concern (*cura*) to both Rome and Parthia. In the same way Rome could have been a *cura* to Horace. So the traditional interpretation – and only that interpretation – is almost certainly right. ('The currents flowing between the shining Cyclades' [19-20] seem to be just a colourful example of 'dangerous waters'. But we do not know exactly what political storms Horace had in mind.)

I come now to another fashionable contention: that our view of a poem is determined by the power-structure of our own society. I want to argue that 'determined' is wrong, though 'influenced' is sometimes the case. In *Epode* 3 Horace inveighs against garlic, which he seems to have been tricked into eating as a practical joke by Maecenas. The poem concludes as follows:

> *at si quid umquam tale concupiveris,*
> *iocose Maecenas, precor*
> *manum puella savio opponat tuo*
> *extrema et in sponda cubet*   (19-22)

This is usually interpreted as 'If you ever take it into your head to play this kind of trick on me again ... I hope your girl wards off your kisses with her hand and sleeps on the edge of the bed'. But how is this supposed to be a retribution for what Maecenas

has done to Horace? And is not *concupiveris* too strongly sensual
a word to mean 'take it into your head'? Might it not mean 'If
you are ever greedy enough to eat such stuff, I hope your girl will
ward off your kisses and sleep on the edge of the bed'? It turns
out that this is not an original idea: apparently it was proposed by
Lambinus in the sixteenth century.[7] But whether the idea is right
or wrong, what happens then to the all-important power-structure?
Politically, Lambinus' world was very different from ours.

Or take another example. Writing about the Hypermestra ode
(3.11), Arnold Bradshaw pointed out that Horace does not actually
say that he is pursuing Lyde (for whose benefit the story is retold);
and that the emphasis of the Hypermestra story is clearly on
marriage.[8] He therefore concluded that Horace was recommending
to Lyde that she should get married. But it seems unlikely that
Horace would invoke the god Mercury and the supernaturally
persuasive power of the lyre simply to convey a piece of avuncular
advice. Moreover, Lyde is not the type of name that one associates
with marriage; in two other odes it belongs to a young woman who
is clearly a *meretrix* or call-girl. So one concludes that Horace is
using the myth in a light-hearted way, saying, 'Lyde, look what
happens to girls like the daughters of Danaus who mistreat men
(they were punished in hell), and look at the glory that Hypermestra
achieved by being loyal and affectionate!' Now Arnold Bradshaw
is, like myself, a white, Dublin, middle-class, atheist, heterosexual,
male, who has lived most of his life in a representative democracy.
So how can the power-structure theory explain the fact that we
hold different views? And that's not all. When I started to draft
a translation of the poem, I took Bradshaw's line; it was only
subsequently that I reverted to the traditional view, which was held
by Porphyrio probably in the fourth century. How can the power-
structure theory account for a change of mind?

In using the scale of probability, above which is truth and below
which is ignorance or falsehood, I am of course following the
traditional, empirical, method of classical humanism. In the last
twenty-five years or so a person reasoning in this way has come
to be called a positivist. I realise that in this context 'positivist' is a
rude word, but I am not quite clear what it means. Does it simply
mean 'one who believes in independent facts'? Take the simple

statement 'De Valera died on 29 August 1975'. Surely that conveys true and meaningful information, regardless of whether a Fianna Fail admirer adds 'after a long and distinguished career', or a Fine Gael supporter adds 'and not before time'. But is positivism *just* a belief in facts? Does its method not also make room for hypotheses? Sometimes, as we have seen, a hypothesis can be proved; but often, although it can be supported by probable arguments, proof is unattainable. Either way, it involves the use of imagination. In *Odes* 2.2.13 we have the memorable epigram *crescit indulgens sibi dirus hydrops* ('The dreaded dropsy *crescit* by indulging itself'). David West translates *crescit* by 'swells'.[9] That is exactly right for dropsy – so right, in fact, that one wonders why Horace didn't write *turget. Dirus* suggests some kind of dreadful monster, *crescit* one that grows. Did Horace not have at the back of his mind the Hydra (water-creature)? Apollodorus (2.5.2) tells us that every time one head was lopped off two more took its place. So the monster literally grew. Finally, in 4.4.61-2, where he explicitly refers to the Hydra, Horace says *firmior ... crevit* ('grew stronger). So the hypothesis has *some s*upport but it falls short of proof; and I don't know how many will be convinced. Incidentally, that kind of idea only became current in literary criticism after Freud's work on the unconscious mind.

I must not give the impression that a commentator is never plagued by doubts. In exceptional cases the precise sense of a word eludes us. In the famous opening of *Odes* 3.30: *Exegi monumentum aere perennius / regalique situ pyramidum altius* ('I have finished a monument more lasting than bronze and higher than the royal *situ* of the pyramids'), what is meant by *situ?* The straightforward translation 'site' seems very unlikely, because, so far from being lofty, the site of the pyramids was flat and this was well known to the Romans, especially after the Alexandrian war. Heinze understood it as meaning 'grave' or 'tomb' – an unattested sense; others take it as 'structure', which is equally unattested. Either of these could be right, as Horace sometimes does extend ordinary usage; but neither can be *proved.* One other suggestion is that *situs* means 'decay'; that *is* an established sense, but it would be odd for Horace to compare the soaring height of his monument with something that was crumbling; and Diodorus, who had recently visited Egypt, says that the blocks of the pyramids show no sign of decay (1.63.5). It is noticeable that Propertius and Martial, who both echo Horace's passage, at this point change the wording.

Later in the same ode we have the opposite problem: *princeps Aeolium carmen ad Italos / deduxisse modos*. Which of the many senses of *deduco* are relevant? Does it mean 'to compose', 'to escort' as in a wedding, 'to lead in triumph', or 'to settle' as with a group of colonists? Perhaps the wisest thing is to translate the basic, general, meaning and say 'to have brought (or transported) Aeolian verse to Italian tunes'. ('Metres', of course, is wrong, for the metres were not Italian but Greek.) Roman readers may have added one or other of the particular meanings but some of those meanings would have been less appropriate than others. 'Compose in accompaniment to' ignores the natural meaning of *ad* in a geographical context; again, it is unlikely that Horace would here have used the vaunting language of conquest (*deduci* in the Cleopatra ode (1.37.31) is a very different matter); finally, Horace could hardly have presented himself as a Greek *oikistes* in this very Italian poem.

As a last example of such doubt, we may take the end of *Odes* 3.26. There Horace is retiring from the campaigns of love but at the end of the poem he asks Venus to raise her whip and give the arrogant Chloe just one flick. Does this mean he wants Chloe to feel desire (however transitory) for him, in which case his resolution falters? Or does he want her to feel desire for some arrogant man who will give her a taste of her own medicine? Readers may remain unsure; or they may feel instinctively inclined to one answer or the other. In the latter case that's a subjective preference which cannot be refuted. However, Horace would not have meant *both*. One has to distinguish a logical contradiction from an interesting ambiguity. As an example of the latter one might take Horace's social attitude, which is both proud and humble – proud *vis à vis* the philistine masses, humble *vis à vis* Maecenas and Augustus. That double attitude is memorably represented in *Sat.* 1.9, the encounter with the pest. Or we could examine Horace's attitude towards his own grander lyrics. He is certainly proud of them; and yet he feels they are on a higher level than his ordinary companionable self – think of his ironical metamorphosis into a swan (*Odes* 2.20), the down-to-earth endings of 2.1 and 3.3, the Matine bee in 4.2.27. What saves this ambiguity from contradiction is the figure of the *vates* or seer, which shows (and in the main justifies) what the normal Horace could achieve under the pressure of great events.

So far we've been concerned only with the explication of single poems. But the method can be extended. Take *Odes* 3.9 – the verbal exchanges between the poet and Lydia, in which *donec ... nec ...vigui* is mimicked by *donec ... neque ... vigui*; and Ilia, the ancestress of Rome, trumps the King of the Persians (1-8). A similar interchange takes place in Catullus 45 between two lovers, Septimius and Acme; the parallels are easily spotted. Here we are concerned only with the differences. Catullus presents a tableau in which Septimius has Acme on his knee; there is no such scene-setting in Horace. Half way through, Acme 'kisses the sweet boy's intoxicated eyes'; there is no physical contact in Horace. With Catullus' pair there are no rivals, no recriminations; the mood of enchanted love remains unchanged throughout, and the weather seems set fair for the indefinite future. Horace's scene, however, is *not* static. We are given a miniature drama which runs from the past through the present and into the future. The participants have changed before and, in spite of their protestations, we suspect they will change again. So we have Catullus' heart against Horace's head, emotion against wit. That much is objectively clear. Which poem you *prefer*, of course, is up to you. Some regard the ode as shallow and cynical; others find Catullus' piece cloyingly sentimental; and perhaps both effects were envisaged by the respective poets. At any rate, analysis can go no further.

We have now come quite a long way without asking what poetry *is* or attempting to define *the nature of literature*. Such questions are impenetrably obscure and endlessly controversial; and they actually take us away from the works themselves. More is said on this topic in Chapter 17 below. Here I would only observe that a competent lecturer on art can say all he wants about a painting's theme, colour, composition, style, history and effect without becoming trapped in the quagmire of aesthetics.

I have been trying to indicate how far the traditional type of classical scholar can be called a positivist. Positivism may have its limitations; but its method is essential for anyone who sets out to edit a text. It is interesting that post-moderns do not produce editions or commentaries. 'Epistemological problems' are sometimes pleaded in excuse. Another, equally insulting, word is 'historicist'. According to Webster's Dictionary, historicism is 'the belief that the student must enter into the mind and attitudes of past periods, accept their point of view, and avoid all intrusion of his own standards or assumptions'. Now one must grant that this doctrine is often unrealistic and at times it is crudely applied. A few years ago Nicholas Horsfall claimed that Virgil's Roman readers regarded Dido with dislike and suspicion.[10] I do not deny that many conservative Roman men – and doubtless some women too – would have held that opinion. (The tradition of *Punica fides* lasted long after 146 BC). However, Horsfall speaks in sweeping terms of 'a Roman reader', 'a Roman's reactions', 'Roman feelings', and 'a Roman' – phrases that imply a unanimous point of view. Yet in the first century AD Ovid tells us that no part of the *Aeneid* was more popular than the tale of Dido and Aeneas (*Tristia* 2.535-6); in the second century the educated lady whom Juvenal regards as an obnoxious type takes Dido's part 'forgiving the doomed Elissa' (*Sat.* 6.435); in the fourth century Macrobius observes how the story was represented in paintings, statues, tapestries, plays and songs (*Sat.* 5.17.5); and there is the famous passage of St Augustine's *Confessions* (1.13). So even in antiquity the Pharisees didn't have things all their own way. The examples also show that we do know how *some* Romans thought about *some* literary questions.

Let us briefly consider Horace's opinions. As we are concerned with the *Odes*, we will ignore his carefully balanced assessment of Lucilius and consider his position *vis à vis* Alcaeus, who was separated from him by over five centuries, belonged to a different country and a higher social class, spent much of his life in armed rebellion, and endured at least two periods of exile. Instead of regarding Alcaeus as 'desperately foreign', Horace concentrated on their common interests – poetry, wine, sex and (to a lesser extent) the vicissitudes of politics (*Odes* 1.32). These shared experiences gave Horace a feeling of affinity with his predecessor, which helped to define and project elements of his own personality. He himself describes such a relationship on three occasions as 'following' an author (*sequor*), on three as 'imitating' (*imitor*), and once as 'emulating' him (*aemulor*). The last is probably the most satisfactory term. Certainly the current vogue-words 'subversion', 'undermining', and 'appropriation' are seriously misleading, The first two carry hostile connotations, and 'appropriation' implies that the original owner has been deprived of his property. Of Alcaeus as a man Horace doubtless knew a good deal more than we do. If he did, he may well have found some of his personal traits disagreeable; but those were irrelevant to Horace's poetic purpose. (Similarly, we can admire and enjoy at least some of Pound, Eliot and Yeats without being dubbed fascists or racists or superstitious snobs.) Within the Roman context, when Horace expresses contempt for huge triumphalist spectacles and for dolled-up pop-stars, while professing admiration for tragic drama (*Epistles* 2.1.188-93, 205-7 and 210-13), we believe him; for he has no reason to misrepresent his opinions.

Horace's attitude to the Emperor is altogether more complex and it has to be considered carefully; for it affects our view of the poet himself. First, Horace knew a good deal about the young revolutionary's rise to power. The proscriptions of 43-2 BC and the treatment of Perusia in 41 must have troubled him; and one cannot assume that he welcomed everything that was done in the next thirty years. Equally, we do not know how whole-heartedly he had embraced the cause of Brutus and Cassius. To judge from *Sat.* 1.6, he was far from enthusiastic about the ways in which the senatorial oligarchy had perpetuated its power. The period between Caesar's murder and the defeat of Antony was one of great confusion. The issues were far from clear. Men of great political significance, like Messalla, Plancus and Dellius changed allegiance more than once; even the independent Pollio came to terms with Augustus. In Horace's case one can argue that, by accepting Maecenas' patronage in 37 BC, he had committed himself to the young Caesar's cause; yet in *Sat.* 1.10 (ca. 35 BC) some Antonians are included among Horace's friends;[11] there is no favourable mention of Octavian until the eve of Actium and even then Horace still speaks primarily as the supporter of Maecenas (*Epode* 1).

It is true, of course, that Horace had been remarkably lucky: he had survived Philippi; he had been pardoned by the victors; and he had been rescued from his work at the treasury by the model of all patrons. Such luck predictably aroused resentment; there were

murmurs of 'good fortune's son!' (*fortunae filius*; *Sat.* 2.6.49).
Such feelings reflected prejudice from above and below against
the freedman's son. Yet even after Actium Horace's respectful
references to Octavian are laced with irony. In *Sat.* 2.1.20 the
Princeps is compared to a nervous horse which must not be
rubbed the wrong way. In *Sat.* 2.5.62 ff. he is mentioned in highly
honorific terms as the lord of land and sea; but those lines are a
parody of an oracle and they are delivered by the rascally Tiresias
in a lecture on legacy-hunting. Ten years later the Emperor is
referred to again in a comic context (*Epistles* 1.13) but he is still
not addressed in any of the *Sermones*. This reticence brought a
letter of complaint from the palace: 'Are you afraid that, if you're
seen to be a friend of mine, it will blight your reputation with
posterity?'[12] Some gesture was therefore called for and it was
duly made in *Epistles* 2.1. Granted, the poem's opening eulogy is
rather out of place in a *sermo* (conversation). Yet the honours and
altars were real; and, more important, the whole passage is just
an introduction to a self-interested plea for modern poetry. We
may still, of course, find the passage excessively deferential but,
when set beside, say, the *Laus Pisonis*, or Statius' poem on the
equestrian statue of Domitian, or Pliny's interminable *Panegyric*
on Trajan, to say nothing of the addresses prefixed to seventeenth-
and eighteenth-century English works, it seems quite restrained.
Before leaving this topic we should recall the letter from
Augustus in which he asked that Horace should become his
private secretary.[13] What an opportunity! If the poet had been
seriously interested in power and wealth, he would surely have
agreed. In fact he excused himself (his health was *so* unreliable)
and Augustus accepted the refusal with good humour.

So far we have been looking at the relation of Horace to the
Emperor in 'real life', drawing on Suetonius and the informal
Satires. However, when Horace has been disliked in later ages,
it has largely been for his praises of Augustus in the *Odes*. If we
simply take the view that Augustus was an autocrat and Horace,
like some other poets at the time, a creeping sycophant, then all is
easy. Yet one or two points should be borne in mind. First, modern
representative democracy, which allows an exceptional degree of
criticism and ridicule against its rulers, is a rare plant; and even

if we regard it as the least objectionable kind of constitution, it was never an option in ancient Rome. So in trying to assess the character of Cicero or Horace or anyone else, we must ask whether he lived a decent life within the framework of his own day. Secondly, even a modern democracy may, at a time of crisis, prefer dictatorship to anarchy. (In 1958 France called in De Gaulle to save the country from civil war; and that was before civil war started.) Rome had endured the reality of civil war intermittently for sixty years before Augustus emerged.

If we are interested in fairness to Augustus, we have to weigh many contrasting truths against each other, considering the gains and losses that he brought. The first and most conspicuous loss, as we learn from the history books, was the loss of freedom; but what freedoms do we have in mind, and whose? Were the provincials more, or less, free from exploitation under Augustus? Were traders more, or less, free from piracy? Were the *equites* more, or less, free to gain advancement in government service? Were the common people more, or less, free from famine and the danger of fire? Were all classes more, or less, free to inter-marry? Was everyone more, or less, free from the fear of riot and violent death? It is the senator Tacitus who talks about 'servitude' (*servitium*; *Annals* 1.2) – naturally enough; for, although the machinery of the republican constitution continued to function, everyone knew where the important decisions were now being taken. While Tacitus' strictures are understandable, and the long-term outlook was unsettled (as it usually is), the seventeen years between 30 and 13 BC were a period of hope and recovery, not one of grim oppression.

And yes, Horace *does* praise the Emperor in some important odes (though 75% have nothing to do with him). In them the poet is speaking as the national *vates,* voicing sentiments no doubt inspired by the Emperor but also widely endorsed by the community as a whole. Whatever private reservations Horace may have had were irrelevant. For instance, when he declared that Augustus would eventually sip nectar along with Pollux and Hercules (*Odes* 3.3.9 ff.), he never thought of adding, 'Of course, I personally think he will survive only in his fame'.

Ronald Syme, arguably the greatest Roman historian of the last sixty years, devoted most of his efforts to recovering the details of families, careers, and military campaigns. Such purely empirical research was based directly on the ancient sources, without any presuppositions. It is true that, writing in the late 1930s, he tended to see Augustus as a Roman Hitler, and (less plausibly) Maecenas as a Roman Goebbels. Yet if historians' views are actually *determined,* as opposed to *influenced,* by the power-structure of their own society, then all British historians in that period ought to have said much the same thing. They didn't. The late Don Fowler took the same disapproving line as Syme did.[14] But many, like myself, think he was mistaken.

The opposite view is also found today: that no culture has the right to make *any* moral judgments about another. To accept that particular heresy would prevent us from condemning crucifixion (remember those six thousand crosses along the Appian Way after the suppression of Spartacus); the torture of slaves to extract evidence; and, most revolting of all, the murder of human beings to provide public entertainment. So we *are* entitled to observe the shortcomings of the Roman political and social system; but in discussing individuals we can ask only whether they made the best of that system or embodied its worst features. (The glaring faults of our own society need not be enumerated.)

A more sophisticated theory states that in making moral or aesthetic assessments we cannot engage directly with the ancient world; we are obliged to approach it through the opinions of intervening centuries. It's not always clear how many centuries we must take into account; but the theory insists that we must start from our own day. Thus in 1963 H.A. Mason stated 'the royal road to Juvenal is through profound enjoyment of Eliot and Pound';[15] I wonder which contemporary writers would be thought bookish enough to serve as an equivalent? Anyhow, what if one *never* obtained profound enjoyment from Eliot or Pound? Thousands of young people who went to school and university in the 1930s and 40s studied the fourth book of the *Aeneid* without any knowledge of that pair. Their first encounter with criticism may have come when they found T.R. Glover chiding Dido for following inclination rather than duty and T.E. Page condemning Aeneas for his caddish behaviour.[16] So two well-read civilised

Victorians could take sharply different views of the same literary affair. Nor was there unanimity in the eighteenth century (see Charles James Fox's hostile opinion of Aeneas quoted by Page on p.xviii of his Introduction). In the late twentieth century my friend William S. Anderson told me, to my surprise, that he thought Dido deserved to die. He knows all the arguments as well as I do; so our disagreement cannot be resolved. That kind of point would surely be accepted by any positivist.

In the case of Horace's love-poems a clearly-defined personality is projected by the odes themselves. I accept the traditional view that from this projection the main features of the man *(qua lover)* can be inferred, with the important qualification that the *persona* is at times processed or edited for rhetorical effect. Since the same information is available to everyone, forming a picture of Horace's personality is not like composing a view of a living character. At the same time, forming a picture is not the same as experiencing a response. Most people *like* Horace, though not everybody does; and, if you are quite clear why you dislike him and your reasons are well based, no one can prove you wrong. The evidence, then, indicates that in affairs of the heart the poet was somewhat fickle, somewhat hot-tempered, attracted mainly to girls but not immune to the charms of boys, at times jealous of younger rivals, and occasionally vindictive towards ageing women.

When we apply our bi-focal method, assessing Horace's attitude to women in the *Odes* by the standards of our own day, we will probably find we are in certain respects less disapproving than our Victorian forebears. Sex outside marriage, if not universally approved of, is at least reluctantly accepted; homosexual relationships are no longer officially penalised. On the other hand, we are less likely than the Victorians to condone a class system in which women were systematically exploited by men of higher status. Moreover, given the primitive attempts at contraception, we are more likely to speculate uneasily about the hidden lives of even the wealthier and more cultivated *meretrices*: how many abortions did they have to suffer in, say, a five-year period? How often did they resort to infanticide? What miseries awaited them in old age? We do not know what Horace thought about such matters; he may, or may not, have been generous to some of his former mistresses.

There is no sign of any such concern in his poetry; but, as always, we have to bear in mind the requirements of genre.

Our own age, of course, is far from homogeneous in its opinions. There are still people, as there were in ancient Rome, who regard Ovid's erotic poetry as morally objectionable, though there can hardly be any disagreement about its cleverness. If we leave aside adultery, even people who accept all sexual relations between consenting adults usually draw the line at pederasty. Such scruples about the exploitation of the disadvantaged and the young cannot be proved correct in the manner of a geometric theorem; but they can be defended not just with reference to the principles of Christianity but also within the value-system of classical humanism.

I have been maintaining, then, that in the study of Horace's *Odes* some facts can be established by empirical argument; in other cases various degrees of probability can be attained (even post-moderns, who accuse the positivists of dogmatism, often try to persuade us that view X is better than view Y). Finally, there will be cases where, after all the arguments have been presented and exhausted, subjective responses will remain unaltered. I therefore recommend neither pure absolutism nor pure relativism, neither pure dogmatism nor pure scepticism, but a rational mixture of all four. I believe Horace would have agreed.

Related material:

The Satires of Horace (Cambridge, 1966; repr. Bristol, 1982 and 1994).

'Horace' in E.J. Kenney and W.V. Clausen (eds) *The Cambridge History of Classical Literature*, vol. 2 (Cambridge, 1982) 370-404.

Themes in Roman Satire (London, 1986; repr. Bristol, 1998) 132-42.

Horace, Epistles *Book II and* Epistle to the Pisones (Ars Poetica) (Cambridge, 1989).

'Horace as a Moralist' in N. Rudd (ed.) *Horace 2000* (London, 1993) 64-88.

A Commentary on Horace, Odes *Book III* by R.G.M. Nisbet and Niall Rudd (Oxford, 2004)

4 Achilles or Agamemnon?
Horace, *Epistle* 1.2.13

[From *Classical Philology* 75 (1980) 68-9]

Antenor censet belli praecidere causam:
quid Paris? ut salvus regnet vivatque beatus,
cogi posse negat. Nestor componere lites
inter Peliden festinat et inter Atriden:
hunc amor, ira quidem communiter urit utrumque

Antenor proposes at a stroke to remove the cause of the war.
And what is Paris's answer? He declares that nothing will induce him
to reign in safety and live in happiness! Nestor is anxious
to settle the quarrel of Peleus' son with the son of Atreus:
one is ravaged by passion and both alike by anger.

(*Epistles* 1.2.9-13)

Antenor proposes to end the war by having Helen sent home (*Iliad* 7.350-51). Paris (Alexander) refuses to agree, though he offers to hand over treasure that he had brought from Greece (357-64). Earlier Nestor had tried to mediate in the quarrel between Achilles and Agamemnon (*Iliad* 1.275-84). The identity of *hunc* in line 13 of this epistle cannot be decided on linguistic grounds, for *hic* may refer to either the former or the latter of the two people just mentioned.[1] So we turn to the context of Nestor's intervention; and we do so with the assumption that Horace has got it right. (After all, he asks us to believe that he has just been re-reading the poem.) This in turn means that we have to do with the tug of war over Briseis. The fate of the other girl, the daughter of Chryses, has already been settled, much to Agamemnon's indignation: she is to be returned to her father (1.141-4). To restore his prestige he now insists on taking Briseis from Achilles. Although Agamemnon claims to have tender feelings for the daughter of Chryses and to rate her

even above Clytemnestra (1.112-15), there is no suggestion that
he has any positive feelings about Briseis. He demands her from
Achilles simply to assert his own superior status; and later it
appears that their partnership has never been consummated (*Iliad*
9.132-4 and 19.261-3). As for Achilles, while it is true that in
this same passage we hear virtually nothing about his attitude to
Briseis either, he does refer to her later on as his ἄλοχον θυμαρέα
('his darling wife'; 9.336) and declares that he loved her 'with
all his heart' ἐκ θυμοῦ φίλεον – (9.343). On the strength of these
phrases, moreover, Achilles became for the Romans the example
par excellence of the epic warrior as a lover. The most significant
instance is Horace, *Odes* 2.4.2-4 (*insolentem / serva Briseis niveo
colore / movit Achillem*; 'the slave-girl Briseis with her snowy
colour moved the arrogant Achilles'); but one also thinks of
Propertius 2.8.35-6; of Ovid, *Amores* 2.8.11 (*Thessalus ancillae
facie Briseidos arsit*; 'the Thessalian took fire at the beauty of the
servant Briseis'); and of *Ars Amatoria* 2.711.

We conclude, therefore, that in our passage the man in love is
Achilles. No doubt the natural thing would have been for Horace
to present Achilles as consumed by passion and Agamemnon by
anger. However, as Achilles' anger was the motif of Homer's whole
epic, that antithesis was impossible; so we hear of one (Achilles)
consumed by passion, and both of them by anger. In this context
amor is seen as a destructive emotion (so the Penguin translation's
'love' is not quite accurate). At the beginning we are reminded that
it was on account of Paris's *amor* that Greece became embroiled
in a weary struggle with a foreign country. The *Iliad* is full of the
feverish passions of foolish kings and peoples, as Horace tells
us (6-7). But after mentioning Paris, Achilles and Agamemnon,
Horace puts the blame primarily on the leaders:

> *quidquid delirant reges, plectuntur Achivi,*
> *seditione dolis scelere atque libidine et ira*
> *Iliacos intra muros peccatur et extra.*

> For every act of royal madness the Achaeans are scourged.
> Sedition, deceit, crime, lust and anger make up
> a tale of sin on either side of the Trojan wall.

> (1.2.14-16)

5 Theme and Imagery in Propertius 2.15

[From *Classical Quarterly* 32 (1982) 152-5]

A glance at P.J. Enk's commentary (Leiden, 1962) vol. 2, 212-14 will show how much dispute there has been about this poem's coherence. In the past several scholars have proposed transpositions but no scheme has won acceptance; and no modern expert advocates that procedure.[1] Another way of understanding the poem's design might be through its modes of expression – exclamation, narrative, threat, etc.[2] However, this also proves unsatisfactory; for, although a number of clear divisions can be made, the sections are too short and fragmented to be regarded as structural units. (We will find, however, that at three important points a change in the mode of expression accompanies and reinforces the divisions suggested by a different method of analysis.) A third approach might be made by following the direction of the poet's address – now to himself, now to Cynthia, now to the reader. However, it is not always clear where the divisions come; and, even when we agree on an approximation ('somewhere between line x and line y'), the break rarely coincides with a break in thought.[3] So it is worth trying instead the approach indicated by my title. In doing so we shall note half a dozen cases where the method supports one textual reading against proposed alternatives.

o me felicem! o nox mihi candida! et o tu / lectule deliciis facte beate meis! (O happy me! O night that shone for me! And O you darling bed blessed by my delight! [Loeb edn]). In this rapturous opening, with its sequence of exclamations and its allusion to Ticida,[4] the most arresting phrase is *nox candida*. Camps rightly reminds us of the practice of marking white days on the calendar; but we should not overlook the paradox of 'radiant night', especially as this sets in motion a series of antithetical images which develop through the first part of the poem and re-emerge at the end. The contrast light / dark is continued in *apposita ... lucerna / sublato lumine* ('with the lamp beside us / when the light was put out'; 3-4); then it changes to revealed / concealed in *nudatis ... papillis / tunica ... operta* ('with breasts bared, covered by her tunic'; 5-6); then to open / closed in *patefecit lapsos ocellos* ('opened my eyes which had closed'; 7) – a sequence which supports *lapsos* against O.'s *lassos*. As this last pair has to do with eyes, we are still closely in touch with the contrast light / dark; and this is confirmed by *caeco / oculi* in 11-12: *non iuvat in caeco Venerem corrumpere motu: / si nescis, oculi sunt in amore duces* ('there is no point in spoiling Venus' pleasure by concealed movements: if you need to be told, in love eyes are the guides'). The thought is then developed in a pair of *exempla* on the theme of nakedness (Paris / Helen, Endymion / Selene). If Cynthia persists in remaining clothed (*vestita*), her dress will be torn (*scissa veste*); she may even have to show bruised arms to her mother. There is no need for such demure behaviour, says the poet, no reason why she should cover her breasts. The lovers' gazing continues with *oculos satiemus* ('let us feast our eyes'; 23). And the whole motif concludes in 24: *nox tibi longa venit, ... nec reditura dies* ('a long night is coming to you, and day will not return'). Here *nox ... dies* recalls *nox ... candida* (1) – except that now the night is death and the daylight life. This contrast tells against Burman's proposal to read *quies* for *dies* in 24.

Propertius then goes on to talk of lifelong attachment; but there is no abrupt change of direction. The clause *dum nos fata sinunt* ('as long as fate allows us'; 23) has already foreshadowed the new theme; and *dies* (26) – now used in its commonest sense – momentarily disguises the fact that the opening theme is over. The syntax of *atque* (25) also indicates progression. Attachment begins as a physical image: *atque utinam <u>haerentis</u> sic nos <u>vincire catena</u> / velles, ut <u>numquam solveret</u> ulla dies*! ('and would that you might wish to bind us with a chain as we embrace that no day might ever put us asunder'). Propertius wishes that he and Cynthia could be bound together; he cites the pair of doves (with interlocking word-order) as an *exemplum* from nature: *exemplo <u>iunctae</u> tibi sint in amore columbae, / masculus et totum femina <u>coniugium</u>* ('let your model be doves linked in love, male and female, a perfect couple'; 27-8). Such love, he says (30), can have no limit. No doubt he is partly thinking of intensity but, in view of 26 (*ut numquam solveret* *ulla dies*; 'that no day may ever put us asunder') and 36 (*huius ero vivus, mortuus huius ero*; 'hers will I be in life, in death will I be hers'), one must also include the idea of time: Propertius will always be Cynthia's. The importance of this assertion is signalled and prepared for in the *adynata* (impossibilities) described in 31-44. Propertius might have concluded the theme of attachment with 36 but instead he searched for further ways of expressing what the love-partnership meant to him: *quod mihi si secum talis concedere noctes / illa velit, vitae longus et annus erit* ('If, then, she were willing grant me nights like this with her, even a year's life would be long'). In view of *illa velit* (38), *tecum* is impossible in 37. The oldest correction is *secum*. Several scholars have thought it otiose; but that is not a good reason for rejecting it, because Propertius, like Catullus, often works by accumulating emphasis. Here *secum* continues the idea of attachment – an important argument in its favour, and one which cannot be used to support the modern conjectures. Nor does any one of those conjectures seem so convincing as to impose itself for other reasons.[5] Propertius, then, claims that, if Cynthia grants him nights like this with her, a year of life will be a long period; if she grants him *many* such nights, he will live for ever; indeed a single night is enough to make a man a god – rhetorical variations on the theme of lifelong passion.

In lines 41-8 we have, as it were, a reply to the criticisms made by respectable public-spirited people – a reply which insists that a life devoted to love and wine is infinitely less harmful than a life devoted to violence and civil war. Future generations will endorse Propertius' claim: *haec certe merito poterunt laudare minores: / laeserunt nullos pocula nostra deos* ('Our wine-cups never offended any gods'). Some editors (such as Camps and Hanslik)[6] have been dissatisfied with *pocula* (48) and have printed Fontein's *proelia* instead. This provides an excellent contrast with the civil wars just mentioned in 43-6, whereas 'our wine cups' as opposed to 'other people's warfare' is admittedly weak. However, if we go back to 42 (*et pressi multo membra iacere mero*; '[if anyone wished] to lie with his limbs weighed down with much wine'), we find a reference to wine and also, by implication, to a dining couch. So lines 47 and 48, with *pocula*, would hark back to 41-2 and so provide a frame for the whole section, just as *nox ... dies*

(24) recalled *nox ... candida* (1). Supporters of Fontein can fairly
point out that *proelia* would link up with the *rixa* described earlier
(3-6); but that argument is balanced by the fact that *pocula*, as we
shall see in a moment, provides an equally impressive link with
what follows.

In line 49 Propertius turns to Cynthia again, urging her to make
the most of love and life while it is still possible. But that is not
what he says. He says: *tu modo, dum lucet, fructum ne desere
vitae*! So, instead of putting the more obvious *dum licet* (while it
is possible'), which Palmer and Housman both wanted to restore,
he recalled the opening images by writing *dum lucet,* ('while it is
light').[7] He also provided an original version of *carpe diem*: 'do not
leave the fruit of life (to wither on the tree)'. Then, prompted by this
idea, he added those sad and beautiful lines describing the leaves
which drop from withered garlands and float strewn (i.e. scattered
and dead) on wine cups:[8] *ac veluti folia arentis liquere corollas. /
quae passim calathis strata natare vides*. This links up with the
previous section (love and wine being better than the struggle for
power and glory) and adds the idea 'even though both ways of life
are brief and uncertain'. The choice between *pocula* and *proelia*
has now become very narrow. I think myself that *pocula* is just
superior, though, even if the balance is equally poised, *pocula*
should still be retained; for the text should be changed only if the
editor is convinced that the conjecture is an improvement. In the
last line (*forsitan includet crastina fata dies*, 'tomorrow's day will
perhaps close our allotted span') *fata* and *dies* recall the slightly
different *fata* and *dies* of 23-4; and *includet* brings us back to the
series developed in 1-24. Therefore, although exact parallels may
be hard to find, the word should not be altered to *inducet* (the
reading preferred by Burman and Ayrmann).

The main divisions of the poem, then, fall at lines 24, 40, and 48.
These divisions coincide with the new wish (*atque utinam*, 25), the
new conditionals (*si cuperent* etc., 41 ff.), and the final exhortation
(*tu ne desere*, 49). There are four related themes: (1) recollections
of and reflections on an experience of rapturous love; (2) a wish
that the relationship may last for ever; (3) a justification of *amor*
in contrast to the life of political engagement; (4) an exhortation to
make the most of the present. Each theme is conveyed and enforced

by an appropriate set of images: (1) light / dark, open / closed etc.; (2) lifelong attachment; (3) passion and wine as opposed to the desolation of war; (4) light, ripeness and love contrasted with darkness, withering and death. According to Butler and Barber, 'the elegy is far from being perfect in point of form, and there are repetitions in the argument'.[9] – a harsh verdict. With a lover's hopefulness (touching and transient) Propertius sees a night of radiant pleasure as analogous to a lifetime of love surrounded by the darkness of death. As in music, the repetitions are part of the form – and hence part of the meaning. If the result is a beautiful and memorable poem, perfection can be left to look after itself.

Related Material:

'Pound and Propertius' in *The Classical Tradition in Operation* (Toronto, 1994) 117-50 and appendix.

6 Echo and Narcissus: a Study in Duality

[From *Classical Views* 30 (1986) 43-8]

In Ovid, *Metamorphoses* 3.339-510 the poet brings together the stories of Echo and Narcissus. Echo, in love with Narcissus and rejected by him, pines away to become a disembodied voice (339-401). Subsequently Narcissus, following a prayer from a similarly rejected lover, falls in love with his own reflection and pines away himself – to be visited at the moment of his death by Echo (402-510).

One could start from the probability, noted by several commentators, that Ovid was the first to bring Echo (auditory reflection) into relation with Narcissus (visual reflection). This brilliant innovation had also a psychological dimension; for, since Echo was pure otherness and Narcissus pure selfhood, neither represented a complete form of human personality.

Asked if the attractive boy would reach old age, the prophet Tiresias answered *si se non noverit* ('if he does not come to know himself'; 348) – an odd inversion of the Delphic 'know thyself', which was usually a recipe for survival. Yet inversion, like correspondence and illusion, is at the heart of the story. The notes that follow try to show how these phenomena are conveyed by certain stylistic features which, though common enough in the *Metamorphoses*, and indeed elsewhere in Ovid, seem to occur here with exceptional frequency. Taken together, they show Ovid at his most ingenious; and they ensure that, instead of feeling sad at the death of a beautiful boy, we will be delighted by the poet's playfulness and athleticism.

In the line *sed fuit in tenera tam dura superbia forma* (354), Teirisias' hint of coming tragedy is strengthened by *superbia* ('arrogance'), which suggests the Greek idea of *hybris*. Narcissus' *dura superbia* ('harsh arrogance') is contained within his *tenera forma* ('soft body') in the chiastic pattern of adjective(1), adjective (2),

69

noun (2), noun (1). On either side of 354 come lines which almost repeat each other: *multi illum iuvenes, multae cupiere puellae* ('many young men, many girls desired him') and *nulli illum iuvenes, nullae tetigere puellae* ('no young men, no girls touched him'). Apart from *multi / nulli*, the difference lies in the verbs *cupiere* and *tetigere* – a crucial distinction in the tale that follows.

The story of Echo's past begins in 356-8: *aspicit hunc ... vocalis nymphe ... resonabilis Echo* (a talkative nymph, resounding Echo, caught sight of him'); when the main story is resumed, *aspicit* is taken up by *vidit* (371). Echo's epithet *resonabilis* is the first of many 'reciprocal' words; it was apparently coined by Ovid as a play on the meaning of her name, which consisted of two very similar vowels (ἠχεῖν 'eh kane').[1] Initially she possessed a full vocal and physical presence but her voice was destined to be first truncated and then disembodied, *vox* ('voice') without *corpus* ('body') representing an aural version of shadow without substance. Her first punishment was incurred by detaining Juno when the goddess was about to surprise a nymph lying *sub Iove* (363) – 'in the open air' or 'beneath Jupiter'. Like other puns, this has a single aural, but a double semantic, element. It is both one and two. As a punishment, her voice is reduced to an echo – an idea conveyed in two different ways: *in fine loquendi / ingeminat voces auditaque verba reportat* ('she reproduces the final words of a speech and repeats the expressions she has heard'; 369).[2]

Echo's falling in love with Narcissus is conveyed in a chiasmus: *incaluit, sequitur ... quoque magis sequitur, flamma propiore calescit* ('she caught fire, followed ... and the more she followed the closer the flame that fired her') – a pattern representing a kind of verbal mirror-image. Again, in 376-8, her nature does not allow her to begin but does allow her to send back *sua verba*, her own words (in that they come from her mouth) but they are not really her own.[3]

In 380 the imperfect dialogue begins. Narcissus' enquiry *ecquis adest?* ('Is anyone there?') is confirmed by Echo's *adest*. Then *voce 'veni!' magna clamat: vocat illa vocantem* ('"Come here" he shouts aloud; she calls the caller'; 382). The two v-sounds at the beginning are answered by two at the end – an effect which cannot be reproduced in English. In 383-4 the echo is conveyed in a different way: 'Why are you running away from me?' he said, and got back[4] as many words as he had spoken (the correlatives *tot / quot*). Narcissus is *deceptus imagine vocis* ('deluded by the reflection of the answering voice'; 385) – a phrase which fore-shadows the climax of the story. He asks Echo to meet him – *huc coeamus* ('here let's get together'). She answers *coeamus* (let's get together') – another double entendre. She moves forward to embrace him, whereupon he exclaims *ante ... emoriar quam sit tibi copia nostri* ('I would die before I would let you possess me'; 391). In her answer poor Echo makes another *faux pas*, 'I would let you possess me' (392). Ashamed at being rejected, she now lives in lonely caves. The witty aetiological point anticipates her metamorphosis, which is caused, as with Narcissus, by passion consuming the body (395-401). In the end, unlike good children, she is heard and not seen.

We now return to Narcissus – a figure of the Hippolytus type. One of his lovers prays for revenge (another kind of reciprocation): *sic amet ipse licet, sic non potiatur amato* ('It is right that he himself should love like this, and like this fail to gain possession of his beloved'; 405). Here *amet* is answered *by amato* but contradicted by *non potiatur*; there is also a subsidiary musical effect whereby *(am)et* is echoed by *(lic)et* and *(poti)atur* is picked up by *(am)ato*. The prayer is heard by Nemesis, goddess of retribution.

The landscape provides a setting for the climactic scene. The spring is clear and silvery – just like a mirror. Its surface has remained unruffled by grazing-men (*pastores*) or their grazed (*pastae*) goats. Grass grows around it, ready to receive a flower. Like Narcissus himself, the place is isolated and without warmth (412). The young hunter is attracted by its appearance (*faciem*) – a word soon to describe another source of attraction ('face'). While he is eager to slake his thirst, a different kind of thirst increases; for he is captivated by the image (*imagine*) of the beautiful shape that he sees, mistaking shadow (*umbra*) for substance (*corpus*). The twin stars at which he gazes are his own eyes, the reflection here being conveyed by apposition – *geminum, sua lumina, sidus* (420). In the boy before him he notices the beautiful combination of red and white (interlocking word-order), which anticipates the coming metamorphosis. He unwittingly desires himself; and the admiration is mutual: *qui probat ipse probatur* (425). The agent / victim simultaneously ignites and burns – transitive *accendit* balanced by intransitive *ardet*. But, as he still fails to recognise himself, his destruction does not begin yet (as Tiresias predicted).

Ovid then turns to the cheating effect of the spring, using this time the non-chiastic correspondence adjective (1), adjective (2), noun (1), noun (2) – *irrita fallaci dedit oscula fonti* ('how often did he give futile kisses to the deceitful spring!'). The same illusion has two effects – mocking his eyes and at the same time urging him on (431). Now the poet's mode changes from narrative to self address: 'Poor dupe, why pursue a fleeing image (*simulacra*)? … What you see is but the shadow of a reflection (*imaginis umbra*); it has no substance of its own; it came with you and stays while you stay; it will leave when you leave – if you can'.

Narcissus now begins his self-pitying lament. The passage is again full of verbal correspondences: *et placet et video: sed quod videoque placetque / non tamen invenio* ('It pleases and I see it; but what I see and what pleases me I fail to find'). Then another piece of word-play. When Narcissus calls the figure before him *puer unice* (454), he means the boy is 'matchless', though the other sense of 'unique' is available to the reader. Whichever sense we apply, is Narcissus right or wrong? In any case, his vanity remains unshaken. More replications follow: 'When I smile, you smile back … when I nod, you return the gesture'.

Then suddenly the fatal recognition (the tragic *anagnorisis*): *iste ego sum!* ('I am that fellow'; 463). At once the illusion vanishes: *nec me mea fallit imago* ('nor does my reflection deceive me'). But the discovery brings a new dilemma in which one possible course of action is cancelled by another: *roger anne rogem? quid deinde rogabo* ('Should I be asked or should I ask? In that case what shall I ask?'; 465). Satisfaction has brought only hunger: *inopem me copia fecit*. Here the antithesis is conveyed by etymology.[5] One who previously delighted in his body now craves separation; he has a strange desire (*votum novum*): the absence of his beloved; and he wishes that the latter might live longer. As it is, *duo concordes anima moriemur in una* ('We two kindred spirits will die in a single breath'; 472).

As he says this, Narcissus' tears ruffle the surface of the water, his image breaks up and his death begins. Now he is willing to gaze without touching; but it is too late for that. He pounds his chest, reddening the marble-like flesh. The colour, which is of course that of blood, shows that feeling has at last come to one who was like a statue (419). And the combination of red and white foreshadows his transformation into a flower.

Echo now returns for the last time, still repeating what he says. When he cries *heu frustra dilecte puer!* ('alas, dear boy, loved in vain!'; 500). she takes up his words; but they now reflect her emotion, not his.[6] There remains just the mutual farewell: *vale! / vale!* The bright eyes close, still admiring the beauty of their owner.

The tale could have ended there; but, as so often, Ovid thinks of one further stroke of cleverness. The scene switches to Hades; and there is Narcissus, still admiring himself in a pool of the river Styx (504-5). His sisters, the water-nymphs, mourn; the dryads mourn (*planxere / planxerunt*); and appropriately (though surely she remains in the world above) Echo repeats their mourning (*plangentibus adsonat*). Up above, Narcissus' body has disappeared; in its place is a flower with white petals surrounding a yellow centre.

Narcissus and Echo is, of course, one of the great 'significant' myths. Thanks to the work of Frederick Goldin and Louise Vinge, we can follow its ramifications from antiquity, through the world of the troubadours, and up to the nineteenth century.[7] Such investigations are endlessly fascinating and they provide the western reader with a cross-section of his own cultural history. However, Ovid's version will not be superseded. Its permanence has to do with the coruscating style which we have been studying. When the performance is over and the smiling magician has stepped off the platform, we are left delighted – but also slightly bemused. To restore our confidence we turn to our neighbour and assure him that it's all done by mirrors.

Related Material:

'Ovid and the Augustan Myth' in *Lines of Enquiry* (Cambridge, 1976) 1-31.

'Pyramus and Thisbe in Ovid and Shakespeare' in D. West and T. Woodman (eds) *Creative Imitation and Latin Literature* (Cambridge, 1979) 173-93

'Daedalus and Icarus' in C. Martindale (ed.) *Ovid Renewed* (Cambridge, 1988) 21-53.

7 The Topicality of Juvenal

[Previously unpublished]

Juvenal may be regarded as topical in two respects. First, he provides an interesting illustration of the current dispute between traditional empirics, who are sometimes accused of assuming that every question ought to have one right answer, and post-modern relativists, who often seem to imply that there is no right answer to anything. Secondly, at the end of the paper I shall note how some of Juvenal's complaints about ancient Rome are highly relevant to our own experience.

I suggest, then, that we begin by standing, as it were, beside Juvenal, entering into his feelings of indignation and disgust. After that, we will move over to the side of his victims, noting some of the charges that they may well have regarded as unfair and offensive. In the third part I shall step back and attempt to see Juvenal and his victims together in the context of Roman society between, say, AD 50 and 150. This, I hope, will bring out how little his contemporaries were to blame for the conditions he describes. (In that respect his satire has a tragic dimension.)

Finally, I shall put the Romans and ourselves together, opposing the idea, usually associated with Moses Finley, that the ancients are 'desperately foreign'. Juvenal, after all, claimed to be dealing with what folks have been doing since the flood – their prayers, fears, anger, pleasure, joys and their to-ing and fro-ing (*Sat.*1.81-6). Are we really so very different?

The first satire begins with a condemnation of poetry-recitals: they have become a social ritual; they concentrate on irrelevant genres like sentimental elegy and mythological epic; and they are an inexcusable waste of time. Juvenal's protest is a retaliation in kind for all the boredom he has endured, in that it, too, is delivered at a recital. There is no exact modern equivalent; but I recall a slightly jaundiced colleague observing, in connection

75

with academic conferences and their lectures, that eventually the people you want to see and hear are outnumbered by those whom you wish to avoid.

The poem goes on to say, in effect, why shouldn't I write? I've had the requisite education:

> *et nos ergo manum ferulae subduximus, et nos*
> *consilium dedimus Sullae, privatus ut altum*
> *dormiret.*

> I too have snatched my hand from under the cane; I too
> have tendered advice to Sulla to retire from public life
> and sleep the sleep of the just. (1.15-17)

Note how the education is described: it consists of learning fanciful speeches by heart, and being caned for one's misdemeanours.

But why write satire? The answer, in brief, is that poetry should focus on life; but life is vicious; so one has to write satire.

> *cum tener uxorem ducat spado, Mevia Tuscum*
> *figat aprum et nuda teneat venabula mamma,*
> *patricios omnis opibus cum provocet unus*
> *quo tondente gravis iuveni mihi barba sonabat*
> *cum pars Niliacae plebis, cum verna Canopi*
> *Crispinus Tyrias umero revocante lacernas*
> *ventilet aestivum digitis sudantibus aurum,*
> *nec sufferre queat maioris pondera gemmae,*
> *difficile est saturam non scribere.*

> When a soft eunuch marries, and Mevia takes to sticking
> a Tuscan boar, with a spear beside her naked breast,
> when a fellow who made my stiff young beard crunch with
> his clippers
> can challenge the whole upper class with his millions single-
> handed,
> when Crispinus, a blob of Nilotic scum, bred in Canopus,
> hitches a cloak of Tyrian purple onto his shoulder
> and flutters a simple ring of gold on his sweaty finger
> (in summer he cannot bear the weight of a heavy stone),
> it's hard *not* to write satire.   1.22-30)

The common feature of married eunuch, pig-sticking lady, millionaire barber, and powerful Egyptian is that they are all seen as grotesque violations of the natural order. The form of the sentence is that when *a*, *b*, *c* and *d* happen one has to cry out in protest. We now stand in the street watching a parade of successful undesirables. The form remains the same: who could contain himself when *e*, *f* and *g* come by (a grossly over-rich lawyer, a political informer and a number of gigolos)? Then how can I suppress my fury at the sight of *h* and *i* (a guardian who has prostituted his ward and a fraudulent provincial governor)? Is not satire demanded when *j* and *k* are active (a husband who accepts money from his wife's lover and a worthless young aristocrat who expects a military command)? Shall I not fill my notebooks when *l* and *m* happen (when a forger makes a fortune and a wife poisons her husband)? Then, summing up:

> *si natura negat, facit indignatio versum*
> *qualemcumque potest, quales ego vel Cluvienus*

> If nature fails, then indignation generates verse,
> doing the best it can, like mine – or like Cluvienus'.
>   (1.79-80)

Cluvienus, presumably some second-rate ranter, has vanished into oblivion. The second half of the poem centres on the kinds of people that now enjoy money, status, and power. It is clear that, unlike Horace who wants to influence people's moral awareness, Juvenal rarely has such thoughts, and certainly no hopes of general reform:

> *nil erit ulterius quod nostris moribus addat*
> *posteritas, eadem facient cupientque minores;*
> *omne in praecipiti vitium stetit. utere velis,*
> *totos pande sinus.*

> There'll be no scope for new generations to add to our record
> of rottenness; they'll be just the same in their deeds and desires.
> Every evil has reached a precipice. Up with the sail, then,
> crowd on every stitch of canvas.   (1.147-50)

The large ship under sail is a symbol of the grand rhetorical style.

Satire 2 is about male homosexuals who dress and talk like austere
moralists. Their hypocrisy is seen in their household decoration:

> The nearest any of them comes to culture
> is to buy a copy of Aristotle's head or Pittacus' portrait,
> or to have an original bust of Cleanthes[1] placed on the side-
> board   (2.5-7)

At one point Juvenal abandons invective in favour of a teasing
sarcasm, which he puts into the mouth of a woman called Laronia,
who is no better than she ought to be but is at least 'straight':[2]

> When one of those grim-faced ascetics was crying
> 'O Julian law,[3]
> where are you now? Wake up!'Laronia couldn't endure it,
> and answered thus with a smile: 'It's a happy age that has you, sir,
> to reform its morals; Rome had better clean itself up!
> A third Cato has dropped from the sky! But seriously, tell me –
> Where did you get that lovely scent that is wafted in waves
> from your hairy neck? You mustn't be shy about naming the
> shop'.   (2.36-42)

Satire 3 reverts to the manifold evils of the big city: the destruction
of beauty in the name of progress; the dangers of fire and falling
houses; the squalor of rack-rent lodgings; the crippling cost of
living; the noise of traffic even at night; the continual burglaries
and muggings. A special target is presented by immigrants from
Greece and Asia minor. Their language, dress, musical instruments
and names are no less obnoxious than their sycophancy, lechery,
hypocrisy and dishonesty. They are simply a pollutant blown in by
the wind or washed in like sewage. Life for the good old Roman
has become unbearable. Hence Juvenal's friend Umbricius, who
delivers much of the indictment, is now on the point of leaving.

Satire 6, the longest and most elaborate piece, is an attack on women
– an attack so violent and unrelenting that many have taken it as
proof of an almost pathological misogyny. In reply it can be pointed
out that in the other fifteen poems Juvenal's targets are male; and
it may indeed be that, like Hamlet, Juvenal is proclaiming 'Man
delights not me, no, nor women neither'. Yet *Sat.* 6 differs from

the rest in that, while men are exposed as greedy, vainglorious, lecherous and dishonest, women are attacked solely in their capacity as females. Perhaps this was inevitable. Since upper-class women's activities were virtually limited to private life, it followed that their delinquencies had to be domestic. However, Juvenal narrowed the restriction still further by concentrating on upper-class *wives*. It is worth adding that while Juvenal castigates women for being unfaithful to their husbands, he never takes men to task for betraying their wives. A man may be ridiculed for adulterous behaviour but it is always on prudential grounds – the disproportionate cost, the dreadful inconvenience, the danger of detection and the consequent disgrace. In this respect Juvenal was in line with the other satirists. One has to bear in mind that in a strictly patrilinear society, without reliable contraception, the father had to rely on the fidelity of his wife in order to be sure that the child who would inherit his name and property was really his. Hence the double standard prevailed.

From the little said so far it will be clear that Juvenal's satire, with its onslaught on race, class and gender, is a veritable bible of political incorrectness. Yet it is more than that; for it also attacks the rich and aristocratic. The former are selfish, gluttonous and philistine; in every case their wealth is based, not on ability, but on crime (1.75-6). As for the aristocracy, a patrician name really means nothing. Moral excellence is the only true nobility: *nobilitas sola est atque unica virtus* ('virtue is the one and only nobility'; 8.20). This might sound like a modern egalitarian sentiment, but Juvenal is really implying, not that the aristocracy should be abolished, but rather that the present lot are a disgrace to their ancestors. At one point the poet imagines the Emperor's representative enjoying a social evening:

Send your lieutenant, Caesar,
to Ostia, send him. But look for him first in a roomy bodega.
You will find him lying cheek by jowl beside an assassin,
enjoying the company of sailors, thieves, and runaway slaves,
on his right a hangman and a fellow who hammers coffins together,
on his left the silent drums of a sprawling eunuch priest.
(8.171-6)

The idea of degeneracy might seem to imply that in itself the aristocratic class had once been a good thing. But Juvenal does not go in for such positive affirmations; and there is a characteristic sting in the tail:

> However far back you care to go in tracing your name,
> the fact remains that your clan began in a haven for outlaws.
> The first of all your line, whatever his name may have been,
> was either a shepherd – or else a thing I'd rather not mention.
>
>   (8.272-5)

In other words he was a crook. For Rome is supposed to have started as a sanctuary for men on the run. In terms of tact, that is the equivalent of Barry Humphreys telling some old Australian families that their ancestors were convicts.

So far we have been taking Juvenal on his own terms, sharing his scorn, enjoying his vivid scenes and savouring the extravagance of his satirical wit. All those features are surely objective and uncontroversial, as the positivists would say. What we have not done, however, is to examine his logic or to question the fairness of his judgements.

For that we must move to another viewpoint, taking our stand beside the writer's victims. This procedure acknowledges that, as the post-moderns insist, there can be more than one response to Juvenal's allegations. At the moment, however, we are going to discuss *ancient* responses; and that would be deprecated by post-moderns; for they believe that the claim to see the world through the eyes of the ancients is a historicist's illusion. Let us see if the attempt is really so futile.

Going back to *Sat.* 1, we recall that recitations were the standard way of publicising poetry; they were not *by definition* excruciatingly boring occasions. As for the genres dismissed by Juvenal, elegy had its own strengths and mythological epic could convey a deeper criticism of life than satire. (One thinks of the *Aeneid*, though admittedly Juvenal had more recent work in his sights.) The rhetorical education mocked in those lines had existed for well over two centuries. It was designed to train a governing class, not by making youngsters write essays, but by teaching them to speak effectively – an ability central to a public career at the bar, in the senate, in provincial government or in military councils. It was, in fact, an efficient system.[4]

As for the eunuch in line 22, his inability to father children was no reason why he had to forego the comforts of marriage (anyway, adoption was a common procedure). Equally there was no reason why a barber should not make money (though in the case alluded to the man seems not to have acquired his fortune by cutting hair).[5] Consider now the bitter words of the departing Umbricius:

> Let Artorius live there and Catulus too;
> let those remain who are able to turn black into white,
> happily winning contracts for temple, river, and harbour,
> for draining flooded land, and carrying corpses to the pyre.
>
> (1.29-32)

Observe how the accusation of dishonesty (turning black into white) spills over, so as to discredit the essential occupations of contractor and undertaker – sheer social prejudice.

As for Greeks and other immigrants, their presence in Rome was not illegal. It was often involuntary, in that many had been brought there as prisoners and slaves. Many of those had been emancipated and finished their days as freedmen. Their descendants were born and bred in the capital and knew no other home. Others came as refugees, others to find jobs; and over the centuries some of these people made an enormous contribution to Rome's commercial and cultural life.[6] Thanks to the snobbery of the senatorial class, many occupations were open to newcomers in trade; also in teaching, medicine and the arts; at the top of the scale a number of Greeks held important posts in public life. In the case of women, many immigrants or their daughters worked in the clothes-trade (making, dyeing or mending), or in laundries. Others were active as bakers, hairdressers, shop-assistants, waitresses and barmaids. A few with special skills ran businesses or found employment as clerks or midwives.[7] Juvenal gives the absurd impression that most female immigrants were involved in prostitution. Another of Juvenal's targets was the arrogant and selfish patron. Now the patron / client relationship had developed over many centuries and, in the absence of state welfare schemes, it was a central and necessary feature

of Roman life.⁸ The client was expected to support his patron
at elections and to enhance his prestige by waiting on him at
morning salutations, escorting him down town and performing a
multitude of minor personal services. In return the patron might
provide a testimonial for a job; or he might act as a solicitor,
helping the client in a lawsuit or property deal; as a banker,
providing a loan or perhaps a dowry for the client's daughter; as a
matchmaker, finding a suitable husband or wife; as a hotel-keeper,
offering occasional accommodation; or even as publisher's agent,
arranging introductions, advertising, and recitals. Charitable gifts
ranged from a ticket for the games to an item of clothing or even
a piece of property. To present the patron as invariably cold and
insensitive or, like Virro in *Sat.* 5, as actually malevolent, was
a distortion of the truth; for a kindly patron, one need look no
further than the younger Pliny.

I am arguing, then, that although there is no proof, it is only
common sense to assume that *some* members of these categories
would have been annoyed with Juvenal. However, the picture
now becomes more complex. After reading *Satires* 5 and 7, some
patrons might have been implacably hostile; some Roman matrons
might never have forgiven him for *Sat.* 6. Others might have had
mixed opinions. Soldiers could have applauded the remarks about
homosexuals in *Sat.* 2, while resenting the imputations against the
army in *Sat.*16. Rich lawyers might have disliked the recurrent
attacks on wealth, yet welcomed the insulting remarks on Greek
immigrants in *Sat.* 3. So no simple account is available about the
satires' reception.

This brings us to a few problematic features of Juvenal's style.
We are told that every rich man's wealth is based on crime (*Sat.*
1.75); that a virtuous wife is simply not to be found (*Sat.* 6.19-20)
and that every street contains a Clytemnestra (6.656). Elsewhere it
is proclaimed that there are barely seven honest men in the world
(*Sat.* 13.26-7). Such hyperbole raises doubts about the writer's
seriousness. Sometimes he refuses to distinguish degrees of evil.
Thus we hear of a woman who thrashes her next-door neighbour
because his dog barks (*Sat.* 6.415-18), then later vomits in the
presence of her guests. Even more offensive – yes, *more* offensive
– is the blue-stocking who defends the unfortunate Dido, compares

Virgil and Homer, and dominates the conversation (6.434-40).
Such passages make us pause.

Perhaps most disconcerting of all is the handful of passages
where the speaker seems to undermine his own moral integrity.
In *Sat.* 3, for example, Umbricius complains bitterly about Greek
flatterers but then adds, 'We, of course, can pay identical compli-
ments; yes, but / *they* are *believed*' (3.92-3). So what has happened
to the carefully built-up contrast between insincere Greek and
old-fashioned honest Roman? Or again, when moaning about a
client's duties, Umbricius says, in effect, 'What's the point of
getting up before dawn to dance attendance on some rich old lady,
if you're beaten to it by a senior judge?' (3.127-30). Such cases, to
be sure, are very rare but they raise awkward questions about the
satirist's moral seriousness.

One answer is that, since Juvenal was primarily a joker, he did
not wish to direct our attention to real situations.[9] Yet this leaves
too much out. Here is a country scene from the same satire:

> On grand occasions,
> when a public holiday is being held in a grassy theatre,
> and the well-known farce, so long awaited, returns to the
> platform,
> when the peasant child in its mother's arms cowers in
> fear
> confronted by the gaping mouth of the whitened mask,
> even then you will see similar clothes being worn
> by the stalls and the rest alike; as robes of their lofty office,
> the highest officials are content to appear in plain white
> tunics.
> Here (in Rome) the style of the people's clothes is beyond
> their means. (3.172-80)

Examples of serious comment occur at all stages of Juvenal's
work: the vignette of the true poet (7.53-65); the tribute to the
non-aristocratic Cicero (8.236-41); the sombre lines on 'glorious
war' (10.133-41); the writer's simple menu (11.64-76); the
agonies of a guilty conscience (13.196-226); the importance of
parental training (14.1-85); and the noble reminder that no man
is an island:

> (Our creator) intended
> that our fellow-feeling should lead us to ask and offer help;
> to gather scattered inhabitants into communities, leaving
> the ancient woods, deserting the groves where our ancestors
> lived;
> to put up houses, placing another man's dwelling beside
> our own abode, ensuring that we all slept safe and sound
> in the knowledge that each had a friend next door; to
> shield with our weapons
> a fallen comrade or one who reeled from a shocking wound;
> to sound the call on a common trumpet; to man the turrets
> in joint defence, and fasten the gate with a single key.
>
> (15.148-58)

True, such passages usually stand in contrast to satirical material, but in themselves they do not convey rage or contempt; nor are they particularly witty. In their different ways they are all lively and effective pieces of preaching, reminding us vividly of truths we have always known. One recalls that in medieval times Juvenal was often referred to simply as *ethicus* ('the moralist').

So our assessment of Juvenal's personal attitudes cannot hope to be precise or conclusive. Some have gone so far as to maintain that we have only the mask and know nothing of the man. I think this is too pessimistic; the inconsistencies are not numerous enough or deep enough to prevent a general conception from emerging. There are also numerous indications that his antipathies were not merely humorous fantasies but were based on the realities of Roman life.

This takes us to our third standpoint. From here we view Juvenal and his targets together in their social context. Unlike Horace, Juvenal belonged to a class whose fortunes were declining. Though educated for government service, there is no sign that he ever held any official post. In his thirties his friend Martial (7.91.1) called him 'eloquent' (*disertus*), which suggests that he may have performed as a declaimer. (This meant speaking in public in a brilliant style on various set themes.) However he never enjoyed anything like the prestige of Quintilian, who was a successful barrister and a professor of rhetoric. Martial also reveals that Juvenal would pay his respects to a number of important houses (12.18.1-6). So he knew something of the life of a client. Yet he does not imply that he was on close terms with any important patron.

All this means that, while he criticised Roman life, Juvenal himself was part of it, writing as a disgruntled *rentier* within the system. Though he frequently exaggerates, there is usually a kernel of truth in what he says. Speaking of the tenement-dweller's habit of hurling broken pots out the window, he writes:

> *Respice nunc alia ac diversa pericula noctis:*
> *quod spatium tectis sublimibus unde cerebrum*
> *testa ferit, quotiens rimosa et curta fenestris*
> *vasa cadant, quanto percussum pondere signent*
> *et laedant silicem. possis ignavus haberi*
> *et subiti casus improvidus, ad cenam si*
> *intestatus eas.*

> Consider now the various other nocturnal perils:
> how far it is up to those towering floors from which a potsherd
> mashes your brains; how often leaky and broken fragments
> fall from the windows, and with what impact they strike the pavement
> leaving it chipped and shattered. You may well be regarded as slack
> and heedless of sudden disaster if you fail to make a will
> before going out to dinner.   (3.268-74)

A piece of human fantasy? Not so. Certain passages of the *Digest* show that there were laws against throwing pots in that rather basic sense.[10]

Again, Juvenal speaks of *lapsus / tectorum adsiduos* ('the continuous collapse of buildings'; 3.7-8; cf. 190-96) as if the air was always filled with the rumble of falling masonry. That, of course, is going too far. Yet the height of Roman tenements, along with their weak structure, was a constant source of worry, as it was in eighteenth-century London – and often for the same reason: builders and landlords in search of a quick profit. Fire was also a menace (3.7; cf.197-202). Everyone knows of the disastrous fire for which Nero blamed the Christians, while reputedly playing his fiddle. In the generation after Juvenal a fire destroyed 340 houses.[11]

Traffic was horrendous.[12] Seneca, who was neither a fantasist nor a joker, describes the mass of humanity ceaselessly flowing through the streets and being crushed whenever it encountered an obstacle (*De Clementia* 1.6.1); and that was during the day, when vehicular traffic was forbidden. The law had been passed long ago by Julius Caesar and (except for a couple of categories of vehicle) it was still in force.[13] This meant that at sundown the wagons and herds that had been waiting at the gates came pouring in. The resulting pandemonium, says Juvenal, made sleep impossible (3.232-5). Nothing incredible there. Again, there was no street lighting. So conditions favoured burglars and muggers. No statistics, of course, are available; but *a priori* one would expect a high level of crime in a city where there was such a gulf between rich and poor and where policing was inadequate. As usual, the rich were less concerned. They lived outside the centre and they had large numbers of attendants with torches, unlike the poor man with his guttering candle (3.283-8).

On other aspects of Roman life, a useful control is supplied by the younger Pliny, a contemporary of Juvenal but of an altogether more sanguine and complacent disposition. Several of his letters show that he valued recitations – especially those given by himself (*Epistles* 1.13.1; 7.17; and 8.12). Even he admitted that people were often reluctant to attend and that, when they did, they complained it was a waste of time (1.13.2-4). In another letter Pliny criticises those who serve one class of wine to themselves and their important guests, another to lesser friends and a third to their freedmen (2.6). That, of course, was one of the techniques of humiliation practised by the unspeakable Virro in Juvenal 5.24-37. Pliny congratulates himself on avoiding such invidious distinctions; he just serves poor wine to everyone. In general, Pliny is far more kindly disposed to foreigners. He praises the philosophers Euphrates and Artemidorus (1.10 and 3.11) and admires the eloquence of the Assyrian Isaeus (2.3), whom Juvenal mocks as 'torrential' (*Sat.* 3.74). There is also a respectful and sensitive letter (echoing Cicero, *ad Q. fratrem* 1.1) addressed to a man who is going out to govern Achaea, 'the pure and authentic Greece' (*Epistles* 8.24.2). Nevertheless, his philhellenism does not inhibit Pliny from becoming impatient at the volubility of Greek advocates (5.20.4; cf.4.9.14). Similarly his easy-going and charitable nature does not inhibit him from describing the rascally manoeuvres of Regulus in a letter (2.20) which corroborates everything Juvenal says about legacy-hunting (e.g. *Satires* 1.37-41; 4.18-19; 5.137-40; 12.93-101; and 16.54-6). Juvenal's satire, then, may be drastically selective and biased but it is not fanciful. He presents what can best be described as a faithful caricature of Roman life.

These glimpses of social history bring out another contrast with Horace. As remarked above, Horace's satire aimed to heighten the individual's moral awareness; he believed that by taking thought a person could reduce his worries and live a more contented life. But several of the phenomena attacked by Juvenal, however objectionable, were part of a huge process which had begun three centuries earlier and could not be arrested by any individual. Much of this process can be summed up in one word – Romanisation. This happened in various ways. It was sometimes done through communities: in Augustus' time citizenship was given to more than a score of Spanish towns. Or it might be done through the army: auxiliary soldiers were entitled to become citizens after 25 years' service, accounting, it seems, for 10,000 men a year. Or again, the free population was continually growing as a result of the emancipation of slaves. As a consequence of all this, in AD 212, only about eighty years after Juvenal's death, every free inhabitant of the empire was made a Roman citizen.

Extension inevitably meant dilution. Under Trajan the senate was already 34.2% provincial; under Hadrian that figure increased to 43.6%. Of that provincial element 34.6% was from the East under Trajan, under Hadrian 46.5%.[14] One must also take account of the numerous non-senatorial officials of foreign origin who were appointed by the emperor to important secretaryships, procurator-ships and so on. All this reflects the growing importance of the Greek East.[15] The most famous examples of the successful Greek were probably Plutarch, Dio Chrysostom, Epictetus and Lucian. Plutarch, about twenty years older than Juvenal, belonged to a distinguished Greek family. On coming to Rome, he had friends in common with Tacitus and Pliny. He was honoured by Trajan;

and Hadrian made him Procurator of Greece. Dio Chrysostom, rhetorician and philosopher, who was some fifteen years older than Juvenal, enjoyed the friendship of Trajan, whom he praised in several of his speeches. He was not dishonourable; but when he boasts that he has 'known the houses and tables of the rich, and not of private persons only but of powerful officials and kings' (*Oration* 7.66), we believe him. Epictetus, Juvenal's contemporary, became a friend of Hadrian. In his Manual he advises the ambitious reader to prepare for rebuffs: 'When you go to see an influential man, imagine that ... you will be shut out and the door slammed in your face' (33.13). Clearly Epictetus, a former slave, had survived such indignities and outstripped most of his Roman competitors. The essayist Lucian, half a century younger than Juvenal, was appointed to an important post in Egypt. However, in his *Nigrinus* and *Dependent Scholars*, he confirms much of what Juvenal says about Greeks on the make. These four men, then, represent Greek influence in the highest quarters – and they are not the only examples. The emperor Hadrian himself was so devoted to Greek pursuits that some people referred to him as a *Graeculus* ('Greekling') – a term used by Juvenal as one of contempt (3.78).

Sir Ronald Syme, one of the most distinguished Roman histor-ians of the last century, claimed that 'Juvenal does not attack any person or category that commands influence in his own time'.[16] That is certainly true of persons. Juvenal himself says he will attack only the dead (*Sat.* 1.170-71). What he does, in fact, is to use notorious characters from the recent past (and earlier) to illustrate current crimes and vices. However, he does attack Greeks; and within that category there were substantial numbers who did command influence. What would cultivated Greeks, important and less important, have felt about *Sat.* 3? Surely not all of them would have been ignorant of Juvenal.

We have been concentrating on the Greek East; but Spain, too, demands attention. To start at the top, the emperors Trajan, Hadrian and Marcus Aurelius all had Spanish roots. If we think of teachers, rhetoricians and writers, then Seneca, Lucan, Martial and Quintilian all came from there. In Gaul, too, there were influential schools – in Marseilles, Autun, Toulouse, Bordeaux and other centres.[17] With a mixture of resentment and grudging respect, Juvenal says: *Gallia causidicos docuit facunda Britannos* ('smooth-tongued Gaul has been coaching British barristers'; 15.111). In the case of Africa the big names come a bit later – Apuleius, Tertullian, Lactantius and Augustine. Yet Juvenal (7.148) can already call Africa *nutricula causidicorum* ('the nurse-maid of shysters'). From these countries, too, we may be sure that many intellectuals had made their way to Rome. Not all would have had private means; so how were they to maintain themselves? After all, there was no book-trade, as we understand it, to provide contracts and royalties. The only answer was patronage.

Unfortunately, while writers were becoming more numerous, rich and cultivated, patrons were becoming rarer.[18] Patricians of republican ancestry had failed to reproduce themselves. At the death of Domitian (AD 96) such men made up only 1% of the senate. In the second century emperors had to ennoble plebeian families. 'After the reign of Septimius Severus (AD 193-211), senators were rare whose rank went back more than one or two generations'.[19] According to Juvenal, hopes for patronage centred entirely on Caesar (*Sat.* 7.1), that is to say, on Hadrian himself. This points to a further problem. Such patrons who did exist could not run the risk of rivalling the emperor. Other sources of employment were not abundant. Thanks to Hadrian's peaceful foreign policy, fewer careers were available in the army. At home, even if commerce had been able to absorb these educated men, there was a massive inhibition on the part of the upper class against engaging directly in trade. Any manual work was ruled out. So the difficulty remained. Even the position of successful writers was becoming precarious. According to Juvenal (*Sat.* 7.82-7), Statius' popularity did not bring him wealth;[20] and Martial (11.3) complains that, although his verses are read from Britain to the Black Sea, 'his purse knows nothing about it'. Again, the general point is confirmed by Pliny: after paying Martial's fare back to Spain, he adds, 'In the past it was normal to reward poets who had praised individuals or cities with offices or with money; but in our day this was one of the first practices to become obsolete' (*Epistles* 3.21.3).

From our standpoint, then, it is clear that Juvenal was caught in a trap. Not an actual poverty trap, perhaps, if poverty is taken to mean destitution, but certainly a trap which held him within the confines of the shabby genteel. Perhaps this was not wholly surprising; for what patron would have assisted a man who castigated patrons with such bitterness? Even if some tolerant patron had been inclined to help, the idea might not have appealed to his wife. An analogous trap constrained educated women. A career in law, government or finance simply did not exist. There was nothing available in the higher levels of administration. Midwifery was a working-class occupation and there were no opportunities available in teaching. It followed that, if a cultivated well-off lady could not find fulfilment within her traditional sphere (home, family and polite accomplishments), she was condemned to frivolity.

From this external perspective Juvenal's satire can be seen as tragic. The evils which he exposed were real; and yet they were, in a sense, inevitable and incurable. Ironically, they came in large part as a result of Rome's spectacular success. And Juvenal knew it: *nunc patimur longae pacis mala, saevior armis / luxuria incubuit victumque ulciscitur orbem* ('Now we are paying for a lengthy peace; more deadly than armies, luxury has fallen upon us, avenging the world we conquered'; *Sat.* 6.292-3). In other words, the life which Juvenal and his fellow-Romans had to endure was to a large extent the nemesis of empire.

Our final position is alongside Juvenal and his fellow-citizens. Here we think first, perhaps, of the famous *Satire* 10 on the futility of aspirations or, as Dr Johnson called it, 'The Vanity of Human Wishes'. Like Johnson, we may reject the bleakness of its final message;[21] and yet the poem may be seen as a salutary corrective to the attitude which expects life (even the lives of the great) to be easy and pleasant. However, the relevance of Juvenal's satires goes much further than this. Let us list briefly the liberal aims (whether Christian or humanist) which have been cherished increasingly in the west over the last two hundred years: (1) to reduce unfairness resulting from birth, wealth, religion or class; (2) to reduce suspicion of other races; (3) to reduce unfair discrepancies between the roles of men and women; (4) to reduce the disadvantages of the handicapped; (5) to reduce antagonism towards homosexuals. Even if we embrace all these ideals, we may still see the force of many of Juvenal's complaints.

In *Sat.* 3 he points to an attractive area outside the Porta Capena which has now been ruined by modernisation (3.12-20). We can all cite examples. Some years ago, when I was studying the myth of Daedalus and Icarus, I visited the old town of Malmesbury; there, in the eleventh century, the famous Elmer had leapt off the tower of the Abbey wearing a pair of home-made wings. Elmer, I had read, was still commemorated by a historic fifteenth-century pub called 'The Flying Monk'; but on arrival I found it had been bulldozed to make way for a supermarket. In the last thirty years we have become all too familiar with officially sanctified greed. Juvenal says: *inter nos sanctissima divitiarum / maiestas, etsi funesta Pecunia templo / nondum habitat, nullas nummorum ereximus aras* ('In our society nothing is held in such veneration / as the grandeur of riches, although as yet there stands no temple / for murderous Money to dwell in, no altar erected to Cash'; *Sat.* 1.112-14). It is now a truism that all our enterprises are 'finance-led'; and, if they are not 'cost-effective', then they are abandoned; for we must always give 'value for money'. Then there is the cost of accommodation, especially in the capital. Readers will have their own examples. I simply cite the fact that one may well have to pay over £170,000 in a very modest district for a house which fifty years ago cost £1700. Fires, no doubt, are less frequent; and yet we have all read of cases where someone has set fire to his premises to collect the insurance. There was no insurance in Rome; but Juvenal does say that, when a rich man's house burns down, he is loaded with so many presents that he is justly suspected of starting the fire himself (*Sat.* 3.220-2). As for traffic, one recalls that the M25 was constructed at enormous expense to ease the flow of traffic in the city centre; it is now known as 'the biggest car-park in England'. It is clear that legislation along the lines of that imposed by Julius Caesar will soon need to be passed. (Ken Livingstone's 'congestion charge' goes half way there.)

With regard to occupations and their rewards, it takes, according to Juvenal, a year for a schoolmaster, working in a blackboard jungle, to earn what a gladiator picks up in a single fight (*Sat.* 7.242-3). Substitute boxer for gladiator and Juvenal appears guilty of understatement. (I say nothing of soccer-stars, snooker-players, golfers *et hoc genus omne.*) In recent years a certain figure has became familiar – the chairman, say, of a privatised industry who is paid over half a million. When things go badly, he is not 'sacked';

he 'steps down' and is rewarded with a seven-figure cheque for his failure. Solicitors are supposed to ensure that we live in a fair, well-regulated society; but people of modest means are often afraid to consult them, being unwilling to pay £100 for each letter – and that's cheap in comparison with the rate charged by barristers. Juvenal's cameo of Matho, filling his brand-new litter, foreshadows modern equivalents in their Mercs and Rollers. The structure of the medical profession is equally unbalanced, with a group of grossly overpaid consultants at the top and crowds of young doctors at the bottom, afraid of making a mistake through lack of sleep.

Spending can be as offensive as acquisition. One thinks of people who buy an important picture as an investment, paying so many hundreds of thousands that they have to consign it to a bank vault, after employing a student at a pittance to paint a copy for their wall. And what of those who buy old wine at auction for so astronomical a sum that they can never afford to drink it? Examples are countless, ranging in recent times from Imelda Marcos' shoes and Sir Elton John's flowers, to the palaces of Saddam Hussein.

Other kinds of fraudulence bring us closer to home. What can one say of academics who are paid to teach, then assure their students that there are no independent facts, no such thing as objective knowledge? Even an honest atheist is offended by Christian priests who reject the incarnation and the resurrection, and in some cases, apparently, even the existence of God. How often have we heard of children in schools and orphanages being sexually abused by those whose duty it was to protect them? Banks, we used to believe, were respectable places; now they vie with one another in persuading young people to borrow money, then confiscate all they have, in order to swell their own inflated profits and to pay for their wall-to-wall carpets. Then there are policemen who extort false confessions. And there are politicians who … well, the less said the better.

Everyone knows that non-Caucasian immigrants are often in a wretched plight. As they were admitted to do essential work which the native British turned down, it is clearly wrong that they should be undervalued. Yet, just occasionally one catches a glimpse of the other side of the picture. Not long ago a letter appeared in a national newspaper from an executive who had been made redundant in his fifties; after trying for months to find another job he went down to the job-centre. There he explained his predicament to a turban-wearing Sikh who told him his case was hopeless and he'd better emigrate. Juvenal would have relished that.

Again, the modern liberal supports women's claims for equality in the work place; but he may still want to retain the concept of femininity. In that case, he will regret the fact that so many progressive women have taken over the more objectionable habits of men, like foul language and reckless driving. Juvenal speaks of the lady who goes pig-sticking in the amphitheatre. Even that seems more appealing than the mud-wrestling, which apparently has its headquarters in Hamburg. And then there is the hysterical adulation given to pop-stars and other talentless exhibitionists. Bits of their clothing are much sought after; relics of Elvis Presley fetch especially high prices. Cheaper, no doubt, would be the sweaty shirts which Wimbledon victors now toss into the crowd. Items selected by Juvenal as the focus of Roman female interest are mentioned in *Sat.* 6:

> Others, whenever the curtains are quietly stowed away,
> when the theatre's locked and empty and only the courts
> are heard,
> when the People's Games are over and Cybele's far in the future,
> sadly fondle Accius' mask, and his staff, and his loin-cloth.'
> (*Sat.* 6.67-70)

Now I grant that some of these illustrations have been in questionable taste; but good taste is not Juvenal's strong-point. In adopting this final position *beside* him and his Romans, we can at least appreciate that the problems of the megalopolis are not new; also that, however horrifying and intractable they may be, such problems can, against all the odds, be made entertaining. That is the paradox of Juvenal's art.

Related Material:

'Poets and Patrons in Juvenal's Seventh Satire' in *Lines of Enquiry* (Cambridge, 1976; repr. 2004) 84-118.

Juvenal, Satires I, III and X (with E. Courtney) (Bristol, 1977; repr. London 1994).

Themes in Roman Satire (London, 1986; repr. Bristol, 1988).

Juvenal, the Satires (a verse tr.) (repr. Oxford, 1999).

8 The Classical Presence in *Titus Andronicus*

[From *Shakespeare Survey* 55 (2002) 199-208]

This paper has to do with the play's *Romanitas*. By that I mean, not its tenuous relation to historical fact, but rather the characters' awareness of Rome's cultural traditions.[1] The plural is needed, because there were two such traditions. When, as Horace said, 'Captive Greece made her rough conqueror captive' *(Epistles* 2.1.156), she brought to Latium her poetry and mythology (along with much else). The point is so familiar that one tends to forget its exceptional nature. In the annals of imperialism how many victors have learned the language of the vanquished and set about acquiring their culture? From Homer and his successors the Romans learned about Priam, Hecuba, and the rest; and, when, with their growing sense of power, they looked for a pedigree that would rival that of the Greeks in age and prestige, they found it in Troy. The link was supplied by the story of Aeneas, that was eventually given its classic form by Virgil. However, the contribution of Aeneas had first to be reconciled with the other, native, tradition that Rome was founded by her eponymous ancestor Romulus.[2] This was achieved by making Aeneas' descendant Rhea Silvia, also called Ilia ('Trojan woman'), Romulus' mother. Rome's subsequent fortunes, as they passed gradually from legend to history, were recounted by Livy, and the two traditions together were presented by Ovid and Plutarch.

As a result, when Titus makes his entry in Shakespeare's play, he can salute Jupiter Capitolinus – the central symbol of Rome's power (Act 1, Sc.1, 80); then, without any sense of incongruity, go on to speak of his own 'five and twenty valiant sons, / Half of the number that King Priam had' (82-3). We have already heard something of the moral context in which he is expected to operate: the senatorial order is seen as the noble defender of justice (2) and its members are addressed as the guardians of virtue, justice, continence and nobility, to which Jupiter's temple is consecrated (15-16). The speeches of

95

Saturninus and Bassianus are, of course, pieces of undisguised flattery, though they do reflect the standards which the senate was supposed to uphold[3] – standards that form an ironic background to what is about to happen.

We have also been told something about Titus. His surname is Pius and he has been chosen Emperor 'for many good and great deserts to Rome' (23-4). In view of the numerous Virgilian analogies that follow, it is fair to see 'Pius' as a reminiscence of Virgil's *pius Aeneas*; however, the use of Pius as an emperor's *surname* is made easier by the fact that from AD 138 to161 Rome was ruled by Antoninus Pius. The origins of 'Andronicus' are less clear, but perhaps the important thing to remember is that 'Conqueror of men' was a suitable name for a victorious general.[4]

Before taking any political action, however, Titus must discharge a religious duty: he must bury his dead sons. As he has just compared himself to Priam, one recalls that Priam's last achievement in the *Iliad* was to recover the body of Hector for decent burial. Likewise in Virgil's epic, before entering the underworld, Aeneas must bury his comrade Misenus (*Aen.* 6.149-235). Later the Sibyl explains that, unless they have been buried, the souls of the dead cannot be transported across the Styx: *centum errant annos volitantque haec litora circum* ('They wander for a hundred years and *hover* about these *shores*'; 6.329). That is what Titus has in mind when he says, 'Why suffer'st thou thy sons unburied yet / To *hover* on the dreadful *shore* of Styx?' The theme of burial points forward to the altercation about the dead Mutius (352-95); and, ultimately, to the fate of Tamora at the end of the play.

Respect for the dead takes a more sinister form when Lucius demands that Tamora's son, Alarbus, be hacked to pieces and sacrificed '*Ad manes fratrum* ('to the spirits of our brothers') ... / That so the *shadows* be not unappeas'd' (98-100). George Hunter[5] refers us to an early precedent, related in Livy 1.25.12, where the last of the Horatii kills the last of the Curiatii, saying *Duos* fratrum manibus *dedi: tertium causae belli huiusce, ut Romanus Albano imperet, dabo* ('I have offered two *to the spirits of my brothers*, I shall offer the third to the purpose of this war, that Roman should rule over Alban'). Ovid (*Metamorphoses* 13.443 ff.) tells how earlier still Achilles' ghost demanded that Polyxena, Hecuba's daughter, be sacrificed to his *spirit* (*manes*); the Greeks duly obeyed the pitiless *shadow* (*umbrae*). The words 'spirit' and 'shadow' are not in Golding's version (529-39). As Lucius indicated, there might be harmful consequences if the shadows were not appeased;[6] but his demand is made in excessively bloodthirsty terms. When Titus consents, Tamora makes a passionate and reasoned protest in words that foreshadow Portia's speech in *The Merchant of Venice*. Titus is somewhat uneasy and, with half an apology ('pardon me'), he insists that Lucius and his brothers are asking 'religiously' for a sacrifice 'T'appease the groaning *shadows* that are gone' (129). This and Lucius' impatient pressure justify Tamora's bitter response, 'O cruel, irreligious piety!' (130). Andronicus has disgraced his name. Chiron adds, 'Was never *Scythia* half so barbarous!' In Seneca's *Troades* Andromache, hearing of Astyanax's death, cries, 'What Colchian, what *Scythian* with his shifting home has committed such a crime?' (*Troades* 1104-5). This is the verdict of one of 'the barbarous Goths' (28), whose hands so far are clean. Demetrius, however, now takes a step on the downward path, reminding his mother of Hecuba who took a 'sharp revenge / Upon the *Thracian tyrant* in his tent' (138). '*Sharp* revenge' is a pregnant phrase; for Golding, describing Hecuba's revenge on Polymestor for murdering her son, says she 'Did in the traitor's face bestowe *her nayles,* and scratched out / His eyes' (*Met.* 13.673-4).[7] 'The *Thracian tyrant*' also comes from Golding, who at line 678 translates Ovid (565) quite literally: 'The *Thracians* at theyr *Tyrannes* harme for anger waxing wood'. Like Shakespeare's Goths, the Thracian race is also *pronum ...in Venerem* (Ovid, *Met.* 6.459-60).

As his sons are buried, Titus delivers a short but noble speech of committal (151-6). Soon after, he is greeted by Marcus, who speaks of 'this funeral pomp (presumably in the sense of the Latin *pompa*, 'procession') / That hath aspired to Solon's happiness' (179-80). In Herodotus 1.32 Solon tells Croesus that a fortunate man should not be called 'blessed' until his life is finished. Shakespeare could have found this in Plutarch's *Life of Solon* (North's translation): 'When the goddes have continued a man's good fortune to his end, then we think that man happy and blessed, and never before' (Nonesuch edn [1929] vol. l, p. 270). Marcus' elliptical reference shows his erudition and his wish to console Titus but it rather misrepresents

Solon; for it suggests that the sons have achieved happiness simply in virtue of being killed. Solon's dictum applies only to those who have been fortunate throughout life and in their death.[8]

When Saturninus declares that he will marry Titus' daughter, Lavinia (244-7), he bids Tamora, who is obviously glowering, to brighten up: 'Thou com'st not to be made a scorn in Rome' (269). Bearing in mind that Tamora has already said, 'We are brought to Rome / To beautify thy triumphs' (112-13), one suspects that Shakespeare is thinking of Cleopatra, who was determined not to be displayed in a triumph (Livy, fragment 54 – *non triumphabor*, reflected in Plutarch's *Life of Antony* 84.4; cf. Horace, *Odes* 1.37.30-32 with Porphyrion's Greek note); one thinks of her defiant speech in *Antony and Cleopatra* (Act 5, Sc. 2, 55 ff. – 'Shall they hoist me up,/ And show me to the shouting varletry / Of censuring Rome?' (cf. 209-13 in the same scene). Saturninus then makes a noble gesture: '*Ransomeless* here we set our prisoners free' (278). A similar gesture was made by Scipio, as recorded in Plutarch, *Life of Scipio Africanus*: 'Scipio gave them (all the Spanish prisoners) libertie to depart *without* paying of *ransome*' (North [1603] p.1088).

In consenting to the marriage of Lavinia to Saturninus, Titus has taken no account of Bassianus, who breaks in: 'Lord Titus, by your leave, this maid is mine' (280). Marcus supports him, appealing to one of the fundamental principles of Roman law, *suum cuique* ('to each his own')[9] – a phrase that, like several other references to law and justice, sounds an ironical note in a play where the only law is the *lex talionis*. This interchange recalls a Virgilian dispute in which another Lavinia had been betrothed to Turnus (*Aen.* 7.366) but was then assigned by her father to Aeneas (*Aen.* 7.268-73; cf. *coniuge praerepta* in 9.138) – an action which precipitated a full-scale war: *pactaque* furit pro *coniuge* Turnus' ('And Turnus fights furiously for his *promised bride*'; Ovid, *Met.*14.451). Doubtless the Virgilian precedent was responsible for the name of Titus' daughter, who was '*betroth'd*' to Bassianus (290). As Lavinia is dragged away, Mutius tries to prevent pursuit and is killed by Titus for dishonouring his father. The episode may be set beside a famous case at the beginniing of the republic. Brutus, the first consul, superintended the execution of his two sons, who had plotted to restore the Tarquins. Livy (2.3.8) mentions the anguish on the father's face but does not suggest for a moment that he had any choice.[10] Titus' action, however, was committed in a fit of rage arising from wounded *amour-propre*.

After this fracas, Saturninus decides that he doesn't want Lavinia after all; he turns to 'lovely Tamora, Queen of the Goths / That like the stately *Phoebe* 'mongst her *nymphs* / Dost *overshine* the gallant'st dames of Rome' (321-2). It has been noticed that in *Aen.* 1.498 ff. (in Phaer's translation, first published in 1573) the lovely Dido is 'most like vnto *Diana bright* when she to hunt goeth out ... / Whom thousands of the lady *Nimphes* await to do her will, / She on her armes her quiuer beares, and all them *overshines*'.[11] Virgil in turn is indebted to Homer, who says that Nausicaa, like Artemis, outshone her attendants (*Odyssey* 6.109).

Lucius now begs that Mutius be buried with his brothers in the family tomb (352-3). Titus angrily refuses: the tomb is for 'none basely slain in brawls' (358). He seems unaware that it takes two to make a brawl. As the wrangle continues, Marcus appeals to Titus as 'more than *half my soul*' (378). The phrase comes, directly or otherwise, from Horace, who in *Odes* 1.3.8 addresses Virgil as *animae dimidium meae*. As so often, the imitator goes one step further than his source: '*more than* half my soul'; similarly Lavinia loses her hands as well as her tongue. Marcus then pleads, 'Thou art a Roman, be not barbarous' (383), and he finally cites the action of the Greeks who, on Ulysses' advice, buried Ajax (384-6). This information could have come from Lambinus' note on Horace, *Satires* 2.3.187: *Ulysses ... Agamemnonem ... exoravit ut Aiacem sineret sepeliri* ('Ulysses prevailed on Agamemnon to allow Ajax to be buried'). Given the focus of this paper, it is fair to point out that the appeals to Titus' Graeco-Roman heritage are placed at the climax of the speech and succeed in tipping the scales. Saturninus, cast in the role of Agamemnon, agrees with ill grace.

In the short scene that follows Saturninus accuses his brother of 'rape' in the sense of 'abduction' (409), as in Claudian, *De Raptu Proserpinae*. This somewhat absurd overstatement prefaces the theme of 'rape' in the full sense, acted out in the rape of Lavinia. The ensuing altercation is stilled by 'the subtle Queen of Goths', who excuses Titus for not dissembling his fury and then urges Saturninus to dissemble his, whispering 'I'll find a day to massacre them all' (455). As a result, the hunt scheduled for the morrow arouses

feelings of foreboding, whether or not one remembers the hunt in
Aeneid 4.

In line 500 Aaron speaks for the first time. He proves to be quite
at ease in Graeco-Roman culture, declaring in Marlovian hyperbole
that his mistress is climbing Olympus' top and that she is bound to
him as tightly as Prometheus is to Caucasus (516) – a rather odd
simile, foreshadowing the brutal instances of bondage that are to
follow. Tamora is likened to a goddess, Semiramis, a nymph and a
siren – all alluring females and the last of them, at least, potentially
murderous.[12] Aaron then separates Chiron and Demetrius, who
are quarreling over Lavinia. He does so by diverting them from
adulterous seduction (for Lavinia is as chaste as Lucrece) to joint
rape, Lavinia being seen as 'a dainty doe' (617; cf. 593 and Act 2,
Sc.1, 26). Secrecy must be observed but, as 'The Emperor's court
is like the house of Fame' (626) – Ovid, *Met.*12.39 ff., by way of
Chaucer[13] – the youths are to take Lavinia quietly into a wood,
where they will be 'shadow'd from heaven's *eye*' (630). This,
of course, is quite intelligible in itself; but it also represents the
remnant of an earlier allusion in which Bassianus is visualised as
wearing 'Vulcan's badge' (589), meaning horns. The adultery of
Mars and Venus was reported to Vulcan (Venus' husband) by the
sun who, as the original spy in the sky, sees everything – a famous
story from *Odyssey* 8.266 ff., recounted by Ovid, *Met.* 4.171 ff .
Ovid does not refer to an eye but his translator, Golding (206-8),
does: 'It is reported how this god [the Sunne] did first of all espie, /
(For everie thing in Heaven and Earth is open to his *eie*) / How
Venus with the warlike Mars advoutrie did commit'.

Demetrius claims that, until (right or wrong) he satisfies his
lust, he is going through hell. 'Be it right or wrong' seems to be the
intended meaning of *Sit, fas aut nefas* (633).The normal Latin for
this would be *sive fas sit sive nefas* – a phrase apparently without
previous example; so the writer may be improvising. In the words
per Stygia, per manes vehor (635), *Stygia* seems intelligible enough,
though I have not noticed this neuter plural adjective being used as
a noun for 'the Stygian regions'. The reading of F4 (*Per Styga*,
'through the Styx') deserves consideration. The words will then
be scanned quite regularly as the beginning of an English iambic
pentameter, like the shorter phrase *Sit fas aut nefas* in 633. The

source is acknowledged to be Seneca's iambic trimeter *per Styga, per amnes igneos, amens sequar* ('through the Styx, through the river of fire, I will follow in my madness'; *Phaedra* 1180), spoken by the heroine in an agony of guilt. A copyist unfamiliar with the Greek accusative singular might well have altered *Styga* into a Latin neuter plural *Stygia* (cf. the misprint in Hughes' note), whereas the opposite process would have been most unlikely. It seems more probable, however, that the change was made deliberately by Shakespeare; for the general *Stygia* would have combined with the general *manes* ('spirits'), which he substituted for the other river (i.e. Phlegethon).

In Act 2, Sc. 2 Tamora, who is by now the emperor's wife, conveniently forgets her pledge of devotion given in Act 1, Sc. 1, 334-7. She tries to seduce Aaron: 'let us sit, / And whilst the *babbling* echo mocks the hounds ... ' (16-17). Echo was called *a vocalis nymphe* in Ovid (*Met.* 3.357), which Golding (443) rendered as 'a *babling* nymph'. (One recalls that for such babbling Echo had been deprived of speech.) Tamora proposes that they follow the example of Virgil's Aeneas and Dido in the cave (*Aen.* 4.165ff.); Aaron, however, declines; for 'Blood and revenge are hammering in my head' (39). He looks forward to Bassianus' death and the violation of Lavinia: 'His Philomel must lose her tongue today, / Thy sons make pillage of her chastity' (43-4). This is the first sign that Ovid's story is about to be woven into the action of the play.

There follows an exchange of discourtesies. Bassianus opens: 'Who have we here? Rome's royal empress / ... Or is it Dian, habited like her?' (55-7). In the Greek romances it was common for a young man, on meeting a young woman, to ask in admiration whether she was a goddess. The earliest example comes in the source of all romances, where Odysseus addresses Nausicaa (*Odyssey* 6.151-2). More to the point, in *Aeneid* Book 1 Aeneas encounters a female figure dressed in hunting garb and wonders if it is Diana (329); actually it is Venus in the disguise of a huntress. To Bassianus' sarcastic question, Tamora retorts, 'Had I the pow'r that some say Dian had, / Thy temples should be planted presently / With horns, as was Actaeon's'. At this Lavinia reveals an unexpectedly coarse side of her character: 'Tis thought you have a goodly gift in horning', i.e. in making men cuckolds; Saturninus will surely have horns now;

let's hope his hounds don't catch sight of him! The horrifying story of Actaeon was to be found in Ovid, *Met.* 3.138 ff. As A.B.Taylor remarks, 'The invocation of Actaeon is ominous in a play where men and women are about to turn predators'.[14] Bassianus then refers insultingly to Aaron's colour, despising as 'a barbarous Moor' (78) the man whom Tamora had called her 'sweet Moor' (51). As Shakespeare has been thinking of the *Aeneid*, it is possible that he has in mind Virgil's Iarbas, another member of 'the Moorish race' (*Aen.* 4.206-7), who is motivated, because of his intentions towards Dido, by malevolence towards Aeneas. Virgil never mentions *his* colour but the phrase *Gaetulus Iarbas* (4.326) has connotations of wildness and savagery.

Tamora now tells her sons that Bassianus and Lavinia have enticed her to 'A barren detested vale' (93). As her account develops it becomes harder to remember that this is the *locus amoenus* described in such idyllic terms to Aaron (12-18). She alleges that they intended to tie her to a tree (the bondage theme again) and leave her to die. Her sons therefore murder Bassianus and make to drag Lavinia away, telling Tamora to ignore her pleas. Lavinia then cries, 'When did the tiger's young ones teach the dam?' – a clever adaptation of Ovid's straightforward comparison of Procne to a tigress in *Met.* 6.637. Bassianus' body is then flung into a pit, as Aaron had instructed. In describing the pit Shakespeare's imagination runs riot.[15] Just a few points are relevant here. First, the place is 'As hateful as Cocytus' misty mouth' (236). The mist may owe something to the sulphurous vapour (*halitus*) that issued from the cave at the entrance to the underworld in *Aeneid* 6.240. Again, Shakespeare is thinking of hell in terms of its rivers; for not only does he use 'Cocytus' but also, with the adjective 'hateful', he alludes to 'abhorred Styx'. Later the pit is a '*gaping* hollow of the earth' (249); likewise Virgil's cave yawns 'with a vast *gape*' (*vasto hiatu, Aen.* 6.237). Finally, with 'a swallowing womb' we have a grotesque inversion of *Terra Mater.* (Housman had something similar in mind when he wrote: 'Now to her lap the incestuous earth / The son she bore has ta'en' (*Additional Poems* 8). Inside the pit the dim light given out by the carbuncle ring on Bassianus' corpse reminds Martius of Pyramus – 'When he by night lay bathed in *maiden blood*' (232). This is the view that Thisbe had of the dead Pyramus by moonlight. It comes, not directly from

Ovid's *Metamorphoses*,but from Golding's translation: 'And there beweltred in his *maiden bloud* hir lover she espide' (4.162).

As Shakespeare could not represent the rape and mutilation on stage, the atrocities are described in Act 2, Sc. 3, first brutally by Demetrius and Chiron, then sympathetically by Marcus. However, Marcus' sympathy rings false as he dwells in loving detail on the girl's injuries (especially in 23-5). Equally false in this situation are his Ovidian allusions. He infers that 'some Tereus hath deflowered thee' (26), then describes her blood coming 'As from *a conduit* with three issuing spouts' (30). This goes beyond what Ovid had said about the bleeding Pyramus: 'As when a *Conduite* pipe is crackt, the water bursting out / Doth shote it selfe a great way off and pierce the Ayre about' (Golding 4.148-9). As the story was supposed to explain how the berries of the mulberry tree became red, the blood *had* to spurt into the air. Yet the image of the cracked pipe has been much criticised as a lapse of taste. Gower left it out (*Confessio Amantis*, 3.4.2); Chaucer took it in his stride: 'The blod out of the wounde as brode sterte / As water, whan the *condit* broken is' (*The Legend of Good Women*, 851-2); Shakespeare multiplied it by three.

Marcus also notices that the loss of Lavinia's hands prevented her from revealing the crime in the manner employed by Philomel, who 'in a tedious sampler sewed her mind' (39). Had Lavinia's tongue not been cut out, she could have charmed her attacker, who would have fallen asleep 'As *Cerberus* at the Thracian poet's feet' (51). As often, Shakespeare is blending two passages. In the story of Orpheus ('the Thracian poet') and Eurydice, Cerberus, on hearing Orpheus' song, ceases to bark (Virgil, *Georgics* 4.483) but does not fall asleep. In *Aeneid* 6, however, he does fall asleep after devouring the drugged cake thrown to him by another *vates* – not a poet, but a prophetess (419-23). When Marcus leads in the wounded Lavinia he compares her to a wounded deer (Act 3, Sc. 1, 90-1) – a simile taken up by Titus in one of those puns that make the modern reader uncomfortable.[16] The figure itself picks up the 'dainty doe' mentioned by Aaron (Act 1, Sc.1, 617) and by Demetrius (Act 2, Sc. 1, .26). Dido, too, had been likened by Virgil to a stricken doe (*Aen.* 4.68-73) and the immediate cause of the war in Italy was the wounding of a pet stag (*Aen.* 7.483 ff.).

In Act 3, Sc. 1 Titus tries to save his sons' lives by allowing Aaron to chop off his hand, but the hand is returned to him along with the young men's heads. Here, as the editors point out, Shakespeare is indebted to Bandello, *Novelle* 3.21. The severed heads, however, come from Seneca's *Thyestes*, in which Atreus removes the cover of a dish, revealing the heads of the sons whose bodies Thyestes has just eaten (*Thyestes* 1004-5). In both plays the moment is a terrific *coup de théâtre*; but, by using the severed heads here at this half-way point, Shakespeare forfeited the chance of using them later on and so had to fall back on a less plausible alternative.

At the end of Act 3, Sc. 1 Lucius departs to persuade the Goths to attack Rome, 'And make proud Saturnine and his empress / Beg at the gates like Tarquin and his queen' (298-9). According to Livy (1.59.1), following the death of Lucretia, Brutus swore 'to hunt down L.Tarquinius Superbus along with his wicked wife'; in 1.60.2 he adds that 'the gates were closed against Tarquinius'; and in 2.6.2 Tarquin pleads to the Etruscans that he is an exile and 'in poverty' (*egentem*). Shakespeare has combined these elements to form a picture of the royal pair begging at the gate.[17]

In Act 3, Sc. 2, 52 ff. comes the scene where Marcus kills a fly with his knife. Titus claims, 'Out on thee, murderer! Thou kill'st my heart; / Mine eyes are cloy'd with view of tyranny'. The combination of sharp instrument, fly and tyranny raises the possibility that Shakespeare may have half remembered how the tyrant Domitian 'at the beginning of his reign ... used to do nothing more than catch flies and run them through with a sharp pen' (Suetonius, *Life of Domitian*, 3.1). Shakespeare's scene, of course, may be entirely original: one thinks of 'As willingly as one would kill a fly' (Act 5, Sc. 1, 142) and 'As flies to wanton boys'. Although Philemon Holland's translation of Suetonius (1606) was probably too late, Domitian's behaviour was so odd that Shakespeare might have heard of it through another channel, perhaps even his schoolmaster. However that may be, he builds this trivial scene into a vicious attack on the Moor (67-79). As the Act closes, Titus leads Lavinia and the boy Lucius away to read 'Sad stories chanced in the times of old' (84).

This is immediately taken up in Act 4, Sc. 1, where young Lucius is told that 'Cornelia never with more *care* / Read to her sons than she hath read to thee / Sweet poetry and Tully's Orator'

(12-14). Cornelia's care in educating the Gracchi is recorded at the beginning of Plutarch's *Life of Tiberius Gracchus*; North's translation uses the phrase 'so *carefully*'. The commentaries may be right in referring to Cicero's *Orator* and *De Oratore*, but it is worth mentioning that in another rhetorical work, the *Brutus*, Cicero twice reports Cornelia's activities as a mother (*Brutus* 104 and 211). Of these passages the former is the more interesting in that it too refers to her *care* (*diligentia*).

Lavinia is now in a highly agitated condition – so much so that Lucius recalls reading how 'Hecuba of Troy / Ran *mad* for sorrow' (20-21) – perhaps a rather distant echo of Golding, who speaks of Hecuba being 'dumb for sorrow' (13.645), but Nørgaard (see note 24 below) may be right in pointing to Cooper's *Thesaurus*, where '[Hecuba] finally waxed *madde*, and did bite and strike all men she met'. Lavinia now seizes a copy of the 'Metamorphosis' (so entitled by Golding) and manages, with some help, to find 'the tragic tale of Philomel' (47). From this we infer that the 'sweet poetry', which she used to read to Lucius, included Ovid's masterpiece. Titus, beginning to understand what has happened, suspects she was 'Forc'd in the ruthless, vast, and *gloomy woods* '. Ovid had written *in stabula alta trahit, silvis obscura vetustis* ('drags her into deep *stabula, darkly hidden* by ancient *woods*'; *Met.* 6.521); there he was using *stabula* in the sense of 'dens', as Virgil did in *Aen.* 6.179, where Aeneas made his way *in antiquam silvam, stabula alta ferarum* ('into an ancient forest, the deep *dens of* wild beasts'). In view of this, it is perhaps significant that Marcus asks, 'O why should nature build so foul *a den?*' (59). Golding (6.663) mistranslates *alta stabula* as 'a pelting graunge' – a small barn. Yet he has some excuse; for, unlike Shakespeare, Ovid later says that Philomela was locked up in a building: *structa rigent solido stabulorum moenia saxo* ('the walls of the building (*stabulorum*) were firmly constructed out of solid stone'; *Met.* 6.573; cf. 596). Titus now urges Lavinia to indicate in some way who did the deed. Could it have been Saturnine 'as Tarquin erst / That left the camp to sin in Lucrece' bed?' (63-4). This, of course, was not Tarquinius Superbus but his son Sextus, whose crime was recounted in Livy 1.57.6-58.12 and described in *The Rape of Lucrece* (512 ff.). Marcus traces his own name in a sandy plot.[18] Now comes the moment of recognition (Aristotle's tragic *anagnôrisis*). Fulfilling Chiron's taunt, 'An if thy stumps will let thee, play the scribe' (Act 2, Sc. 3, 4), Lavinia writes (in Latin, one notes) '*Stuprum*. Chiron. Demetrius' (78). The dramatic impact of this can be assessed when we contrast it with the chap book, in which Lavinia succeeds in composing a rhyming couplet: 'The lustful Sons of the proud Emperess / Are doers of this hateful wickedness'.

At the sight of the names, Titus, according to the transmitted text, exclaims: *Magni dominator poli, / Tam lentus audis scelera? tam lentus vides?* ('Ruler of great heaven, are you so insensitive when you hear of crimes? So insensitive when you witness them?' [81-2]). *Magni*, however, is a misquotation, as Theobald saw; for Seneca does not admit a long syllable at that point in the line. The second line undoubtedly comes from Seneca, *Phaedra* 672, and there line 671 ends *Magne* (sic) *regnator deum*; similarly in Seneca's *Thyestes* 1077 Jupiter is addressed as *summe caeli rector* ('Highest ruler of heaven', not 'Ruler of highest heaven'); and in the very next line we find *dominator*. Again one wonders whether it is Shakespeare's change or that of a copyist.[19]

Marcus kneels down with Titus, Lavinia and young Lucius who is now 'the Roman Hector's hope' (88), his father, who has gone to enlist the help of the Goths in saving the city, being now 'the Roman Hector'. They swear an oath of vengeance, which Titus wishes to engrave on 'a leaf of brass' (102). This phrase has nothing to do with the myth of the ages. It refers to the durability of brass (cf. Horace, *Odes* 3.30.1: *monumentum aere perennius*, 'a monument more lasting than bronze'). Titus mentions this material, because the sands on which Marcus and Lavinia have just written will be blown by the *wind* 'like Sibyl's *leaves* abroad' (105); in *Aen*. 6.74-5 Aeneas begs the Sibyl not to entrust her prophecies to *leaves* that will be scattered by the *winds*.

In Act 4, Sc. 2, 20 young Lucius delivers to Chiron and Demetrius weapons sent by Titus ostensibly for their protection (15-16). The accompanying scroll reads *Integer vitae scelerisque purus / Non eget Mauri iaculis nec arcu* ('The man who is unblemished in his life and free from crime has no need of a Moor's javelins or bow'). Spelled out, the message means, I take it, 'An *honest* man needs no weapons, least of all those of a Moor'. Chiron recalls reading Horace's lines (*Odes* 1.22.1-2) 'in the grammar'; but he fails to see their significance.[20] Aaron, however, does see the point and comments, in an aside, on Chiron's stupidity: 'Now, what a thing it is to be an ass' (25).

Tamora's black baby is now brought in and Aaron, in high style, refuses to allow Demetrius to kill it, casting himself as Jupiter against the giant Enceladus and 'Typhon's brood'[21] – even, if need be, against Hercules and Mars (97). He sets about ensuring the baby's safety by murdering its nurse, then carries it away for protection to the Goths, remarking good-humouredly: 'I'll make you … suck the goat, / And cabin in a cave' (179-81). This only makes sense if we remember that in Greek mythology the infant Zeus was hidden in a Cretan cave to prevent Cronus (the original child-eater) from devouring him; there he was suckled by the goat Amalthea.[22] (One thinks of Poussin's beautiful picture in the Dulwich Gallery.)[23] The parallel gains relevance from the fact that the Italian counterpart of Cronus was Saturn and this baby is being smuggled away to escape the wrath of *Saturn*inus.

In the myth of the metals Astraea (Justice) eventually tired of men's wickedness and rose to the skies, where she became the constellation Virgo. In Aratus' account (*Phaenomena* 129-36) this happened with the arrival of the bronze age; Ovid says that it was in the age of iron that *terras Astraea reliquit* ('Astraea quit the Earth'; *Met.* 1.141-50). When in Act 4, Sc. 3, 4 Titus quoted the phrase, no doubt the more learned would have remembered Ovid's context. Yet it is the *consequences* of Astraea's departure that are emphasised. In what follows, the main concern is absent Justice; between line 9 in this scene and 23 in the next the word itself occurs eleven times. So, at the risk of being 'reductive', it seems a mistake to give too much attention to the myth, which is not actually mentioned.[24]

In Act 4. Sc. 3, 54 ff. Titus distributes arrows destined for half a dozen divinities. The conceits about hitting Virgo, Taurus, Aries and the rest (which were perhaps thought of as being represented on the wall of the court) are based, as Maxwell says, on Seneca, *Thyestes* 844 ff., where the chorus predicts that the signs of the zodiac will fall down. Later (Act 4, Sc. 4, 61 ff.) news comes that Lucius is leading an army against Rome, as Coriolanus had done so long before . In Act 5, Sc. 1 he makes a noble entry, but before long is clamouring that Aaron and his baby be hanged (47-8 and 51-2). In return for the safety of the child, Aaron proceeds to tell all that has happened. He treats the rape and mutilation of Lavinia as acts of entertainment (91-6), whereupon Lucius cries out that her two attackers were '*barbarous beastly* villains like thyself' (97). (Golding in 6.655 calls the intention of Tereus '*barbrous and beastly*'.) Finally Lucius orders Aaron to be gagged (151).

Taking a hint from Ovid's Procne, who disguises herself as a Bacchanal (*Met.* 6.589 ff.), Tamora now dresses herself as Revenge (Act 5, Sc. 2, 3); Chiron and Demetrius are Rape and Murder. Titus is not deceived but Tamora thinks he is mad and plans to use him 'to scatter and disperse the giddy Goths' (78). In due course Titus orders Chiron and Demetrius to be tied up and gagged (160-61). After rehearsing their crimes, he proceeds to tell them his grisly plans: 'For worse than Philomel you used my daughter, / And worse than Progne I will be revenged' (194-5). The banquet will prove 'More stern and bloody than the Centaurs' feast' (203) – an ambitious claim; for at that feast, recounted by Ovid in the most gruesome detail (*Met.* 12.210-535), well over fifty lives were lost.

In the preparation and description of the meal Shakespeare diverged from his sources, as noted above. Unlike Ovid and Seneca, he included even the sons' heads in the dish (189 and 200). We are to imagine the skulls being ground to dust and then made into a paste. In Ovid, when Tereus sends for his son, Procne says, 'You have within the one whom you want' (*Met.* 6.655). When he asks again, Philomela bursts in and hurls the child's head at his father, who immediately pursues the women; before he can catch them they are transformed into birds. In Seneca, when Thyestes calls for his sons, Atreus with a flourish uncovers the dish, revealing their heads (*Thyestes* 1005). In Shakespeare, Titus serves the meal dressed as a chef (Act 5, Sc. 3, 30). Before it begins he asks Saturninus if Virginius was right to kill his daughter. Livy (3.44) tells how Appius Claudius was seized with a desire to debauch Verginius' daughter (*virginis ... stuprandae libido*). By employing a legalistic device he was about to succeed in doing so when her father, Verginius, intervened and killed the girl. Shakespeare draws on a later version, which says she was actually 'enforced, stained, and deflowered' (38).[25] Saturninus says

Virginius' action was justified, whereupon Titus kills Lavinia (45-6), explaining that she had been raped by Chiron and Demetrius.

> *Saturninus:*   Go fetch them hither to us presently.
> *Titus:*   Why, there they are, both baked in this pie;
>   Whereof their mother daintily hath *fed*,
>   Eating the flesh that she herself hath *bred.*
>   (60-61)

The rhyme seems to come from Golding: 'King Tereus ... *fed* / And swallowed downe the selfsame flesh that of his bowels *bred*' (6.824-5). Yet the picture of a mother eating her own children is doubly revolting, because she seems to be taking them back into her body. The point is made by Shakespeare himself when he makes Titus say 'and bid that strumpet ... , / Like to the earth, swallow her own increase' (Act 5, Sc. 2, 190-91). Instead of gloating over Tamora's horror, Titus kills her. In Seneca the victim reacts with a typical flight of rhetoric, addressing Jupiter as *tu, summe caeli rector, aetheriae potens / dominator aulae* ('Thou, highest ruler of heaven, powerful master of the celestial court'; *Thyestes* 1077-8). Thyestes urges the god to bring cosmic chaos.

With Tamora, Titus and Saturninus all dead, a speaker urges Marcus to re-enact the role of Aeneas recounting the fall of Priam's Troy to Dido; he is to tell what new Sinon has bewitched the citizens (for Sinon, see *Aen.* 2.57-198, especially the reference to his tricks and craftiness at 195-6) and who has brought 'the *fatal engine* in (*fatalis machina* describes the horse in *Aen.* 2.237) / That gives our Troy, our Rome, the fatal wound' (Act 5, Sc. 3, 79-86). 'Our Troy, our Rome' – the presence of the past could not be more concisely explicit. Marcus at first sight complies: like Aeneas, he cannot *utter* all the bitter *grief* (88) – *infandum, regina, iubes renovare dolorem* ('*Unutterable,* o queen, is *the grief* that you bid me recall'); but, unlike Aeneas, he really *is* unable to face the task and passes it on to Lucius, who summarises the events, speaking of his own part once again in terms that recall Coriolanus.[26]

After being hailed as emperor, he promises to bring reconciliation; but first he passes a cruel sentence on the defiant Aaron:

'Set him breast-deep in earth and famish him; / There let him stand and rave and cry for food' (178-9). Many of the audience would, no doubt, have recalled the fate of Tantalus. In Homer (*Odyssey* 11.582 ff.) he stands in a pool and is plagued by thirst; he is also 'tantalised' by fruit, figs and olives. In Horace, *Epodes* 17.66 he is tortured by the sight of an ample meal; and in a similar passage a young boy is to be buried up to his neck and starved within the sight of food (*Epodes* 5.31 ff.). But how is Tantalus connected with Shakespeare's play? In Seneca's *Thyestes* Tantalus' ghost appears in the opening scene, complaining about the tortures of both hunger and thirst (*Thyestes* 1-6; cf. 152 ff.). He is, we are reminded, the grandfather of both Atreus and Thyestes; and his crime? He carved up his son Pelops and served him as food to the gods. So there seems ample reason why he should have occurred to Shakespeare at this point in the play. Moreover, one of Thyestes' murdered sons was also called Tantalus.

As for Tamora, she is to be denied burial; instead she will be thrown 'to *beasts* and *birds* to prey' (197). Such a fate is mentioned several times in ancient literature; but, since we know that Shakespeare had been reading the *Thyestes,* it is reasonable to cite lines 1032-3 of that play. There, realising that his sons are dead but not that he himself has eaten them, Thyestes asks Atreus: *utrumne saevis pabulum alitibus iacent, / an beluis servantur, an pascunt feras?* ('Do they lie there as *prey* for cruel *birds*, or are they reserved for sea-monsters? Or are they food for *beasts?*'). Such, then, is the fate in store for Tamora. The last word of the play is 'pity'; but it is the kind of pity associated with vultures.

Although there have been various attempts to moralise the *Metamorphoses,* it is now generally accepted that the various effects – comic, pathetic, horrific, bizarre – are all parts of an ever-moving narrative, all facets of the poet's iridescent imagination. Occasionally we find his brutality sensational or even absurd, and his sentimental descriptions of cruelty repellent; but Ovid himself is not deeply involved and does not invite us to pause and ponder. Unlike Virgil, he has little to offer the earnest. This cast of mind is surely what appealed to Shakespeare at this stage of his career. Opinion about Seneca's tragedies is still divided. Can they be seen, not just as an orgy of horrors, but as a Stoic's attempt to show what happens when reason is overthrown by lawless passions? Are their emotional passages noble rhetoric or overblown bombast? The various controversies surrounding *Titus Andronicus* also seem set to continue. However, as we watch the writer's memory at work – taking now from Virgil, Ovid or Plutarch, now from Livy, Horace or Seneca, combining or altering what is taken to suit his dramatic purpose – we can hardly deny that, in addition to much else, the play is a brilliant display of creative reminiscence.

Related Material:

'Pyramus and Thisbe in Shakespeare and Ovid' in D. West and
   T. Woodman (eds) *Creative Imitation and Latin Literature*
   (Cambridge, 1979) ch. 10.
'Two Twin Comedies' in *The Classical Tradition in Operation*
   (Toronto, 1994) ch. 2.

9 *The Taming of the Shrew*:
Some Classical Points of Reference

[From *Hermathena* 129 (1980) 23-8]

Second Servant: Dost thou love pictures? we will fetch
thee straight
Adonis painted by a running brook,
And Cytherea all in *sedges hid.*
(Induction 2, 49-51)[1]

The story of Venus and Adonis is recounted by Ovid in *Metamor-phoses* 10.525-59 and 708-39; but there is there no running brook and no attempt at concealment on Venus' part. As J.A.K. Thomson and others have seen, the playwright has in mind the story of Salmacis and Hermaphroditus as told in *Metamorphoses* 4. There the young Hermaphroditus comes to a pool in Caria: *non illic canna palustris / nec steriles ulvae nec acuta cuspide iunci* (298-9); Golding translates: 'No fennie *sedge*, no barren recke, no reede / Nor rush with pricking poynt was there, nor other moorish weede' (362-3). The nymph of the pool, Salmacis, was filled with desire for Hermaphroditus, but the boy rejected her; so she pretended to go away. In fact, however, she concealed herself behind a thicket: *fruticumque recondita silva / delituit* (339-40), which Golding translates as 'She *hides* hir in a bushie queach' (418). When Hermaphroditus dived into the pool, she followed and clung to him so hard that their male and female bodies merged into one.

In *The Passionate Pilgrim*, no.6 we read:

Cytherea, all in love forlorn,
A longing *tarriance* for Adonis made
Under an osier growing by a brook,
A brook where Adon us'd to *cool* his spleen ...

113

> Anon he comes, and throws his mantle by,
> And stood stark naked on the brook's green brim:
> *The sun* look'd on the world with glorious eye,
> Yet not so wistly as this queen on him.

In his version of the Salmacis / Hermaphroditus episode Golding
says:

> he tooke so great delight
> In *coolenesse* of the pleasant spring, that streight he stripped
> quight
> His garments from his tender skin. When Salmacis behilde
> His naked beautie, such strong pangs so ardently hir hilde,
> That utterly she was astraught. And even as *Phebus beames*
> Against a myrrour pure and clere rebound with broken
> gleames:
> Even so hir eys did sparcle fire. Scarce could she *tarrience*
> make.   (10.424-30)

The general picture, combined with correspondences like 'tarriance' /
'tarrience'[2], 'cool' / 'coolenesse' and 'sun' / 'Phebus beames', makes
it virtually certain that the writer had Golding's passage in mind. So
the sonnet and the lines of the play have a common source. However,
since in each case a brook is substituted for Ovid's pool and Venus
and Adonis are confused with Salmacis and Hermaphroditus, it
seems likely that the two passages are by the same man.

In view of the uncertainties surrounding *The Taming of the Shrew*,
it may perhaps be denied that the man in question was Shakespeare.
A further application of the same method will make the sceptic's
position rather more difficult. At Act 1, Sc. 1, 166 ff. Lucentio says:

> O yes, I saw sweet beauty in her face,
> Such as the daughter of Agenor had,
> That made great Jove to humble him to her hand,
> When with his knees he kissed the Cretan strand.

Ovid, recounting the abduction of Europa, writes: *miratur
Agenore nata / ... flores ad candida porrigit ora ... oscula dat
manibus ... / nunc latus in fulvis niveum deponit harenis* (*Met.* 2.858
ff.); Golding translates: 'Agenors daughter marveld much ... / Annon

she reaches to his mouth hir hand with herbes and flowres ... / He lickes hir hands ... / Annon he layes his snowie side against the golden sand' (2.1075 ff.). So far so good. But in Ovid this is not 'the Cretan strand'; it is the coast of Sidon (line 840). The writer has made a very understandable slip; for Crete is where Jupiter and Europa arrive a few lines later (*Met.* 3.2 ff.).[3] It so happens that the very same mistake occurs in *A Midsummer Night's Dream.* At Act 4, Sc. 1, 111 ff., remembering that Cadmus went in search of his sister Europa (*Met.* 3.3 ff.) and mistakenly thinking that Europa was abducted in Crete, Hippolyta assumes that at some stage Cadmus must have been in Crete: 'I was with Hercules and Cadmus once, / When in a wood of Crete they bay'd the bear'. Since no one doubts that Shakespeare wrote *A Midsummer Night's Dream*, it seems likely that he also wrote the corresponding passage in *The Taming of the Shrew.*

For the next argument we must start from another position. In Act 4, Sc. 5, 27 ff. Petruchio addresses Vincentio: 'Good morrow, gentle mistress, where away?' Then, turning to Katharina, he says:

> Tell me, sweet Kate, and tell me truly too,
> Hast thou beheld a *fresher* gentlewoman?
> Such war of *white* and *red* within her cheeks! ...

Katharina then greets Vincentio:

> Young budding virgin, fair and *fresh* and sweet,
> Whither away, or where is thy abode?
> *Happy* the parents of so fair a child;
> Happier the man, whom favourable stars
> Allot thee for his lovely *bed-fellow!*

In his comment on line 30, Warwick Bond refers to *Venus and Adonis* 345 f. ('To note the fighting conflict of her hue, / How *white* and *red* each other did destroy') and also to *The Rape of Lucrece* 71 f. ('This silent war of lilies and of roses, / Which Tarquin view'd in her fair face's field'). It certainly looks as if the playwright half remembered those earlier lines. If so, he seems to have been led, by association, to another passage of Golding's Ovid:

> For in his face the colour *fresh* appeared like the same
> That is in Apples which doe hang upon the Sunnie side:
> Or Ivorie shadowed with a *red*: or such as is espide
> Of *white* and *scarlet* colours mixt appearing in the Moone.

What makes this suggestion likely is the fact that these lines of Golding are preceded by a greeting to a beautiful young person:

> Or if thou be a mortall wight, right *happie* folke are they,
> By whome thou camste into this worlde, right *happy* is (I say)
> Thy mother and thy sister too (if any bee): good hap
> That woman had that was thy Nurce and gave thy mouth hir pap.
> But farre above all other, far more blist than these is shee
> Whome thou vouchsafest for the wife and *bedfellow* for to bee.

It only remains to add that *this* white and scarlet face belongs to Hermaphroditus and the girl addressing him is Salmacis (*Met.* 4.392 ff.).[4]

To sum up: Induction 2. 49-51 is linked to *The Passionate Pilgrim* no.6 by the shared confusion of Venus and Adonis with Salmacis and Hermaphroditus; Act 1, Sc. 1, 166 ff. is linked to *A Midsummer Night's Dream* by the shared confusion of Sidon with Crete; Act 4, Sc. 5, 30 is linked to *Venus and Adonis* and to *The Rape of Lucrece*, and also to the story of Salmacis and Hermaphroditus; while lines 39 ff. of the same scene are similarly linked to the story of Salmacis and Hermaphroditus. Admittedly not all these connections have the same degree of probability; and when taken together they do not establish beyond doubt that all the passages in question are by Shakespeare; but they do lend some additional weight to that assumption.

   If the foregoing argument is considered reasonable, then the following points may throw a little more light on that fascinating subject, Shakespeare's mind at work.

1. *Tranio:*   Let's be no stoics nor no stocks I pray,
                  Or so devote to Aristotle's checks,
                  As Ovid be an outcast quite abjured.
                              (Act 1, Sc. 1, 31 ff.)

In view of the witty nature of the lines (e.g. stoics / stocks), we must surely be meant to think of Ovid not just as an outcast from a stern moral system but as an outcast from the Augustan world; cf 'honest Ovid ... among the Goths' (*As You Like It*, Act 3, Sc. 3, 10), an allusion which is also relevant to our last point.

2. *Lucentio*   As Anna to the Queen of Carthage was
                              (Act 1, Sc. 1, 153)

An editor might well comment: 'Anna was the sister of Dido, Queen of Carthage; see Virgil, *Aeneid* 4'. Yet this would not adequately indicate what is happening. We must go further back, to 147 ff.:

      Lucentio: O Tranio, till I found it to be true,
                    I never thought it possible or likely;
                    But see, while idly I stood looking on,
                    I found the effect of love in idleness.

So a character suddenly finds himself in love – against all expectation. This puts the writer in mind of Dido, who, against all expectation, suddenly found herself in love with Aeneas. He remembers that Dido confided in the sister whom she loved: *Anna fatebor enim, ...* ('For Anna, I shall confess...'; *Aen.* 4.20) and *o luce magis dilecta sorori* ('O dearer to your sister than the light'; 4.31). So he writes:

    And now in plainness do *confess* to thee
    That art to me as secret and as *dear*
    As *Anna* to the Queen of Carthage was.

So the reminiscence is not just of a character, but of a character in a dramatic situation. As the situation is recalled, so are the appropriate words. It seems a little harsh, then, to speak of a 'rather forced introduction of a classical reference', as the Cambridge editors do. At least we will have to find some other reason for regarding the passage as non-Shakespearian.

3. The same considerations apply to the lines immediately following. On line161, *Redime te captum quam queas minimo* ('Ransom yourself from captivity as cheaply as you can'), Dr Johnson remarked, 'Our author had this line from Lily, which I mention, that it may not be brought as an argument of his learning'. It is true, as T.W. Baldwin points out, that the actual wording comes from Lily[5] rather than from Terence, who in *The Eunuch* (1.1.29 f.) has *ut te redimas captum quam queas / minimo*. Yet Dr Johnson may have been ungenerous; for it seems that Shakespeare was not merely repeating a Latin tag but remembering, however dimly, a comic situation. In *The Eunuch* Phaedria, a young lover, is talking to his older and wiser servant, Parmeno (27-9):

> *Phaedria:*   *et taedet et amore ardeo, et prudens sciens,*
>   *vivus vidensque pereo, nec quid agam scio*

I am sick of it and yet *I burn* with love; knowingly and consciously, living and with my eyes open, *I perish,* and I don't know what to do.

> *Parmeno:*   *quid agas nisi ut te redimas captum quam*
>   *queas minimo?*

What should you do except ransom yourself from captivity as cheaply as you can?

This reappears, slightly modified, in Lucentio's dialogue with *his* servant Tranio: 'Tranio, *I burn,* I pine, *I perish,* Tranio ...' (154) and 'Assist me, Tranio, for I know thou wilt' (157)

> *Tranio:*   If love have touched you, nought remains
>   but so –
>   *Redime te captum quam queas minimo.*
>   (160 f.)

The reminiscence, therefore, is less simple and less mechanical than Johnson seems to have thought.

Related Material:

'Pyramus and Thisbe in Shakespeare and Ovid' in D. West and T. Woodman (eds) *Creative Imitation and Latin Literature* (Cambridge, 1979) ch. 10.

'Two Twin Comedies' in *The Classical Tradition in Operation* (Toronto, 1994) ch. 2.

10 Milton, *Sonnet* 17 (Carey no. 87):
an Avoidable Controversy

[From *Hermathena* 158 (1995) 109-15]

Lawrence of virtuous father virtuous son,
Now that the fields are dank, and ways are mire,
Where shall we sometimes meet, and by the fire
Help waste a sullen day, what may be won
From the hard season gaining? Time will run
On smoother till Favonius reinspire
The frozen earth; and clothe in fresh attire
The lily and the rose, that neither sowed nor spun.
What neat repast shall feast us, light and choice,
Of Attic taste, with wine, whence we may rise
To hear the lute well touched, or artful voice
Warble immortal notes and Tuscan air?
He who of those delights can judge, and spare
To interpose them oft, is not unwise.

For two hundred years or so after its publication, there is no evience, so far as I know, that the sonnet caused any perplexity.[1] The controversy about the last two lines (which affects, of course, the interpretation of the whole poem) seems to have begun in 1859, when Thomas Keightly wrote '*spare,* sc. time'.[2] In 1882 he was contradicted by David Masson, who said 'surely the opposite – "refrain from interposing them oft".'[3] Subsequently, at least a dozen editors and critics followed Masson's lead; but, according to F. Neiman, writing in 1949, they did so 'uncritically'.[4] After that the debate expanded and ramified. In the *Variorum Commentary* (1972), A.S.P. Woodhouse argued for 'spare' in the sense of 'refrain'; but in the same place his old friend, Douglas Bush, maintained that 'spare time to' was at least as logical as 'forbear to' and perhaps more so.[5] Before that work appeared, John Carey had given up the struggle, simply commenting 'the word (i.e. 'spare') is ambiguous'.[6] In earlier times such a conclusion would have been reached with regret; and Milton might have been criticized for an expression which left itself open to contradictory interpretations. But not now; indeed Stanley Fish welcomes the alleged ambiguity. 'The lines,' he says, 'first generate a pressure for judgment – "He who of those delights can judge" – and then decline to deliver it. The responsibility of deciding when and how often – if at all – to indulge in "those delights" is transferred from the text to its readers.'[7] 'Judge for yourselves', then, is what the verses mean in Fish's terms. Fish also believes, in line with this view, that the double negative 'not unwise' means neither 'unwise' nor 'wise'.[8] What, then, *does* Milton mean by 'spare to interpose'?

1. *Lexical Evidence*

Under '*spare*' (II.6) *OED*, vol. 16.115 gives 'to abstain or refrain from using, employing, exercising etc.; to forbear, omit, or avoid the use or occasion of'. The dictionary then adds under II.6c, 'Const. *to* and infinitive. Frequent from the 14th to the 17th century; now *rare*'. About a score of examples follow, including: (1637) 'I shall spare to bee so injurious to your patience'; and (1686) 'The Controller ... would not spare to inform the worst he could against him'. This use, of course, is parallel to that of the Latin *parco* with the infinitive (*OLD*, sense 2c).

Under '*spare*' 8c *OED* gives 'to set apart, save, or give (time) from one's usual or ordinary duties or avocations'. One clear case with the infinitive is (1833) 'Can you spare a minute just to look out of this window?' – a use which, of course, has continued to our own day. However – and surely this is the crucial point – in this last instance, as in all the other cases cited, a noun like 'minute' or 'time' is actually included. Hence there is no possibility of confusion with sense 6c noted above. By the same token, 8c has no parallel in the Latin *parco*. If, therefore, those who advocate 'spare', as meaning 'afford time' wish to command any attention, they must adduce examples of 'spare' used in that sense *with the infinitive*, and *without* any noun like 'time'. So far they have not done so.

Bush tries to escape from this obligation by saying, 'Milton's use of words and idioms is notoriously bold and his usages cannot be limited by examples in *OED*'. However, in this case the innovation would be quite unique (there are no previous, and no subsequent, examples); it would also contradict a well-established usage. In spite of Humpty Dumpty's famous principle, a critic has no right to invent a meaning, and then foist it onto a passage which clearly says something quite different.

There is further evidence from another dictionary. In 1963 J.A.W. Bennett wrote to the *Times Literary Supplement*[9], pointing out that one of the *Disticha Catonis* had probably been in Milton's mind when he was writing the concluding lines of *Sonnet* 17 – *interpone tuis interdum gaudia curis, / ut possis animo quemvis sufferre laborem* (*Catonis Disticha* 3.6, *Minor Latin Poets* [Loeb edn] 610). This convincing letter brought forth a brief, authoritatively worded, comment from J.C. Maxwell, asserting that the lines from 'Cato' refuted the old view that 'spare / To interpose them oft' meant 'refrain from interposing them often'.[10] In fact, of course, the distich *confirmed* that view: 'Interpose pleasures *occasionally* among your serious concerns, so that you may be able to bear any trouble whatsoever'. The point was noted politely two weeks later by V. Scholderer.[11] Instead of admitting his careless error, Maxwell replied with an evasive and disingenuous letter which did him no credit.[12] And there, for the time being, the matter was allowed to rest.

The next surprise came when Bush published his edition in 1965 and appealed to the distich in support of 'spare' meaning 'spare time'.[13] As we have seen, the distich gave no such support, unless, of course, *interdum* (sometimes) was to be understood in the sense of *saepe* (frequently) on the grounds that the author of the *Disticha* was, too, notoriously bold and enjoyed a freedom which was not to be limited by examples from *Lewis and Short*. A year later – another surprise – Bush's mistake was repeated by Honigmann in his edition of the Sonnets.[14]

2. *Evidence from within the Poem*

The sonnet is, as everyone admits, an invitation to enjoyment. However, it is a *judicious* invitation. The recipient, though a young man, is not a frivolous hedonist but a virtuous friend.[15] Such convivial hours will not be frequent ('Where shall we *sometimes* meet?'; line 3). The food and wine, like the music, will be such as to win the approval of discriminating people – an idea reinforced by the adjective 'Attic' (*OED* sense 2, 'simple and refined'); but they will not be over-lavish (lines 9-12). The final couplet (omitting the controversial phrase) is equally measured: he who of those delights can judge (i.e. assess their worth and the position which they should occupy in the life of a good man) ... is not unwise. The place and validity of civilised pleasure is therefore acknowledged; but it is carefully limited, as we would expect from a writer of Milton's outlook. Into this sequence of thought 'refrain from interposing them oft' fits smoothly and harmoniously. To defend the other view, Honigmann has to maintain that the question addressed to Lawrence ('Where shall we sometimes meet?') is superseded when the poem concludes with 'interpose them oft'. So, instead of reinforcing what goes before, the concluding lines significantly alter the rhetorical thrust of the poem. Even in Honigmann's terms (i.e. a contrast between line 3 and lines 13-14) this is unsatisfactory. As we have just seen, the difficulty goes further than this; for the recommendation of frequent parties is also at odds with 'a ... day' (line 4), with the tone of lines 9-12 and with the prudent phrasing of the last two lines. Here, however, we are at least dealing with serious structural arguments. One editor, who shall be nameless, welcomes the erroneous view because it presents us with a merry Milton instead of the traditional sober-sides. It would, I fear, take more than the misinterpretation of 'spare' to turn the puritan poet into a soul-mate of Old King Cole.

3. *Evidence from Horace*

Anyone who writes about English poetry from a Latin background must beware of grinding his own axe. But in Milton's case we are dealing with a writer who could think and compose in Latin, and had a greater mastery of the language than any of today's professional scholars. The Horatian spirit of Sonnet 17 has often been observed. The form of the opening line recalls *o matre pulchra filia pulchrior* ('You of beautiful mother more beautiful daughter'; *Odes* 1.16.1). The call for relaxation in the face of bleak weather is reminiscent of poems like *Horrida tempestas* ('a rough storm has drawn down the sky'; *Epode* 13) and *Vides ut alta* ('see how Soracte is shining, piled high with snow'; *Odes* 1.9). The 'neat repast' comes from the invitation to Maecenas in *Odes* 3.29.14-15, where Horace observes that many rich and busy men like to relax over a simple but elegantly served meal (*mundae cenae*).[16] The construction of *parco* with the infinitive occurs in another invitation to Maecenas (*Odes* 3.8.26), where the statesman is urged to refrain from worrying overmuch (*parce ... nimium cavere*) about public affairs. So it is fair to assume that Milton meant this to be read as a Horatian poem.

Whatever his actual *practice* may have been, in his hospitality poems Horace never suggests that his parties should be frequent. Almost all the odes in question are composed, or purport to have been composed, to suit some special occasion. Outside the *Odes,* there is one case where the speaker says explicitly that such celebrations should take place occasionally rather than often. According to the 'unprofessional philosopher' Ofellus in *Sat.*2.2, the wise man (*sapiens*, line 63) will be fastidious (*mundus*) in his dining habits (65). Normally he will live frugally; but sometimes (*aliquando*, line 82)[17] he will indulge himself more freely. Later Ofellus describes his simple diet, then adds how in special circumstances he would offer something more choice (116-25). A more familiar passage comes from *Odes* 4.12: there, after inviting Virgil to a party, Horace concludes: *misce stultitiam consiliis brevem: / dulce est desipere in loco* ('mingle a brief moment of folly with your serious concerns; it is sweet to take an occasional holiday from sense; 4.12.27-8) – a *brief* moment; an *occasional* holiday.

One must not, of course, give the impression that this sensible idea was confined to Horace. Phaedrus, for example, in the first century AD tells how Aesop was ridiculed for playing games with children. In answer he put an unstrung bow on the ground. The moral runs (3.14.12-13): *sic lusus animo debent aliquando dari, / ad cogitandum melior ut redeat tibi* ('So *from time to time* your mind should be allowed some forms of recreation, so that it may think more effectively when it resumes its work for you').[18]

4. *Evidence from* Sonnet *18 (Carey)*

> Cyriack, whose grandsire on the royal bench
>   Of British Themis with no mean applause
>   Pronounced and in his volumes taught our laws,
>   Which others at their bar so often wrench;
> Today deep thoughts resolve with me to drench
>   In mirth, that after no repenting draws;
>   Let Euclid rest and Archimedes pause,
>   And what the Swede intend, and what the French.
> To measure life, learn thou betimes, and know
>   Toward solid good what leads the nearest way;
>   For other things mild heaven a time ordains,
> And disapproves that care, though wise in show,
>   That with superfluous burden loads the day,
>   And when God sends a cheerful hour, refrains.

It is generally agreed that Sonnets 17 and 18 come from the same period, and that the two poems are related. But how? Addressing Mr Cyriack Skinner, grandson of Chief Justice Coke, Milton invites him to drench deep thoughts in mirth *today* (my italics throughout this paragraph) and to leave aside *for the time being* the problems of geometry, science and politics (that is the implication of 'rest' and 'pause' in line 7). In pondering on life, one should know what leads directly to solid good. For other, less serious, activities heaven sets aside *a time* (11); it does not approve of the worry that oppresses the day with an *unnecessary* burden, and that, when God sends *a cheerful hour,* refuses to enjoy it (lines 12-14). Such a negative, cheerless attitude is not really, but only apparently, wise.

Again the spirit is Horatian. In view of line 8 ('And what the Swede intend, and what the French'), one thinks of *Odes* 2.11, where a friend is urged to stop worrying about 'what the warlike Cantabrian and the Scythian are plotting' (2.11.1-2); and of *Odes* 3.29, where Maecenas is worrying about 'what the Chinese and Bactra ... and the unruly Don may be preparing' (3.29.26-8). 'To measure life' (line 9) may recall *verae numerosque modosque ediscere vitae* ('to learn the rhythms and measures of an upright life'; *Epistles* 2.2.144). And the heaven which disapproves of excessive worry is surely a less pagan and less cynical version of the god who laughs if a mortal is unduly anxious (*ridetque si mortalis ultra / fas trepidat*; *Odes* 3.29.31-2).

So the two poems make essentially the same point; but they conclude with different emphases. *Sonnet* 18 says 'when the right occasion occurs for convivial pleasures, *enjoy* them; to forego them is unwise'; *Sonnet* 17 says 'enjoy convivial pleasures, *when* the right occasion occurs; to indulge in them frequently is unwise'. Thus each sonnet affirms the principle of the golden mean; but, while the end of 18 advises against the defect of the mean, i.e. dullness, the end of 17 advises against the excess of the mean, i.e. frivolity. Neither, however, recommends *frequent* entertainments.

To sum up: one view of the phrase 'spare / To interpose them oft' represents an established English usage; the other posits a unique innovation. On one view the phrase is supported directly by its Latin source (Cato's distich); on the other it involves an alteration. One view preserves a uniform sequence of thought throughout the poem; the other requires a sudden change of ideas in the middle of the last two lines. One view allows the Horatian reminiscences to culminate in a piece of Horatian advice; the other does not. Finally, one view assumes a tighter, the other a looser, connection with *Sonnet*18. So, although there are arguments on both sides, all the *good* arguments are on the side of Masson. It also follows that, whatever opinion one may have of Fish's theory of interpretation, such a theory derives no support from Milton's sonnet.

11 Dryden on Horace and Juvenal

[A revised version of
University of Toronto Quarterly 32,2 (1963) 155-69.]

Dryden's comparison of Horace and Juvenal comes in his famous
Discourse Concerning The Original And Progress Of Satire begin-
ning on p.78.[1] There Dryden concedes that Horace was 'the better
poet' but he bases his superiority on the *Epodes* and *Odes,* which he
rightly excludes from his discussion of satire. His reasons for doing
so, however, are not satisfactory. 'Horace,' he says, 'has written
many of them satirically, against his private enemies ... but he had
purged himself of this choler before he entered on those discourses
which are more properly called the Roman Satire. He has not now
to do with a Lyce, a Canidia, a Cassius Severus, or a Menas; but
is to correct the vices and follies of his time.' No doubt the error is
largely due to the editors' habit of printing the *Odes* and *Epodes*
before the the the *Satires* and *Epistles.* The first book of satires was
published about 35 BC, the second about 30.[2] The *Epodes* were
written in the same decade and were published in 30. As for the
Odes, the first collection, comprising books 1-3, did not appear
until 23 and there is no proof that any of these poems was written
before 30 BC. So we cannot speak of Horace purging himself of his
choler before undertaking the *Satires.*

Then there is the question of names. Cassius Severus, in spite
of what Dryden says on p. 90, is not mentioned in the *Epodes* or
indeed anywhere else in Horace. His presence in the tradition is
due to the imagination of some ancient scribe who prefixed his
name to the anonymous sixth epode, forgetting that the poem did
not suit his character and was, in all probability, written before he
was born.[3] The same kind of speculation made Pompeius Menas
the object of *Epode* 4, although, unlike Horace's target in line
20, he was never a tribune. Those are both historical persons;
but the same cannot quite be said of Canidia, who is probably

a composite character, based on someone known to Horace but heavily overlaid with fiction. Even if she is counted as a private enemy, this will not help Dryden's case; for she also appears in three of the satires. The distinction which Dryden had in mind would therefore be more clearly stated by saying that, whereas the *Epodes* contain eight lampoons (four of them anonymous, two aimed at Canidia, one at the poet Mevius and one at the heartless Neaera), the *Satires* have none. By 'lampoon' I mean a poem referring to a person named or unnamed with the sole object of abusing him or her. Thus, for instance, *Epode* 9 would not count as a lampoon, in spite of the passing swipes at Sextus Pompeius, Antony and Cleopatra.

Dryden goes on to maintain that personal attacks are defensible when the character in question is a 'public nuisance'. 'All those, whom Horace in his *Satires*, and Persius and Juvenal have mentioned in theirs, with a brand of infamy, are wholly such.' (p. 80). Now the only satirist who was in a position to attack 'public nuisances' with a 'brand of infamy' was Gaius Lucilius, who was a member of the upper class in the free republic of the second century BC and enjoyed the protection of the powerful Scipio Aemilianus. Horace uses various kinds of figure to illustrate his satire (some living, some dead, some merely types); none could be called 'a public nuisance', if that means a vicious person of social or political importance. In Persius there are even fewer individual targets. As for Juvenal, the vices he castigates are contemporary but the names are mostly of 'those whose ashes lie under the Flaminian and Latin Roads' (*Sat.* 1.170 f.). To use the dead as *exempla* is a very different thing from making an example of the living.[4] Those living individuals who are attacked do not represent a threat. More will be said on this point below.

From the human targets of satire Dryden now turns to its general objects, developing the view that 'folly was the proper quarry of Horace and not vice' (p. 83). Folly, he says, was the more difficult; for 'as there are but few notoriously wicked men, in comparison with a shoal of fools and fops, so 'tis a harder thing to make a man wise than to make him honest; for the will is only to be reclaimed in the one, but the understanding is to be informed in the other'. Instead of examining this very questionable reasoning, we shall concentrate on the proposition that Horace's chief concern was not vice but folly. It sounds attractive, offering as it does a neat contrast between the aims of the two satirists; for this reason, it has been accepted by generations of readers and is sometimes found in handbooks today.[5] Unfortunately it is not true. Let us glance quickly at the subjects of the relevant Horatian satires. First Book: (1) greed and envy; (2) adultery; (3) cruelty and intolerance; (4) back-biting and malice; (5) snobbery and ambition; (8) witchcraft and superstition; (9) ill-mannered place-seeking. Second Book: (2) gluttony and meanness; (3) avarice, meanness, murder, prodigality, megalomania, erotic obsession, superstition; (4) gluttony; (5) legacy-hunting; (7) the tyranny of lust and gluttony. One shudders to contemplate the moral system of a man to whom these are but follies.

One of the factors behind this misconception may be a passage of Persius:

> *secuit Lucilius urbem*
> *te Lupe, te Muci, et genuinum fregit in illis,*
> *omne vafer vitium ridenti Flaccus amico*
> *tangit et admissus circum praecordia ludit,*
> *callidus excusso populum suspendere naso.*
> (*Sat.* 1.114-18)

Lucilius cut into the city – you Lupus and you Mucius – and smashed his molar on them. Horace cunningly puts his finger on all the faults of his laughing friend, and after gaining access plays around his conscience, clever as he is at hanging the public on the end of his critical nose.

Dryden prints the third and fourth lines only (p. 83); he then proceeds as follows: 'This was the commendation which Persius gave [Horace]: where, by *vitium,* he means those little vices which we call follies, the defects of human understanding, or, at most, the peccadillos of life, rather than the tragical vices, to which men are hurried by their unruly passions and exorbitant desires'. Now Persius was steeped in Horace's *Satires* (and his *Epistles*);[6] he knew perfectly well that teasing his friends about their foibles was not Horace's practice. So Persius must be interpreted backwards: first he criticises people in general; by doing so in an an entertaining way he cleverly gains access to the conscience of his friends and reminds them amusingly of their faults. The process is described by Horace himself: after describing the greed of an Athenian miser and then the sufferings of Tantalus, Horace suddenly breaks off: *quid rides? mutato nomine de te / fabula narratur* ('What are you laughing at? Change the name and the story is about *you*'; *Sat.* 1.1.69-70). Within the poem the 'you' is addressed to the miser; but indirectly the reader is induced to think of himself.

The main reason for the misconception, however, is undoubtedly the attitude and tone of the two satirists. Horace's basic objection to greed, lust, ambition and so on is that they make the man himself unhappy and bring consequences which may ruin his life. To the Christian, who is aware that other people also suffer from the man's vice and who bears in mind his offence against God, this outlook is bound to appear superficial. Moreover, since Horace's tone is one of sensible ridicule ('Don't be such a fool, man! Can't you see that you're making yourself miserable?'), the Christian reader tends to forget that most of the faults attacked by Horace really are vices. Take, for example, these lines from the first satire (70-9):

> You scrape your money-bags together from every side and fall asleep on top of them, with your mouth still gaping open. You have to keep them inviolate like sacred objects and only enjoy them as you would a painted tablet. Don't you know what money is for? What use it offers? You can buy bread, vegetables and half a litre of wine, and other things too which human nature cannot conveniently do without. Or perhaps you *enjoy* lying awake half dead with fright, spending your days and nights in terror of wicked burglars or fires or slaves who might clean you out and then disappear? I should always hope to be very badly off in goods of that sort!

Here the miser is undoubtedly vicious by Roman and Christian standards alike but Horace portrays him as a ludicrous, slightly pathetic, fool.

It should not be inferred from this that Horace's subjects were always the same as Juvenals's. There are a few very notable differences. First, in every period of his work Juvenal is concerned, not only with vice, but also with crime. He constantly inveighs against forgery, robbery, perjury, adultery, fraud, murder and treason. In Horace such material is far less frequent. Secondly, we do not find any Horatian satire devoted to homosexuality, male prostitution or cannibalism, whereas Juvenal does handle such themes. Finally, while Horace's conception of *nugae* ('trifles') can be inferred from pieces like the seventh and eighth satires of Book 1, the only 'trifle' in Juvenal is an account of how a giant turbot was received at the court of Domitian. There is certainly humour there; but it is humour of a grim kind and an atmosphere of dread hangs over the scene. Juvenal's own comment is this:

> *atque utinam his potius nugis tota illa dedisset*
> *tempora saevitiae, claras quibus abstulit urbi*
> *illustresque animas impune et vindice nullo*
> (Sat. 4.150-2)

> Yes, and what a blessing it would have been if trifles
> of this kind had filled
> all those cruel years in which he robbed the city of its noblest
> and most distinguished souls, with none to punish or avenge.

Nevertheless, in a number of cases the poets' subjects are broadly similar, and there it is the contrast in treatment that proves instructive. Nasidienus (Horace 2.8) and Virro (Juvenal 5) are both hosts. The former, however, in spite of his vanity, vulgarity and naked social ambition, does try (anxiously) to please his guests, treating them all with the same consideration. Virro, on the other hand, constantly humiliates his guests, giving them inferior food and wine, served by ugly and contemptuous waiters; even the water is different; and always there is the threat of violence. These indignities are recounted with a bitter resentment and a hyperbolical wit quite alien to Horace's temper. In another satire (11) Juvenal does plan a pleasant dinner party for his friend, Persicus. In lines 56-76 he describes the simple menu, comparing it with the diet of the men of old. He then continues: 'I will not invite the sort of people who will sneer at my modest circumstances; the meat will not be carved by a graduate of Trypherus' school for chefs; there will be no pretty waiters; and you needn't expect a performance from a troop of Spanish belly-dancers'. That is not Horace's voice. Concluding his invitation, Juvenal urges Persicus to forget his business troubles and enjoy a day's holiday. Horace could easily have written that, but he would never have gone on to say: 'Don't let your wife cause you secret anger because she goes out at dawn and comes home at night with her fine-spun clothes damp and suspiciously creased, her hair rumpled and her face and ears burning'.

Other poems offer similar contrasts. In 2.6 Horace tells how glad he is to get out of Rome, because he enjoys a rest from the noisy merry-go-round of social life. Juvenal's Umbricius is leaving for ever (*Sat.* 3), because the old virtues have disappeared and Rome has passed into the hands of charlatans, pimps and gangsters. In Juvenal's eyes an adulterous lady typifies the avarice, dishonesty and utter rottenness of Roman womanhood (*Sat.* 6); she is a monster, a creature of abhorrence. To Horace (1.2) she is simply a hazard which can easily be avoided with a little common sense. In 1.6 Horace declines to take part in the struggle for office against men who rely on their aristocratic birth and, in doing so, gives a memorable account of his upbringing and his present way of life. In Juvenal (*Sat.* 8) the informal personal note is missing; instead the theme of ambition develops into a long tirade against the aristocracy, who in the recent past have sunk so low as to make a spectacle of themselves in public.

The difference in treatment implies a different attitude on the part of the satirist. Like the Epicureans (and all sensible men), Horace recognised various degrees of bad behaviour. Stealing a cabbage is not the same as robbing a temple (*Sat.* 1.3.115-7). Each case must be judged on its merits. Juvenal's attitude, however, is more like that of the doctrinaire Stoic who regards all sins as equally culpable. The suggestion of philosophical rigour is perhaps misleading; but it is true that Juvenal does not invite us to make distinctions. In his 3.58-112, for instance, we are asked to believe that the clothes, the complaisance and the lechery of the immigrant Greek are all equally reprehensible. Again, in his most elaborate poem – the invective against Roman women – we find the following sequence (6.379 ff.): 'If your wife is musical she will plan adultery with professional singers; but let her be musical (with all it entails) rather than a chatterbox in male company; no less insufferable is the woman who gives her plebeian neighbour a brutal beating; worse still is the blue-stocking who holds the floor on literature, history and philosophy, and corrects her husband's grammar'. In synopsis this sounds merely funny but in the full version of the passage, which runs for nearly eighty lines, there is no suggestion of anticlimax.

In 8.21 ff. Juvenal contrasts Nero with Orestes: both killed their mothers, but Orestes was avenging his father's death, and Orestes never murdered his sister or wife, never sang on the stage, never composed an epic on Troy. Juvenal knows we will naturally take this as satiric bathos; so he hastens to cancel this effect by insisting that Nero's artistic performances were as damnable as anything he ever did. In 3.7-9, what could be worse, says Juvenal, than living in fear of fires, falling houses, and the thousand and one dangers of the savage city, and poets reciting in the month of August? Here the bathos is not cancelled; but, like many famous quotations, this is quite untypical; for although Juvenal often contrives an anticlimax in order to belittle the person he is speaking of – as in the lines on Hannibal (10.166-7) – in this case he has undermined the force of his own argument; for the reader begins to suspect that Umbricius is not so appalled by the other dangers as he pretends. Nevertheless, if we allow for this and a handful of other exceptions, it still remains true that while Horace encourages discrimination, which is an exercise of the reason, Juvenal often overpowers the reason altogether.

This brings us back to Dryden's remark about the informing of the understanding being harder than reclaiming of the will. Apart from its dubious validity, it is for the most part irrelevant to Juvenal. In most of his famous satires Juvenal is not concerned to reclaim the will. His object is to provoke the same scorn, indignation and disgust as he feels himself. His technique suits that purpose; for its effectiveness depends less on the development of a consecutive argument than on presenting a series of lurid pictures, accompanied by emotive comments, which are designed to play on our deepest fears, resentments and taboos. We meet an extended example in the first satire; a section (22-30) was quoted in Chapter 7 (p. 76 f.) above, in which sexual scorn, male arrogance, social snobbery, xenophobia, jealousy and physical revulsion are all piled one on top of the other, until the satirist explodes in a shout of fury and contempt. That is why the cause of Juvenal's fiercest satire is identified as an efficient cause: *facit indignatio versum* ('indignation generates verse'; 1.79). The savage laughter brings a kind of emotional release; but there is no constructive purpose, no thought of healing the disease of the time, because for a man with Juvenal's attitude the state of Roman life is irremediable: *nil erit ulterius quod nostris moribus addat / posteritas, eadem facient cupientque minores* ('There will be nothing further that posterity can add to our behaviour; our descendants will be just the same in their deeds and desires'; 1.147-8).

The same gloomy spirit is visible even in poems which do not appear to be prompted by indignation.[7] The resignation to which the tenth satire leads is a wisdom reserved for the view. The rest of Rome and the rest of mankind will continue their misguided dreams. Satire thirteen, though different from the tenth in tone and strategy, takes the same pessimistic view of human virtue: *rari quippe boni: numera; vix sunt totidem quot / Thebarum portae vel divitis ostia Nili* ('Good men are scarce. Count them – they are hardly as many as the gates of Thebes or the mouths of the rich Nile' – i.e. seven; 13.26-7).

Turning back to Horace, we find that the cause of his satire is a final cause: *ridentem dicere verum* ('to tell the truth with a smile'). The smile is vital; for, as well as being enjoyable in its own right, it makes the truth palatable and therefore easy to ingest. In Horace's own words: 'Great difficulties are usually cut away more forcefully and more effectively by laughter than by vituperation' *(Sat.* 1.10.14-15). This must always be the motto of the reforming satirist. It is basically optimistic in outlook; for it implies that the major cause of human unhappiness is a defect of vision and that, once the satirist has made his diagnosis, the remedy is in the patient's hands.

This brings us to the question of style. Dryden takes issue with Casaubon over the alleged vulgarity of Horace's style, maintaining quite rightly that it 'is constantly accommodated to his subject, either high or low' (p. 78). Later, however, he seems to revise this position, asserting that 'the low style of Horace is according to his subject, that is, generally grovelling' (p. 85). This remark suggests that Dryden has overlooked many of those subtle gradations

which make Horatian satire such a delight. When it is taken in
conjunction with his praise of Juvenal, whose expressions are
'sonorous and more noble', whose words are 'suitable to his
thoughts, sublime and lofty' (p. 85), then it becomes clear that
once again Dryden has distorted the picture in his endeavour to
produce a striking contrast. For Juvenal's sonorous and vehement
rhetoric is inseparable from another feature of his style, one
which Dryden has seen fit to ignore, namely his brilliant use of
demeaning detail. Indeed Juvenal's most characteristic effects
result from the tension set up by these two forces operating
within the same phrase or sentence – or succeeding one another
in violent alternation. An exception which comes to mind is that
magnificent passage in the fifteenth satire beginning 'When
nature gave tears to man, she showed that she was giving him a
tender heart' (131 ff.). The rarity of such cases, however, refutes
Dryden's point. Far more typical is an example like this, picked at
random from the seventh satire:

> *frange miser calamum vigilataque proelia dele,*
> *qui facis in parva sublimia carmina cella,*
> *ut dignus venias hederis et imagine macra*
> (7.27-9)

(If you are looking for any patron other than the emperor)
break your pen, you poor wretch, and destroy the battles
that have kept you awake, you who fashion lofty poems
in a tiny garret in the hope of emerging worthy of an ivy
crown and a skinny bust.

For further evidence of this polarity in Juvenal's style one can
hardly do better than read the tenth satire along with Johnson's *The
Vanity of Human Wishes*.[8] If, therefore, we have to generalise on
the styles of the two poets, it would be safer to say that, whereas
Horace rises and falls between relatively narrow limits, Juvenal
shoots up and down at a speed which leaves us breathless and
exhilarated – and sometimes slightly sick.

Then there is the matter of wit. Here again we are disconcerted
by Dryden's vacillations. It will be recalled that at the outset
he chose Horace for his instruction and Juvenal for his delight

(p. 81-2). Then, finding that Horace's instruction consisted of ridiculing men's follies, he asserted that 'the divine wit of Horace left nothing untouched' (p. 83) and that 'Horace laughs to shame all follies, and insinuates virtue, by familiar examples rather than by the severity of precepts' (p. 84). By now it looks as if Dryden has received as much delight as instruction. But no. He now states that the delight which Horace gives him is 'but languishing'; and that the poet's wit (which a page ago was 'divine') is 'faint' and his salt 'almost insipid'. Juvenal on the other hand 'is of a more vigorous and masculine wit'. 'He gives me,' says Dryden, 'as much pleasure as I can bear; he fully satisfies my expectation; he treats his subject home; his spleen is raised, and so is mine.' As far as it goes, this is a fair assessment of Juvenal's wit; and since preferences in wit are highly subjective, we are willing to let Dryden keep his opinion of Horace, an opinion which, after some bewilderment, we think we have finally grasped: Horace's wit is feeble and intermittent. But Dryden has not yet finished. On p. 92 he takes up Barten Holyday's silly remark that 'a perpetual grin like that of Horace rather angers than emends a man'. Rallying to Horace's defence he says: 'Let the chastisement of Juvenal be never so necessary for this new kind of satire; let him declaim as wittily and sharply as he pleases; yet still the nicest and most delicate touches of satire consist in fine raillery'. There follows a delightful and justly famous account of what Dryden means by 'fine raillery'. It is the ability 'to make a man appear a fool, a blockhead, or a knave, without using any of those opprobrious terms'; it is 'the fineness of a stroke that separates the head from the body and leaves it standing in its place'; or again it is a method which effects 'a pleasant cure with all the limbs preserved entire'. Has Horace, then, been once more reinstated? Alas no, because we are now told that 'fine raillery', as described by Dryden, represents only Horace's *intention*; his *performance* was sadly inferior (pp. 94-5). We shall not stop to ask whether Dryden thinks he has now answered Holyday's objection; or how he himself can ever have enjoyed the instruction of so feeble a wit. It is more important to inquire where his analysis has gone wrong.

In the first place Horace has been credited with a purpose which he never conceived; for Dryden's 'fine raillery' not only involves an attack on living people but also, to judge from the character of Zimri in *Absolom*,[9] entails a great deal more than the passing thrust which was Horace's favourite technique. Secondly the two pairs of characters chosen by Dryden as illustrations of Horace's incompetence can scarcely be called satiric figures at all. Sarmentus and Cicirrus in *Sat.* 1.5 and Persius and Rex in 1.7 are really neither vicious nor foolish; they are merely meant to be funny. Their humour, which consists of an *altercatio* or exchange of insults, was of a kind dear to the Italian heart, as may be seen from Plautine comedy. Some of Cicero's anecdotes, too, would suggest that such humour managed to reach as high as the Roman law-courts without gaining greatly in sophistication. I shall not quote the Horatian passages, which to us fall well short of the uproarious; but Dryden's verdict is certainly unjust: 'I am sorry to say it for Horace's sake; but certain it is, he has no fine palate who can feed so heartily on garbage'. Unjust, because it is not *Horace's* garbage. Although amused at the sallies of Sarmentus and Cicirrus, Horace is careful to dissociate himself from what is said. To ensure that we see this point, he presents the whole incident in the form of a Homeric combat. Thus the primitive slanging-match is heralded by an invocation of the Muse in the true heroic style and by a formal announcement of the names and lineage of the two champions. So, too, in *Sat.* 1.7 the Greek merchant Persius quells the Roman Rex as his ancestor Achilles humbled the Trojan Hector. In the second case it is worth noting that, while the air is supposed to be thick with poisonous taunts, we are only allowed to see two of them. What matters is the scene itself – and the personalities of the two actors. By overlooking the element of parody Dryden seems to have been misled into equating Horace's humour with that of his characters.

The last point which I wish to take up concerns the historical background of the two poets and its effect on their satire. After asserting that Juvenal is the greater satirist, Dryden goes on to say:

> His spirit has more of the commonwealth genius; he treats tyranny, and all the vices attending it, with the utmost rigour; and consequently, a noble soul is better pleased with a zealous vindicator of Roman liberty, than with a temporising poet, a well-mannered court-slave, and a man who is often afraid of laughing in the right place; who is

> ever decent because he is naturally servile ... There was
> more need of a Brutus in Domitian's days, to redeem or
> mend, than of a Horace, if he had then been living, to
> laugh at a fly-catcher.[10] This reflection at the same time
> excuses Horace, but exalts Juvenal.   (pp. 86-7)

In fact the reflection does neither, because it is entirely miscon-
ceived. Dryden (pp. 88-9) relies heavily on the case of Cassius
Severus, who was banished for his attacks on distinguished men
and women (Tacitus, *Annals* 1.72); yet Cassius' exile took place
some forty years after the publication of Horace's satires. Even
the first two decades of Augustus' reign, to judge from Suetonius
and Dio,[11] do not seem to have been particulary illiberal. But
what matters is the time between 38 BC and the eve of Actium in
31. In those years Horace drew closer to Maecenas and hence to
Augustus.Why should anyone sneer at him for not attacking his
own friends and benefactors? The test of his 'servility' is whether,
at their command, he used his pen to satirise their enemies. In the
years immediately preceding Actium the air was thick with abusive
pamphlets. If Horace was pressed to join in, he must have declined
to do so. In fact, the more security he achieved, the milder his
satires became, until in the end he abandoned the genre.[12]

In the case of Juvenal, Dryden's history is equally inaccurate.
From what he says (pp. 87 and 91), it is clear that he thinks Juvenal
wrote his satires in the time of Domitian, which ended in a reign of
terror. A few men, who might fairly be called 'zealous vindicators
of Roman liberty', protested and suffered accordingly. Juvenal
was not among them. Very sensibly he waited for the assassin
to strike. Tacitus, the only contemporary writer of comparable
power, chose the same course. Nerva became emperor in AD
69 and was followed two years later by Trajan. 'Now at last our
spirits are reviving,' says Tacitus. 'Nerva has harmonised the old
discord between the principate and liberty, and every day Trajan
is increasing the happiness of our times' (*Agricola* 3). Later he
speaks of 'the rare good fortune of this age in which we can feel
what we like and say what we feel' (*Histories* 1.1). The new spirit
is also attested by Dio (68.6.4), who stresses Trajan's indifference
to slander, and by Pliny the Younger, who in his panegyric on the
emperor (66.4) says, 'You are urging us to be free, and so we shall

be; you are urging us to express our feelings, and so we shall'. Such liberty was, of course, a privilege rather than a right; and no doubt it fell short of what we would regard as tolerable today. Nevertheless, it did represent a significant easing of tension and it meant that the regime of Domitian was no longer immune from criticism. Several years passed, however, before Juvenal published his first book of satires (about AD 110).

As successive books appeared, it became clear that Juvenal meant what he said about avoiding Lucilian polemic. According to Syme, 'Juvenal does not attack any person or category that commands influence in his own time'.[13] The second part of this statement is open to question, in that any Greeks who read Juvenal must have been offended by the third satire; and some Greeks did command influence in his time. Again, even if Juvenal was not in serious danger, some people must have been annoyed by his censure. Yet obviously he survived.[14] The odd thing is that, in spite of the power of his writing, we have almost no evidence about its reception. There is a gap in our knowledge until the fourth century, by which time Juvenal had become popular. It looks, therefore, as if the satires cannot have had the direct and immediate impact which Dryden imagined.

Finally, in view of Dryden's remark about Juvenal having 'more of the commonwealth genius', we should perhaps recall that, in spite of his invective against Nero and Domitian, there is no sign that he wanted the principate abolished. Still less did he envisage anything like our own form of democracy. As Highet points out, 'Juvenal does not say that the poor are exploited by the governing class or that the middle class is being crushed out of existence'. He does not say that 'the system should be changed to put a different social class on top'.[15] What he does deplore is that, as a result or Rome's imperial power, the old social order has been upset; unscrupulous blackguards with no breeding (many of them Greeks or Syrians) have acquired money and prestige, while decent Romans like himself have been reduced to poverty and humiliation. Thus Juvenal's angriest satires proceed from a vague sort of reactionary idealism enforced by feelings of personal injustice.

The type of analysis which we have been conducting is often unsympathetic, and it may be urged in defence of Dryden that he had few of the scholarly resources available to the modern critic. He could not walk into a library and inspect the serried ranks of Pauly-Wissowa; and seventeenth-century commentaries, admirable as they were, had not experienced the long process of scrutiny and sifting that lies behind the works of Lejay and Courtney. Moreover, Dryden was in no way eccentric in holding such views. They were shared not only by his contemporaries but also by his successors in the eighteenth century; and indeed some of them were still to be found in the twentieth. Yet, however important these considerations may be (and they are of primary importance for an understanding of Dryden's own approach to satire), they ought not to obscure the fact that, as far as Horace and Juvenal are concerned, Dryden's essay is wrong or misleading on almost every major point.

12 Problems of Patronage:
Horace, *Epistles* 1.7.46-98 and Swift's Imitation

[Previously unpublished]

Two thousand years after his death the name 'Maecenas' is still synonymous with a generous patron.[1] A great deal is known about him, but only a few relevant points can be noted here. In addition to his command of Greek he had a wide-ranging intellectual curiosity, being cited by the Elder Pliny as an authority on aquatic creatures and on precious stones. He wrote a *Symposium* – an event at which Virgil and Horace were guests – and a mysterious piece entitled *Prometheus*. A fragment of jewelled verse addressed to Horace in affectionate terms further testifies to his interest in precious stones; it also represents the very antithesis of its recipient's classicism; and it led to his being teased by Augustus. A few other examples of his writing come from Seneca, who quoted them to prove the utter decadence of his character.[2]

Maecenas came from an old and distinguished Etruscan family; Horace, *Odes* 1.1, refers to them as 'kings'. So some of his wealth was no doubt inherited. A substantial amount, however, probably came from what to us is an embarrassing source – the property of men proscribed by the triumvirate of Antony, Octavian and Lepidus (43-2 BC). Though he was with Octavian (later Augustus) at Mutina, Philippi, Perusia, Naulochus and Actium, he was more than a loyal lieutenant. He was a key figure in the negotiations at Brundisium in 40 BC, went as an envoy to ask Antony's help against Sextus Pompeius in 38, and contributed to the peace of Tarentum in 37. He was in charge of Rome and Italy for three periods during Augustus' absence. In 30 BC he used his power quite ruthlessly to put down a rebellion by the younger Lepidus. Yet his position was without precedent. He never commanded an army, never fought an election, never sat in the senate. He remained an *eques* (a 'knight') all his life – not wholly, perhaps, out of modesty. If one had the right friends, constitutional niceties could be overlooked. So, in addition to patron, we now have scholar, writer, soldier, diplomat and governor.[3]

There is also some information of a more personal kind. It was Maecenas who arranged Octavian's marriage to Scribonia in 40 BC. Later, when the emperor was ill (as he often was), he would sleep, and was probably nursed, at Maecenas' house; for it was much more comfortable than the imperial residence. Again, according to Dio, Maecenas often used his influence to calm Augustus' outbursts of rage; and his interventions were accepted with good grace.[4]

There is one further dimension to the character of this extraordinary man: he was a dedicated voluptuary, whose private habits were a total negation of Augustus' official programme of simplicity and restraint. He lived on the Esquiline in a towering mansion set in a park. He reputedly walked with a slouch, attended by eunuchs, or was carried sprawling in a litter with its curtains open. He bathed in a heated swimming pool. His clothes were conspicuously informal – a sloppy tunic and a cloak pulled over his head, leaving his ears sticking out. He kept a choice cellar, and bizarre items (like baby donkey) appeared on his menus. He was also, like many other Romans, bisexual and adulterous. Augustus must have disapproved of this extravagant life-style but he did not interfere, because he liked the man and found him indispensable.[5]

Maecenas, however, paid a price for his complexity. In particu-lar, his hugely responsible job caused incessant worries. Hence the insomnia which he tried to relieve by soft music and trickling water. Pliny speaks of recurrent bouts of fever. Seneca's picture, though no doubt exaggerated, suggests that Maecenas was periodically depressed; one such occasion is mentioned below. There was also at least one serious illness. Worse than all this was an agonising dilemma which confronted him in 22 BC. He was informed that his own brother-in-law was involved in a plot against Augustus. Should he tell his wife, Terentia, who would immediately give her brother a chance to escape? Or should he let events take their course? Perhaps because, as Seneca implies, he was more afraid of his wife than of the emperor, he disclosed the secret. Augustus' anger is thought to account for the fact that Maecenas thereafter held no position of power or trust. When Agrippa was put in charge of Rome in 21 BC, Maecenas' disappointment may be reflected in what he said to Augustus: 'You have made him so important that he must either become your son-in-law or be put to death'. Whatever the truth about Maecenas' indiscretion, he did not permanently forfeit Augustus' good will. During a trial in 12 BC, when Maecenas, who was not himself the defendant, was being abused by the prosecuting counsel, Augustus ordered the lawyer 'to stop slinging mud at his friend'. And a few years later, when Maecenas died, he left all his wealth to Augustus, who 'grieved at his death' and 'missed him sorely'.[6]

The friendship between this Etruscan grandee and Horace, the freedman's son, was even more remarkable. The first steps are well known: the nervous interview (*Sat.* 1.6.55-62), the early exchange of small-talk (*Sat.* 2.6.43-6), the apprehensions of a young man still in his twenties about disturbing his patron's peace (*Sat.* 1.3.63-5), the careful avoidance of political matter in the diary of the journey to Brundisium (*Sat.* 1.5), the emphatic denial of any political aspirations of his own (*Sat.* 1.6.19 ff.). But all the time the relationship was ripening into a deeper kind of *amicitia*, as is shown most fully in *Epodes* 1. Soon Horace felt able to convey his loyalty also indirectly in the form of comic self-deflation, as in the fable of the frog which burst itself in its efforts to rival a calf (*Sat.* 2.3.314-20) or the episode in which the poet, congratulating himself on his simplicity, has decided to have a quiet dinner on his own, when a last-minute invitation comes from Maecenas and he causes uproar in his haste to be gone (*Sat.* 2.7.29-35). In all this there is no question about who was the more dependent party. Horace received money, good dinners and an entrée into the company of interesting and important people; before long he was also given a delightful estate in the Sabine hills. Such kindnesses are fully acknowledged in *Sat.* 2.6, *Odes* 1.1 and many other places.

Yet already there were drawbacks. As early as *Epodes* 14 Maecenas was pressing Horace for the iambics he had promised and, interestingly, the poet felt free to complain: *occidis saepe rogando* ('You'll be the death of me with your nagging'; l. 5). Outsiders were also a problem, wanting Maecenas' signature (*Sat.* 2.6.38), clamouring for inside information about current affairs (*Sat.* 2.6.50-8), looking for introductions (*Sat.* 1.9). Horace was honest enough to admit that he enjoyed such attention: *hoc iuvat et melli est, non mentiar* ('This gives me pleasure and, to tell the truth, it's like honey'). But being a celebrity had another, less attractive, side: many people, from above and below, simply resented his success (*Sat.* 2.6.47-9).

On the other hand many of the rich and famous were now court-ing the poet (*Odes* 2.18.10-11), not only because he belonged to the inner circle, but more particularly because he might be persuaded to write poems in their honour. Later Augustus himself intimated that he would like to be addressed in an epistle and on one occasion went further, urging Horace to become his private secretary. As a result of his growing fame and fortune, Horace's world was expanding. There is a hint that he may have been somewhat irritated by petty criticisms from Maecenas about his uneven haircut, his untidy clothes, his untrimmed nails (*Epistles* 1.1.94-7 and 105). One ode (2.17) is more significant; for it suggests that the emotional balance of the relationship has shifted. In one of his verses Maecenas had asserted that he would cling to life at any price; the ode, however, indicates that he has now been seriously ill; in a mood of depression he has complained to Horace that the dreaded end is not far off. Horace, who had himself survived the injuries received from a falling tree, cheers his friend up, saying in effect, 'These gloomy prognostications worry me to death. You're still alive, and so am I. The stars assure us that when we go, we'll go together. So let's celebrate'.[7]

There had always been one potential source of friction which has not yet been mentioned. Horace directed much of his satire (in the *Odes* as well as the hexameter poems) at wealth and luxury; and it was only to be expected that hostile readers might allege that by doing so he was sniping at Maecenas. There were, however, three features of Maecenas and his wealth which – though they would not impress a modern socialist – did weigh with Horace. First, he was not mean: he subsidised Virgil and Propertius as well as Horace. Secondly, he did not spend his days working in an office or sailing in a ship in order to acquire more money. And thirdly, for all his extravagance, he never looked like ending his days in penury. So it seems unlikely that, when he read about men who failed to obtain happiness by amassing possessions or ruined themselves by profligacy, he took it as a personal affront. Horace himself was not opposed to money *per se*; the same was true of power, glory, fine food, and sex. The crucial question was did these things bring contentment? From his observation they usually didn't. It all depended on whether you dominated them or they you. So Horace ends an attractive poem to Vala (*Epistles* 1.15) very much in the manner of Aristippus with this ironic confession: 'I admire the safe and humble / when funds are low; I'm quite a Stoic with plain fare. / But when something finer and more delectable comes, I say / that truth and the good life are only attained by those, / like you, whose solid wealth is reflected in splendid villas!'.[8]

Yet in the late 20s Horace was making occasional remarks which might have hurt his friend. In *Epistles* 1.18 he advises a client to vary his manner according to the mood of his patron – all amusing enough; but the paragraph begins thus: 'Serving a powerful friend appeals to the uninformed; / others dread it' (86-7); and this lends significance to a couple of lines near the end: 'May I have what I have now, or less, and live for *myself* / what's left of my life, if heaven decides that any is left' (106-7).

These undercurrents have to be kept in mind as we approach *Epistles* 1.7. I summarise the first part which, though omitted by Swift, is immediately relevant: I promised to be out of town for a week and I've been away the whole of August. But you know how unhealthy Rome is at this time of year – and in the autumn. When winter comes, however, (now surely he'll be back; but no) your bard will go down to the seaside. He'll be with you at the beginning of spring, if you will let him (as if Maecenas has not been begging him to come). So the absence has grown from five days to six months. There follows a little dialogue in which a Calabrian host repeatedly offers pears to a guest, who continues to decline them; eventually the host says, 'Suit yourself. If you leave them, the pigs will have them for dinner' (19). Then an impossible condition: if you want me never to leave you (which Maecenas had never asked), you'll have to restore my black hair and my ability to compose love-songs. Then a fable: a little fox crept into a corn bin and ate so much that it couldn't get out. A weasel standing by said, 'You'll have to become as slim as you were when you got in'.

If that story is applied to me, I'll resign everything (as if Horace could ever hand back all he had received from Maecenas). Then a few softer words: I've often called you *pater* and *rex* to your face and in your absence; but I'm still prepared to do without your presents. Finally a polite Homeric precedent: Telemachus declined Menelaus' offer of horses; Ithaca wasn't suitable for them. Small things for the small. Princely Rome doesn't attract me now, rather Tibur (Tivoli) and Tarentum.[9]

Now comes the main parable, which is all that Swift uses (asterisked points are glossed in note[10]):

The distinguished lawyer Philippus,* a dynamic hard-working man,
was returning home from his business at two in the afternoon.
Being no longer young, he was grumbling that the Carinae*
were now too far from the Forum, when they say he noticed a man,
freshly shaven, sitting in a barber's empty booth,   50
penknife in hand, quietly cleaning his own nails.
'Demetrius,' (this was Philippus' lively messenger boy)
'Go and find out who that man is, where he lives,
how well off he is, and who's his father or patron.'
He goes and returns with the answer: 'His name's Volteius Mena;
he's an auctioneer in a small way – quite respectable;
they say he knows when to work and rest, make and spend;
his home is his own; none of his friends are big people;
he enjoys the games, and he goes to the Park when work is finished.'
'I'd like to hear all this from his own lips. So tell him   60
to come to dinner.' Mena really couldn't believe it,
and scratched his head in silence. In the end he answered 'No
thanks.'
'Refuse me, will he?'
                         'Yes. The cheeky devil! He's either
insulting you or has something to hide.'
                         Next morning Philippus
went up to Volteius who was selling some cheap bits and pieces
to folk in their working clothes. 'Good morning,' he opened. At once
Volteius began to apologise for not having called sooner:
he'd been tied up by his business concerns; he was also sorry
for not seeing Philippus first. 'Let's say I'll forget it,
provided you join me for dinner today.'   70
                         'All right.'

'Very well, then,
come about four. In the meantime, carry on coining money!'
At dinner he spoke about all and sundry, regardless of tact,
till at last he was allowed to go home to bed. Thereafter he often
hurried like a fish to the hidden hook. When he'd become
a morning client and a regular guest, Philippus asked him,
when the Latin holiday came,* to come out to his place in the
country.
As he rode in the carriage, Volteius praised the Sabine soil
and air again and again; Philippus watched and smiled.
Looking for light relief and amusement from any quarter,
he offered him seven thousand and guaranteed a loan   80
of as much again, urging him to buy a small holding.
He bought it. (I mustn't keep you too long with a rambling story.)
He changed from a dapper type to a peasant; talked about nothing
but furrows and vineyards; prepared his elms; nearly collapsed
from his strenuous efforts, and wore himself out in his passion for
gain.
But after his sheep were stolen, and his goats died of disease,
and his crops let him down, and his ox died from all the ploughing,
he was driven to despair by his losses. And so, in the middle of the
night
he grabbed a horse and rode to Philippus' house in a rage.
As soon as Philippus saw his rough and shaggy appearance,   90
'Volteius!' he cried, 'you look like a man that's overworked
and over-anxious!'
                    'God help me, sir,' Volteius answered,
'you'd call me a wretch if you wanted to use the proper word.
I beg and implore you by your guardian spirit and your own right
hand
and the gods of your hearth, let me return to my old life!'
When a person sees how his former condition surpasses the one
he is in , he should hurry back, and resume the things he abandoned.
Every man should measure himself by his own foot-rule.

The reader will recognise at once that the story doesn't really fit
Horace's situation. And that is the point. The message to Maecenas
is: 'I have certainly no wish to imitate Volteius; and you, I'm sure,
would not dream of behaving like Philippus'. The strategy is just
the same as in the case of the Calabrian above, though there it is
quite explicit: 'You've made me a precious gift – *not* like the man

from Calabria / who offered pears to his guest' (14-15). So ends a polite but unmistakably firm warning: kindly keep your distance.

Yet whatever their problems may have been, Horace still dedicated the first book of *Epistles* to Maecenas; and he mentions him with respect and affection in his last book of *Odes*. Conversely, when Maecenas died (just two months before his friend), he left the following instruction to the emperor in his will: *Horati Flacci ut mei esto memor* ('Remember Horatius Flaccus as you remember me').[11]

******

Jonathan Swift's misfortunes began early. When he was born in 1667, his father was already dead and his mother took little part in his upbringing; years later he said he had felt the consequences of that marriage during the greatest part of his life. At the age of six he was sent to a boarding school in Kilkenny; in his darker moments he remembered 'the Confinement ten hours a day to nouns and verbs, the terror of the Rod, the bloddy (*sic*) Noses and broken Shins'. He entered Trinity College at fourteen, an age when a boy of that class today is just a year out of prep school. Not surprisingly, he obtained a degree only 'with special favour'.[12]

Yet we are still talking of a member of the English ascendancy. His father had a legal post at the King's Inns; Kilkenny College, however austere, was an elite establishment, founded by the Earl of Ormonde; and a university degree normally led to a life of reasonable comfort and security, if not of wealth. Swift's career seemed assured when his uncle obtained a place for him in the household of Sir William Temple, who treated him like a son. Temple's own career was not without setbacks. In a mood of disenchantment he wrote appreciatively about *The Gardens of Epicurus*; and at Moor Park he acted out Horace's ideal of cultivated retirement; he also praised Horace for declining Augustus' invitation to become his private secretary.[13] The young Swift, however, who was editing Temple's papers, was more impressed by the prominent people he met at Moor Park. On one occasion he was even sent to King William to argue in support of the Triennial Bill. His ambitions grew with his powers, and he expected his patron before long to find him an acceptable place. In 1695, whether or not on Temple's recommendation, he became Vicar of Kilroot on the northern shore of Belfast Lough. It was not a thriving parish. The church was dilapidated and there were few parishioners. Swift, it is said, began one sermon with: 'Dearly beloved Roger'. His stipend was in theory £100 per annum but a sum of £20 was reserved for the previous incumbent 'one, Milne, a Scotchman', who had been dismissed for 'intemperance, incontinency of life, and neglect of his cures'. Not surprisingly, the Vicar returned to Moor Park after a year.[14]

By now Swift had some reservations about Temple: he was at times pompous and condescending; doctrinally he was not quite sound, being tolerant of dissenters, and he was not energetic enough in furthering his protégé's career. After a couple of attempts which failed, Temple claimed to have received a promise from King William of a post for Swift at Canterbury or Westminster; but the promise was never made good. Next year Swift became chaplain to the Lord Justice of Ireland and hoped, with his support, to become Dean of Derry. Yet the records show that he was not even considered for the post. In 1700, however, he did obtain the living of Laracor in County Meath – a place with pleasant rural amenities – and also, shortly after, a prebend at St Patrick's Cathedral, which gave him access to useful contacts in Dublin Castle. He continued to make intermittent visits to England but rose no further in the hierarchy until 1713, when he became Dean of St Patrick's. We shall return presently to the theme of preferment, because it is central to our poem.[15]

First, however, something must be said about the matter of the First Fruits and Twentieth Parts – taxes levied on the clergy by the crown. In 1704 the Queen had agreed that the revenue from these taxes should go towards improving the lot of the poorer parishes in England; so the Irish bishops felt that the same should apply in their country. A petition presented to the Queen received 'a gracious answer' but, as nothing had happened after three years, Swift got permission from Archbishop King to rally support in England. If the project succeeded, it would benefit the poorer Irish clergy and (incidentally, of course) enhance the prospects of the Vicar. By 4 October 1710 the application had got as far John Harley, then Chancellor of the Exchequer, who received Swift effusively

and undertook to show the documents to the Queen. Swift was now
anxious that the matter should be concluded before Ormonde, the new
Lord Lieutenant of Ireland, took office; for that would cause further
complications. Three days later Harley reported that the remission
would be approved 'in a few days'; then, a week later, 'next day'.
After three more weeks of prevarication and procrastination Harley
informed Swift that the remission had taken place and that Swift's
efforts would be acknowledged; the whole affair, however, must
be kept secret. Five days later the new Lord Lieutenant took over,
whereupon the Irish bishops, who were unaware of Swift's success,
renewed the application through *him*. Finally, at the end of July 1711,
the crucial document arrived. The bishops thanked Her Majesty and
Harley and Ormonde; but no one said a word about Swift. To wind
up the whole affair Harley promised to send a letter to the bishops
informing them of the central role played by Swift. He never did.[16]

Back in 1708, when Swift came to London, he was welcomed
into the literary group that included Addison, Steele, and Congreve.
In circles of that kind Horace was never far below the surface.
Once, when Addison was due to arrive in Dublin, he wrote to Swift
saying he was eager 'to eat a dish of bacon and beans in the best
company in the world'. Why 'bacon and beans'? Because they were
on the menu to which Horace looked forward when longing for his
Sabine estate: 'When shall a dish of beans be served (Pythagoras'
kinsmen) / and a few greens sufficiently oiled with fat bacon?' (*Sat.*
2.6.62-3). Pope joined in the Horatian game, contributing a number
of lines to Swift's imitation of that poem, picturing his friends
at table, 'The Beans and Bacon set before 'em, / The Grace-cup
served with all decorum' (137-8), and he later added the opening
section of *Epistles* 1.7 'Imitated in the Manner of Dr Swift'.[17]

At that time Swift was keen to ingratiate himself with the power-
ful Whig junta. For instance, in 1709 he wrote to Lord Halifax,
whom he had flattered in a previous work, reminding him how
'another person of Quality in Horace's time used to serve a sort
of Fellows who had disoblidged him, how he sent them fine
Cloaths and money, which raised their Thoughts and their Hopes,
till these were worn out or spent, and then they were ten times
more miserable than before (the reference is to *Epistles* 1.18.31-6).
Hac ego si compellor imagine cuncta resigno' (in effect 'if this

illustration is applied to me, I withdraw all my requests' – from line 34 of our epistle). He then says he will not bore His Lordship by comparing him to Maecenas, since everyone has done that already. Six months later he adds: 'Remembering I have had the Honor to converse with your Lordship, I say as Horace did when he met your Predecessor (i.e. Maecenas) *cum magnis vixisse invita fatebitur usque / invidia* ('Envy will always have to admit, like it or not, / that I've rubbed shoulders with the great'; *Sat.* 2.1.75-6). Both Swift and Horace took an unabashed pleasure in the company of their superiors. Swift then went on to solicit Halifax's support for the bishopric of Cork.[18]

As the war in Europe dragged on, Tory support for the coalition government began to melt away and the Duke of Marlborough was forced to rely more and more on the Whigs. In 1708 Harley and St John were sacked; Somers and Wharton were brought into the ministry. The Tories now organised themselves into an effective opposition. Marlborough and his colleagues were ridiculed and vilified in the *Examiner* and in a flood of pamphlets, the most mordant contributor being Swift, who had now edged over into the other party. Before long the balance of power shifted in his favour. In the autumn of 1710, with the help of Harley's cousin, Mrs Masham, who had supplanted the Duchess of Marlborough as the Queen's friend and advisor, the Whigs were ousted and a new government under Harley and St John was formed. In the following year Swift's powerful but highly tendentious pamphlet *The Conduct of the Allies* was published; and in 1712 Marlborough was dismissed for embezzlement. For these solid services Swift expected some reward. But though a succession of deaneries fell vacant (Wells, Ely, Lichfield), none came his way. His disap-pointment was most acute over Wells. For as soon as the post became available he had sent a letter to Harley (now Lord Oxford) ending: 'I entirely submit my good fortune to Your Lordship'. His submission was in vain. The deanship went to Oxford's son-in-law. Years earlier Swift had failed to win promotion because he was unknown; now he was known all too well. As he himself said, 'I have many friends and many enemies, and the last are more constant in their nature'.[19]

From his many enemies I select Lord Wharton, since he is

referred to in our poem. It once seemed possible that Swift would go to Ireland as Wharton's chaplain. But, when Swift called to sound him out on his attitude to the First Fruits, he got a chilly reception – and by then Wharton had picked another chaplain. So there were already two reasons for Swift to dislike him. Wharton, moreover, was tolerant of dissenters, whom Swift regarded as a greater threat than catholics to the established church. He had, in addition, the reputation of being 'the greatest rake in England'. Accordingly in the following January (1710) Swift reported as a matter of fact that Wharton had defecated on the high altar of Gloucester Cathedral and presented his fine to church funds. In August, disclaiming any personal animus, Swift declared in his *Short Character*: 'He is a Presbyterian in Politics, and an Atheist in Religion; but he chuseth at present to whore with a Papist'.[20]

At long last, in April 1713, an arrangement was concluded whereby Dean Stearne of St Patrick's should become Bishop of Dromore and Swift should take his place in Dublin. A plan along these lines was first proposed by Judge Coghill, a friend of Swift's; it had to be sanctioned by Archbishop King, the Duke of Ormonde, Lord Oxford and the Queen. After much confusion and delay Swift was installed as Dean on 13 June. The appointment was not universally welcome. A local rhymester spoke for many when he wrote: 'Look down St Patrick, look, we pray / On thine own Church and Steeple; / Convert thy Dean on this Great Day; / Or else God help the people!'. Even Archbishop King could take comfort only because 'a Dean could do less mischief than a Bishop'. Swift himself, to adapt a formula used by Claude Rawson, didn't want St Patrick's and yet didn't *not* want it. Several harsh comments reveal that once again 'the great fish' of contentment had escaped him. I quote one: 'Here I am by way of sinking into utter oblivion; for *hae latebrae* non *dulces*, nec *si mihi credis amoenae'*. ('This retreat is *not* delightful, *nor* if you believe me beautiful'). The words recall, in a negative form, Horace's happy reflection on his Sabine estate in *Epistles* 1.16.15. Swift hopes soon to see Bishop Atterbury and Dr Freind in London, 'though I am an Irish Dean *vervecum in patria, crassoque sub aere natus'* ('born in a land of mutton-heads under a thick sky'). That is Juvenal (*Satires* 10.50) speaking of Democritus. The Thracians, like the Irish, were regarded as a

primitive, hard-drinking lot (*Odes* 1.27.2) and the townsmen of
Abdera had a reputation for stupidity (Cicero, *de Natura Deorum*,
1.120). So at first Swift seems to be laughing at himself. But the
allusion was capable of carrying the opposite nuance; for Juvenal
is saying that Democritus was a great thinker in *spite* of his misty
birthplace. Nevertheless, the implication remains that Ireland and
its atmosphere were dreary and unsatisfactory. The fact is that,
even if Swift had been made Archbishop of Canterbury, he would
still have found something to complain about. At any rate, four
months later he was back in London, attempting to avert a rift
between Oxford and St John (now Bolingbroke). It was at this
period that he wrote his Imitation of Horace's epistle.[21] (Asterisked
points are glossed in note[22].)

> Harley, the nation's great support,*
> Returning home one day from court
> *(His mind with public cares possessed,
> All Europe's business in his breast)*
> Observed a parson near Whitehall,
> Cheapening* old authors on a stall.
> The priest was pretty well in case,*
> And showed some humour in his face;
> Looked with an easy, careless mien,
> A perfect stranger to the spleen;*   10
> Of size that might a pulpit fill,
> But more inclining to sit still.
> My Lord, who (if a man may say't)
> Loves mischief* better than his meat,*
> Was now disposed to crack a jest;*
> And bid friend Lewis* go in quest
> (This Lewis is an arrant shaver,*
> And very much in Harley's favour);
> *In quest, who might this person be,
> What was his name, of what degree: 20
> If possible, to learn his story,
> And whether he were Whig or Tory.
>
> Lewis his patron's humour knows;
> Away upon his errand goes;
> And quickly did the matter sift,

*Found out that it was Dr Swift:
*A clergyman of special note,
For shunning those of his own coat;
Which made his brethren of the gown,
Take care betimes* to run him down: 30
No libertine, nor over-nice,
Addicted to no sort of vice;
Went where he pleased, said what he thought;
Not rich, but owed no man a groat.
In state opinions *à la mode*,
He hated Wharton* like a toad;
Had given the faction* many a wound,
And libelled all the junta* round;
Kept company with men of wit,
*Who often fathered what he writ;   40
His works were hawked in every street,
But seldom rose above a sheet:
Of late indeed the paper-stamp*
Did very much his genius cramp;
And since he could not spend his fire,
He now intended to retire.*

Said Harley, 'I desire to know
From his own mouth if this be so.
Step to the Doctor straight, and say
I'd have him dine with me today.'   50
Swift seemed to wonder what he meant,
Nor would believe my Lord had sent;
So never offered once to stir,
But coldly said, 'Your servant, sir.'
'Does he refuse me?', Harley cried.
*'He does, with insolence and pride.'

Some few days after, Harley spies
The Doctor fastened by the eyes,
At Charing Cross, among the rout,
Where painted monsters* dangle out.   60
He pulled the string, and stopped the coach,
Beckoning the Doctor to approach.

Swift, who could neither fly nor hide,
Came sneaking to the chariot-side,*
And offered many a lame excuse:
He never meant the least abuse –
*'My Lord – the honour you designed –
Extremely proud – but I had dined –
I'm sure I never should neglect –
No man alive has more respect . . . '   70
'Well, I shall think of that no more,
If you'll be sure to come at four.'

The Doctor now obeys the summons,
Likes both his company and commons;*
Displays his talent,* sits till ten;
Next day invited, comes again:
Soon grows domestic,* seldom fails
Either at morning, or at meals;
Comes early and departeth late:
In short, the gudgeon* took the bait.   80
My Lord would carry on the jest,
And down to Windsor takes his guest.
Swift much admires the place and air,
And longs to be a canon* there;
In summer round the park to ride,
In winter – never to reside.*
'A canon! that's a place too mean:
No, Doctor, you shall be a dean;*
*Two dozen canons round your stall,
And you the tyrant o'er them all: 90
You need but cross the Irish seas,
To live in plenty, power and ease.'
Poor Swift departs, and, what is worse,
With borrowed money in his purse;
Travels at least a hundred leagues,
And suffers numberless fatigues.

Suppose him, now, a dean complete,
Demurely* lolling in his seat;
The silver virge,* with decent pride,
Stuck underneath his cushion-side: 100
Suppose him gone through all vexations,

> *Patents, instalments, abjurations,
> First-fruits* and tenths, and chapter-treats,
> Dues, payments, fees, demands and – cheats
> (The wicked laity's contriving,
> To hinder clergymen from thriving),
> Now all the Doctor's money's spent,
> His tenants wrong him in his rent;
> The farmers,* spitefully combined,
> Force him to take his tithes in kind;   110
> And Parvisol* discounts arrears,
> By bills for taxes and repairs.
> Poor Swift, with all his losses vexed,
> Not knowing where to turn him next,
> Above a thousand pounds in debt;
> Takes horse, and in a mighty fret,
> *Rides day and night at such a rate,
> He soon arrives at Harley's gate;
> But was so dirty, pale, and thin,
> Old Read* would hardly let him in.   120

> Said Harley, 'Welcome, reverend Dean!
> What makes your worship look so lean?
> Why sure you won't appear in town,
> In that old wig and rusty gown?
> *I doubt your heart is set on pelf
> So much, that you neglect yourself.
> What! I suppose now stocks are high,
> You've some good purchase in your eye;
> Or is your money out at use?' –

> 'Truce, good my Lord, I beg a truce!'   130
> (The Doctor in a passion cried),
> 'Your raillery is misapplied:
> Experience I have dearly bought,
> You know I am not worth a groat:
> But it's a folly to contest,
> When you resolve to have your jest;
> And since you now have done your worst,
> Pray leave me where you found me first.'*

So then, a delightful poem in neat octosyllabic couplets, effortlessly incorporating the language and rhythms of everyday conversation. Interest centres on the two main figures and on the teasing, ambiguous manner in which their relationship is handled. Is Harley being complimented or taken to task? As we know, for ten years Swift had exerted his rhetorical and satirical powers on behalf of the Tories, Harley in particular, and received nothing in return but promises. As a result he was often bitter: 'I have been used barbarously by the late ministry'. Yet, in spite of all, he was fond of Harley (who was six years his senior) and unwilling to forfeit the *kudos* he enjoyed from the friendship; so he contrived to put the burden of blame for his failures on the bishops. Now Harley has at last delivered, and Swift ascribes the appointment wholly to him, though in fact his was only one voice in the decision. Yet Harley's gesture turns out to be, not a generous if overdue acknowledgement of Swift's services, but simply a malicious joke (15, 81 and 136) – one which left Swift short of the thousand pounds he had been promised to meet the expenses of his new post. As such it earns no gratitude but only an anguished appeal for its cancellation. Whereas Horace was saying 'You, Maecenas, are *not* Philippus, Swift is saying 'You, Harley, *are* Philippus'. And, though elsewhere many of Swift's tributes are couched in the form of a rebuke, here the rebuke is delivered in the form of a tribute.[23]

Nevertheless, Swift remained stubbornly loyal. Two years later he could write to the Earl of Oxford saying, 'I take the liberty of calling you the ablest and faithfullest Minister, and truest lover of Your Country that this Age hath produced'. It may come as a surprise to hear that the recipient was then in the Tower on a charge of high treason. Stranger still, before his trial Swift sent Oxford a translation of Horace, *Odes* 3.2.14-34, which concluded: 'He who betrays his friend shall never be / Under one roof, or in one ship with me. / For, who with traitors would his safety trust, / Lest with the wicked, heaven involve the just? / And, though the villain 'scape a while, he feels / Slow vengeance, like a bloodhound at his heels'. There was at least some substance in the charges; and it may be that vital material was hidden in the French archives. Yet it is hard to believe that Oxford was any more resolute in courting the Pretender than in anything else. At any rate he was released two years later.

As for Swift, it looks as if, in spite of all his experience of Oxford's duplicity, he could not bear the thought that the man whom he was proud to call 'friend' had systematically deceived him on a matter of such gravity. For the Dean's self-esteem Lord Oxford *had* to be innocent; so Swift made him into an unblemished patriot.[24]

Moving finally to the larger picture of Swift's life, we find some points that must command our sympathy: the long series of misfortunes and failures, his dreadful attacks of giddiness (associated with Ménière's disease) and his increasing deafness; above all, the agonies and indignities of his last years, which no human being should have to endure. Conflicting facets of his personality, however, apart from those revealed in the poem, leave us in doubt. In one scale-pan go his unpleasant obsession with scatology and his inability to commit himself to women after obtaining their devotion (unanswerable questions, if you like, about his *psyche*); to them must be added more generally his arrogance, ill-temper and occasional cruelty. In the other scale-pan go his charm, good humour and sense of fun; his friendliness and generosity; and all the practical work he did on behalf of churches, schools and hospitals. There can be no doubt, however, about his legacies: the lunatic asylum to which he devoted his fortune, his campaign against Wood's halfpence, which saved Ireland from financial ruin, and the pleasure he has given to readers over so many generations by his writings, in which *Gulliver's Travels* has a special place. For these services he is still remembered with gratitude by the people whom he so pitied and despised.[25]

Related Material:

'Swift's *On Poetry: A Rhapsody*' forthcoming in *Hermathena* (2006).

13 Variation and Inversion in Pope's *Epistle to Dr Arbuthnot*

[From *Essays in Criticism* 34 (1984) 216-28.]

In theory, Pope's duty as a Christian satirist was clear enough. If attacked, he should not seek personal revenge (that would be return-ing evil for evil); at the same time he had an obligation to speak out against vice. This position was, however, not easy to maintain; what if the attacker was, in Dryden's sense, a public nuisance? Even if he was not, could Pope always be trusted to tell the difference? Again, in dealing with vicious men, the satirist ought, as Dr Arbuthnot had urged in a letter, to 'study more to reform than chastise', though he did admit that 'the one often cannot be effected without the other'.[1] 'General satire' offered no solution; for, in Pope's view, to be effective one had to be specific.[2]

These problems are interestingly illustrated in the *Epistle*, where Pope repeatedly turns the other cheek, and then prevents his oppo-nents from taking advantage of it by bringing over a crashing right hook. Thus Pope claims that his attacks are innocuous (because fools are impervious to satire – Colley, Henley and Sappho remain as vicious as ever); he has frequently suffered from the flattery of fools (in fact their praise is more damaging than their condemnation); his innocent verse was attacked (by the venal Gildon and the furious Dennis), yet he held his peace; he deferred good-naturedly to scholars (the quibbles of pedants like Bentley and Tibald were not worth quarrelling about); he understood and excused the anger of his opponents (their conceit made them unable to bear the truth); how ridiculous to imagine an able writer becoming corroded by jealousy (and how lamentable if Atticus were such a man); he himself never sought adulation (he left such fatuous self-advertisement to Bufo); he has no patron (though patrons are sometimes useful in engaging the attention of dunces); he will never offend the good (but malicious and dishonest creatures like Sporus had better watch out); he has always stood firm in the interests of virtue (attacking vicious men of every station); he has patiently endured abuse directed at himself and his parents (by liars like Welsted, Budgel and Curl).

A great deal has, of course, been done to explain who Pope's victims were and how they had offended him. I have nothing new to offer on that score; but something may perhaps be contributed by examining the poem's classical dimension and studying how Pope varies and inverts his Latin 'models' so as to project the ambiguous attitude outlined above. The result, I believe, will enhance our appreciation of his marvellous expertise.

Some of Horace's major satires begin with an introductory section on a theme which is different from, and yet related to, the main subject. Thus *Sat*.1.1 deals with discontent, before moving on to greed; and the treatment of unfairness in *Sat*.1.3 is prefaced by a passage on inconsistency. In the *Epistle*, before offering his defence as a satirist, Pope comes before us as a literary critic (1-68) – a patient though hard-pressed victim, who is at the same time a man of acknowledged influence in the world. This two-sided figure prepares us for the satirist in the main body of the poem who, while ostensibly a man of great forbearance, is nevertheless prepared to launch wounding attacks. In composing his picture of the beleaguered critic, Pope drew on several passages of Horace. For example Horace had spoken of the mad poet who accosted people in the street and 'killed them by reading' – *occiditque legendo* (*Ars Poetica* 475); Pope renders this as 'If Foes, they write, if Friends, they read me dead' (32). Horace had told how 'the Impertinent' waylaid him in an attempt to get an introduction to Maecenas (*Sat*.1.9); in Pope Pitholeon says, 'You know his Grace, / I want a Patron; ask him for a Place' (50). Describing the general harassment resulting from his friendship with Maecenas, Horace had said:

> 'Roscius would like you to meet him at the Wall by eight tomorrow.'
> 'The Department said be sure to come in today, Quintus; an important matter of common concern has just cropped up.'
> 'Get Maecenas' signature on these papers.' 'I'll try,' you say. 'You can if you want to,' he replies, and won't be put off.   (*Sat*. 2.6 35-9)

Pope develops this lively technique of reportage in lines 49-66. In the whole section both poets are apparently passive targets; but in Pope's case the occasional nuisance has become a crowd. Worse, they 'all fly to Twit'nam' and lay siege to his house. As a result Pope's plight is far graver than Horace's; at the same time his position as a literary authority is more heavily underlined.

This odd picture of exasperated victim and man of influence is given sharper definition by other alterations. In the *Ars Poetica* Horace had advised a young friend to hold on to a poem 'until the ninth year' before publishing it (388).[3] Pope's situation is different. He has been cornered by an incompetent writer and seizes on the Horatian maxim as a means of escape. 'Keep your Piece nine years' (40) is not really a way of saying 'further revision is advisable'; it is a device for postponing publication as long as possible. Later, Horace spoke of stubborn and conceited poets who refused to take the critic Quintilius' advice (*Ars Poetica* 438-44). In Pope the poet is so deferential that he will consent to anything; he even urges Pope to rewrite his work for him: 'I'm all submission, what you'd have it, make it' (45-6). Again, in lines 49-54, Pitholeon (the Hellenist Welsted) is mentioned as both a libeller (who thus contributes to Pope's sufferings) and a place-seeker (who thus testifies to Pope's influence). Here Pope has accepted Bentley's identification of the Grecizing Pitholeon (*Sat.* 1.10.22) with the Pitholaus who libelled Julius Caesar (Suetonius, *Divus Julius* 75); then he has conflated both with 'the Impertinent' of *Sat.* 1.9 who sought a place in Maecenas' circle. Finally, in lines 55-68 Pope describes the supplications of dramatists, which include the submission of 'A Virgin Tragedy' (56). Warton refers to Barford's *Virgin Queen*. This, however, would not exclude the possibility that Pope also had in mind the case of the unfortunate Statius, who, according to Juvenal (*Sat.* 7.87), starves 'unless he sells his virgin *Agave* to Paris'. That allusion, if accepted, would put Pope in a position somewhat like that of Domitian's powerful courtier.

The epistle proper begins with the story of King Midas' barber, to which Pope found an allusion in the first satire of Persius. The king had been given ass's ears as a punishment for preferring Pan's music to that of Apollo. By means of a turban he managed to conceal his ears from everyone except his barber. The latter, unable to keep the terrifying secret, whispered it into a hole in the ground. Persius, who alone realises that everyone in Rome has an ass's ears, eventually confides the secret to his book (120-1).[4] In his use of the myth (60-82) Pope replaces the barber with the king's Minister or, taking a hint from Chaucer,[5] his Queen: 'His very Minister who spy'd them first, / (Some say the Queen) was forc'd to speak or burst' (73-4). Then, going further than Persius, he claims to be in a *worse* position than Midas' barber: 'And is not mine, my Friend, a sorer case, / When ev'ry Coxcomb perks them in my face?' (73-4). Finally Pope draws on the sequel to the story, which is omitted by Persius but supplied by Ovid (*Met.* 11.190-3), whereby the reeds heard the barber's secret and whispered it to one another. Thus, instead of asking his book to keep the secret, as Persius did, Pope urges the *Dunciad* to spread it abroad: 'Out with it, *Dunciad*! let the secret pass, / That secret to each Fool, that he's an Ass' (79-80).

Within this passage something else takes place. Persius mentions a rude gesture made behind the back of a rich poetaster: 'hands which wag in imitation of white ears' (*Sat.* 1.59). Pope, as we have seen, turned this into an open and public gesture against himself: 'ev'ry Coxcomb perks them in my face'. Later in Persius' satire a cautious friend says, 'But why do you feel obliged to rub the rasp of truth / on sensitive ears? Better watch it. You may get a chilly reception / from those baronial porches' (107-9). In Pope the warning comes in lines 75-8: 'Good friend, forbear! you deal in dang'rous things, / I'd never name Queen, Minister, or Kings; / Keep close to ears,[6] and those let Asses prick, / 'Tis nothing" – Nothing? if they bite and kick?'. Maynard Mack referred convincingly to George II's habit of kicking everything in sight when in a temper,[7] (and the line also, of course, includes a swipe at Queen Caroline and Walpole); but, as so often, Pope has contrived a happy blend of history and literature. In *Sat.* 2.1 Horace is urged to write in praise of Caesar (i.e. Octavian) but demurs: 'If the moment isn't right, then Floppy's words won't penetrate / Caesar's pricked-up ear.[8] Rub him the wrong way / and he'll lash out right and left with his hooves in self-defence' (18-20). The crucial difference, of course, is that, whereas Horace's reference to Octavian, though rather cheeky, is fundamentally respectful, Pope's reference to the sovereign is contemptuous and hostile.

So King, Queen, Minister and others are to be branded as asses. The procedure is not cruel, Pope assures us, because 'No creature smarts so little as a Fool' (84). The stupid Codrus has the serene imperturbability of Horace's *iustum et tenacem propositi virum* ('the man who is just and tenacious of his purpose'; *Odes* 3.3.1). Butt in the Twickenham edn (p. 101) directs us to Addison's rendering of the relevant lines:

> Should the whole frame of nature round him break,
> In ruine and confusion hurl'd,
> He, unconcern'd, would hear the mighty crack,
> And stand secure amidst a falling world.

Pope wrote (85-8):

> Let Peals of Laughter, Codrus! round thee break,
> Thou unconcern'd canst hear the mighty Crack.
> Pit, Box and Gall'ry in convulsions hurl'd,
> Thou stand'st unshook amidst a bursting World.

But why Codrus? And why has the scene been changed to that of a performance? The answer, it seems, lies in Juvenal's first satire, where Codrus is among the poets who give recitations – with shattering effects: *convulsaque marmora clamant / semper et adsiduo ruptae lectore columnae* ('The marble statues cry out *in convulsions* and the columns *break* asunder from the succession of readers'; *Sat.* 1.12-13). Near the middle of the poem Pope speaks of the left-handed flattery directed at himself; it is here that the classical dimension becomes quite explicit (116): 'I cough like Horace, and tho' lean, am short'. Horace's shortness is attested in *Epistles* 1.20.24, where he is said to be *corporis exigui* ('of tiny form'); but his cough seems to have no stronger foundation than *Sat.* 1.9.32, where a gypsy predicts that he will not die of consumption. We know nothing of the shape of Ovid's nose; the phrase in line 118 ('such Ovid's nose') is simply a play on the name Publius Ovidius *Naso*. The words 'Sir! you have an Eye ...' (118) must be punctuated as about to run on. The construction would have continued 'like X's'; but it is futile to speculate what ancient figure Pope had in mind. Probably there was no one at all; for, as editors point out, there was nothing wrong with Pope's eyes. In any case Butt's reference to 'the lively eye' of *Epistles* 1.7.45 is unconvincing, because in the present context the eye must be imagined as in some way defective.

Continuing his defence, Pope writes: 'What sin to me unknown / Dipt me in ink, my parents' or my own?'. The question, as Maresca says,[9] recalls that of the disciples: 'Who did this sin, this man or his parents, that he was born blind?' (*John* 9.3). The dipping is therefore a kind of baneful baptism. Yet Pope's 'affliction' is not explained in terms of Jesus' answer that 'the works of God should be made manifest in him'. Instead, the supernatural spirit at work is the pagan Muse: 'As yet a child (*mihi iam puero*) the heavenly mysteries pleased me, and the Muse secretly drew me into her service'. That is Ovid writing about his inborn talent in *Tristia* 4.10.19-20. The lines which immediately follow (21-6) provide the basis for Pope's lines 128-30, as may be seen from Butt's note. As in Ovid's case, Pope's early attempts turned out to be verse; but, unlike Ovid, he did *not* abandon another career for poetry; *nor* did he disobey his father. Christian and classical, then, function harmoniously side by side, though the Christian allusion is quickly past; and, after being established as a point of reference, Ovid is immediately exploited as a contrast.

Pope's second assertion – that poetry helped him to survive (131-2) – comes from that same poem in the *Tristia*: *ergo quod vivo ... / gratia, Musa, tibi: nam te solacia praebes, / tu curae requies, tu medicina venis* ('The fact that I am still alive ... is thanks to you, Muse; for you provide solace; you come as rest and medicine to my trouble'; *Tristia* 4.10.115-18). The Muse's healing function is cleverly presented by Pope as seconding the art of Dr Arbuthnot. Ovid has also helped him, directly or indirectly, to that famous phrase 'this long Disease, my Life'.[10] In the ancient world life was seen as a stage, an inn, a meal, a race-course or a battle, not, so far as I know, as a disease. This may be because in the pagan centuries the cessation of life could not readily be thought of as a cure – except, perhaps, within the mystery religions, which are not well represented in the literary tradition.

Answering his critics in *Epistles* 1.19, Horace says: *non ego ventosae plebis suffragia venor / impensis cenarum et tritae munere vestis* ('I'm not the kind to hunt for the votes of the fickle rabble by standing dinners and giving presents of worn-out clothes'; 37-8). Pope varies this idea in his attack on Gildon: 'Yet then did Gildon draw his venal quill; / I wished the man a dinner, and sate still' (151-2). Horace goes on to say that he never thought it worthwhile *grammaticas ambire tribus et pulpita* ('to canvass the academic critics on their platforms'; 40). Pope, who is still following Horace's sequence of thought, uses this idea as a springboard for his brilliant attack on the pedantry of men like Bentley and Tibbald.

Pope then switches to another source. Other writers, he says, had an excessive notion of their own merit; and they were therefore indignant when Pope assessed them fairly. The private view a man has of his own worth is likely to be unbalanced. One may try to gratify him by flattery but it is hard to guess the extent of his conceit. This seems to be the drift of the passage, though I am not sure that I understand line 177.[11] At any rate, 'a Man's true Merit' and the 'secret Standard in his Mind' come from Persius via Dryden's translation:

> In full assemblies let the crowd prevail:
> I weigh no merit by the common scale.
> The conscience is the test of ev'ry mind;
> 'Seek not thyself, without thyself, to find.'
> *(Sat.* 1.17-19)

In other words, forget about your reputation, simply attend to your own judgement of yourself. Pope once again has turned his classical 'model' upside down.

In lines 215-48 Pope claims he has aimed at no position of eminence in the literary world: 'I sought no homage from the Race that write' (219). This recalls – and inverts – Horace's *multa fero ut placem genus irritabile vatum* ('I put up with much to placate the poets, that rancorous race'; *Epistles* 2.2.102) – a line which is splendidly heightened in Pope's *Imitation*: 'Much do I suffer, much, to keep in peace / This jealous, waspish, wrong-head, rhiming Race (147-8). In Pope's *Epistle* literary prestige is left to

Bufo ('Toad'). This man is seen as the absurd and repellent rival of Apollo, the true judge of poetry, who sits on his 'forked hill', Mt. Parnassus, which Persius calls 'two-peaked' (*biceps*) in the second line of his Prologue. We are told that the toad had already been used by Mallet as the symbol of a conceited patron. However, since Bufo is here flatteringly compared to Maecenas (234), it is worth remembering that the story of the inflated toad or frog was to be found in Horace, *Sat.* 2.3.314-20. It was told there by Damasippus who was criticising Horace for his ludicrous ambition. And what was this ambition? To become like Maecenas. So, according to the critic, Horace has tried to emulate the great patron by puffing himself up. In Pope it is the *patron* who has become the inflated toad; the poet is determined *not* to flatter him.

An extension of Pope's procedure can be seen in the section on malice (283-304). In *Sat.* 1.4 Horace had written, 'The man who traduces a friend behind his back, / who won't defend him when someone else is running him down, / who looks for the big laugh and wants to be thought a wit, / the man who can invent what he never saw but can't keep a secret – / he's the blackguard; beware of him, o son of Rome' (81-5). The argument of these lines, quoted in Latin in the Twickenham edition, was followed by Pope in the version published in 1731-2. Thus the concluding lines read: ''Tis not the sober Sat'rist you should dread, / But such a babling Coxcomb in his Stead'. However, when revising the passage for inclusion in his *Epistle*, Pope adopted an altogether more minatory tone: 'A Lash like mine no honest man shall dread, / But all such babling blockheads in his stead' (303-4). In other words, honest people need not fear my satire, but malicious gossips had better watch out. The warning is immediately given substance by the castigation of Sporus.

The technique which we are studying is not employed solely on Latin literature. When Pope says, 'Three thousand Suns went down on Welsted's Lye' (375), he is combining 'Let not the sun go down upon your wrath' (*Ephesians* 4.26) with the previous verse, 'Wherefore putting away lying, speak every man truth with his neighbour'. Whether or not the combination is fully conscious, it entails an inversion of the original; for 'let not the sun go down on X' has been changed into 'I patiently let the sun go down on

Y'. The reason for Pope's restraint, he tells us (382-3), was the importance which his father attached to another Christian tenet: 'But whosoever shall say, "Thou fool", shall be in danger of hell fire' (*Matthew* 5.22). The reference to his father was prompted, in part at least, by Horace, *Sat.* 1.4.105-26; but, whereas Horace's father pointed to living examples of vice and folly, thus implanting the habit of moral criticism in his son, Pope's father used his influence for the *opposite* purpose, namely to instil charity.

Speaking of his parents, Pope says, 'Unspotted Names! and memorable long, / If there be force in Virtue, or in Song' (386-7). After the death of the young Trojans Nisus and Euryalus, Virgil broke the convention of epic anonymity to write: *fortunati ambo! si quid mea carmina possunt / nulla dies umquam memori vos eximet aeuo* ('O blessed pair! For if my songs possess any power, / no day shall ever remove you from the memory of time'; *Aen.* 9.446-7). The leap from Pope's parents to Virgil's Trojans may seem rather surprising. But a stepping-stone was provided by Ovid in the poem from which we have already quoted. After speaking affectionately of his parents, he wrote *felices ambo* ('happy pair!'; *Tristia* 4.10.81) – a phrase which offered an easy transition to Virgil's *fortunati ambo*.

In his note on line 381 Pope claimed a higher social position for his father than the facts warranted.[12] Some of the same anxiety can be seen in 'Of gentle Blood ... Each Parent sprung' (388-90). Horace, whose rise in the world had been even more dramatic, had chosen the *opposite* strategy. Instead of trying to improve his father's pedigree, he insisted upon what everybody knew, namely that the man had once been a slave (*Sat.* 1.6). This was, no doubt, a courageous declaration but it was not without pride; for the father was portrayed as possessing a noble character. It also meant that in later times Horace's friends could add to his qualities what they took away from his birth (*Epistles* 1.20.22). Pope concludes the lines on his father with another Horatian variation. Ridiculing a Stoic sage who, by gaining mastery over himself, claimed to be as happy as a king, Horace had written *privatusque magis vivam te rege beatus* ('and, though a commoner, I'll live a happier life than Your Majesty'; *Sat.* 1.3.142). Pope turned this into 'Who sprung from Kings shall know less joy than I' (405).

Finally, by writing about his mother (406 ff.), Pope provided a fully independent conclusion. Horace never speaks of his mother; perhaps he never knew her. Again Pope drew on some earlier verses, which are printed by Butt. In doing so he made another significant alteration. The earlier piece included the lines: 'Me, when the Cares my better Years have shown / Another's Age, shall hasten on my own'. This is unfortunate not only in expression but also in sense, for it suggests that the cares (attentions) which Pope has shown to his elderly mother will (as worries) shorten his own life. This may have been one of the things Pope had in mind when he called the lines 'incorrect'.[13] At any rate, when he incorporated them in the *Epistle*, he rewrote them so as to give exactly the *opposite* nuance: 'On Cares like these if Length of days attend, / May Heav'n, to bless those days, preserve my Friend' (414-15). The commandment said 'Honour thy father and thy mother: that thy days may be long upon the land which the Lord thy God giveth thee' (*Exodus* 20.12). So, by attending to his mother, Pope will not shorten but lengthen his life. The version written four years earlier (1731) was addressed to an unidentified young man. Here the passage, which echoes lines 27-8 – 'Friend to my Life (which did you not prolong / The World had wanted many an idle Song') – should refer to Dr Arbuthnot. One notes that in 1751 the last two lines were given to him.

Throughout the *Epistle* Horace is the dominant influence. Pope writes with a Horatian elegance and he has used many of Horace's arguments. But the changes described above have brought him closer in spirit to Lucilius. In lines 342 and 358-9, for instance, Pope claims to have endured everything for the sake of Virtue. This recalls 'To Virtue only and her Friends, a Friend', which is a translation of Horace, *Sat.* 2.1.70: *scilicet uni aequus Virtuti atque eius amicis*.[14] However, Horace is there talking, not of himself but of Lucilius; and he is specifically concerned with the older satirist's courage and pugnacity: 'He indicted the city's leaders, and the city tribe by tribe' (69). If we think of the 'tribe' of statesmen, the 'tribe' of critics etc., that description fits Pope remarkably well. But in one aspect he went (as far as we know) beyond Lucilius, in that he could be at his most aggressive when boasting of his forbearance.

Related Material:

'Pope and Horace on Not Writing Satire' in C. Rawson (ed.) *English Satire and the Satiric Tradition* (Blackwell, Oxford, 1984) 167-82.

'Two Epistles to Augustus' in *The Classical Tradition in Operation* (Toronto, Buffalo and London, 1994) 61-90.

'Pope's Farewell to Horace' forthcoming in *Translation and Literature* 14 (2005).

14 The Optimistic Lines in Johnson's *The Vanity of Human Wishes*

[From *Notes & Queries* 231.1 (March 1986) 99]

But grant, the Virtues of a temp'rate Prime
Bless with an Age exempt from Scorn or Crime;
An Age that melts with unperceiv'd Decay,
And glides in modest Innocence away;
Whose peaceful Day Benevolence endears,
Whose Night congratulating Conscience cheers;
The gen'ral Fav'rite as the gen'ral Friend:
Such Age there is, and who shall wish its End?
[291-8]

We learn from the commentaries that, according to Mrs Piozzi, Johnson had his mother in mind in this passage. What seems to be less widely noticed is the fact that, when Johnson deserted the mordant Juvenal here (as he had to do), he found a very different but no less appropriate source, namely Cicero *On Old Age*.

With the first two lines compare: *libidinosa enim et intemperans adulescentia effetum corpus tradit senectuti* ('A self-indulgent and intemperate prime delivers a worn-out body to old age'; *de Senectute* 29).

With lines 293-4 compare: *non intellegitur quando obrepat senectus, ita sensim sine sensu aetas senescit, nec subito frangitur, sed diuturnitate extinguitur* ('Old age steals upon (the good man) unawares, so gradually and imperceptibly does his age grow old; it does not suddenly fall apart, but fades over a long period of time'; *de Senectute* 38). In view of G.J. Colb's note, cited in the Oxford edn, it would seem that Dryden, *The State of Innocence* i.348-50 was an immediate source.

With lines 295-6 compare: *conscientia bene actae vitae multorumque bene factorum recordatio iucundissima est* ('The consciousness of a life well lived and the memory of many good deeds is exceedingly pleasant'; *de Senectute* 9). This, incidentally, supports the view that 'Benevolence' is the old person's own kindness.

In the next section Johnson resumes his gloomy theme: 'Yet ev'n on this her Load Misfortune flings' (299). And there, too, we find:

> New Forms arise. and diff'rent Views engage,
> Superfluous lags the Vet'ran on the Stage,
> Till pitying Nature signs the last Release,
> And bids afflicted Worth retire to Peace
> (307-10)

With 308 compare: *neque enim histrioni, ut placeat, peragenda fabula est, modo in quocunque fuerit actu probetur; neque sapientibus usque ad 'plaudite' veniendum est* ('To give pleasure it is not necessary for an actor to be on stage throughout the whole of the play, provided he wins approval in the acts where he does appear; similarly, wise men do not need to continue until the audience is bidden to applaud'; *de Senectute* 70); cf. *The Rambler* no. 207, 'The Folly of continuing too long upon the Stage'. And again *senectus autem aetatis peractio tamquam fabulae, cuius defetigationem fugere debemus, praesertim adiuncta satietate* ('Moreover, old age in a person's life is, as it were, the last act of a play; before it brings exhaustion we should hurry away, especially when we have played our part to the point of satiety'; *de Senectute* 85).With lines 309-310 compare: *nam habet natura, ut aliarum omnium rerum, sic vivendi modum* ('For nature has a limit for living as of all other things'; *de Senectute* 85). Also: *vetat Pythagoras iniussu imperatoris, id est dei, de praesidio et statione vitae decedere* ('And Pythagoras says we must not stand down from life's guard-duty and sentry-go until the commander, that is god, has given the order'; *de Senectute* 73).[1]

Cicero does not invite us to inspect these sentiments too critically; for one can hardly 'hurry away' if one has to wait until one is summoned. This inconsistency, however, does not occur in Johnson.

Related Material:

Johnson's Juvenal: London *and* The Vanity of Human Wishes (Bristol, 1981; repr. 1988).
Samuel Johnson: The Latin Poems (Bucknell University Press, Lewisburg, 2005).

15 Two Invitations:

Tennyson *To the Rev. F.D. Maurice* and Horace *to Maecenas* (*Odes* 3.29)

[From *Hermathena* 150 (1991) 5-19]

To the Rev. F.D. Maurice

Come, when no graver cares employ,
Godfather, come and see your boy:
    Your presence will be sun in winter,
Making the little one leap for joy.

For, being of that honest few,
Who give the Fiend himself his due,
    Should eighty-thousand college-councils
Thunder 'Anathema', friend, at you;

Should all our churchmen foam in spite
At you, so careful of the right,
    Yet one lay-hearth would give you welcome
(Take it and come) to the Isle of Wight;

Where, far from noise and smoke of town,
I watch the twilight falling brown
    All round a careless-order'd garden
Close to the ridge of a noble down.

You'll have no scandal while you dine,
But honest talk and wholesome wine,
    And only hear the magpie gossip
Garrulous under a roof of pine:

For groves of pine on either hand,
To break the blast of winter, stand;
    And further on, the hoary Channel
Tumbles a billow on chalk and sand;

Where, if below the milky steep
Some ship of battle slowly creep,
    And thro' zones of light and shadow
Glimmer away to lonely deep,

We might discuss the Northern sin
Which made a selfish war begin;
    Dispute the claims, arrange the chances;
Emperor, Ottoman, which shall win:

Or whether war's avenging rod
Shall lash all Europe into blood;
    Till you should turn to dearer matters,
Dear to the man that is dear to God;

How best to help the slender store,
How mend the dwellings, of the poor;
    How gain in life, as life advances,
Valour and charity more and more.

Come, Maurice, come: the lawn as yet
Is hoar with rime, or spongy-wet;
    But when the wreath of March has blossomed
Crocus, anemone, violet,

Or later, pay one visit here,
For those are few we hold as dear;
    Nor pay but one, but come for many,
Many and many a happy year.

Tyrrhena regum progenies, tibi
non ante verso lene merum cado
    cum flore, Maecenas, rosarum et
        pressa tuis balanus capillis

iamdudum apud me est. eripe te morae,   5
nec semper udum Tibur et Aefulae
    declive contempleris arvum et
        Telegoni iuga parricidae.

fastidiosam desere copiam et
molem propinquam nubibus arduis 10
   omitte mirari beatae
    fumum et opes strepitumque Romae.

plerumque gratae divitibus vices
mundaeque parvo sub lare pauperum
   cenae sine aulaeis et ostro 15
    sollicitam explicuere frontem.

iam clarus occultum Andromedae pater
ostendit ignem, iam Procyon furit
   et stella vesani Leonis,
    sole dies referente siccos: 20

iam pastor umbras cum grege languido
rivumque fessus quaerit et horridi
   dumeta Silvani, caretque
    ripa vagis taciturna ventis.

tu civitatem quis deceat status 25
curas et urbi sollicitus times
   quid Seres et regnata Cyro
    Bactra parent Tanaisque discors.

prudens futuri temporis exitum
caliginosa nocte premit deus, 30
   ridetque si mortalis ultra
    fas trepidat. quod adest memento

componere aequus; cetera fluminis
ritu feruntur, nunc medio alveo
   cum pace delabentis Etruscum 35
    in mare, nunc lapides adesos

stirpesque raptas et pecus et domos
volventis una non sine montium
   clamore vicinaeque silvae,
    cum fera diluvies quietos 40

irritat amnis. ille potens sui
laetusque deget, cui licet in diem
   dixisse 'vixi'. cras vel atra
    nube polum Pater occupato

vel sole puro; non tamen irritum,   45
quodcumque retro est, efficiet neque
   diffinget infectumque reddet,
    quod fugiens semel hora vexit.

Fortuna saevo laeta negotio et
ludum insolentem ludere pertinax   50
   transmutat incertos honores,
    nunc mihi, nunc alii benigna.

laudo manentem; si celeris quatit
pennas, resigno quae dedit et mea
   virtute me involvo probamque   55
    pauperiem sine dote quaero.

non est meum, si mugiat Africis
malus procellis, ad miseras preces
   decurrere et votis pacisci
    ne Cypriae Tyriaeque merces   60

addant avaro divitias mari.
tunc me biremis praesidio scaphae
   tutum per Aegaeos tumultus
    aura feret geminusque Pollux.

Tyrrhenian descendant of kings, I have long had ready for you here a mellow wine in a cask as yet untilted – rose-blooms too, Maecenas, and pomade pressed for your hair. Shake yourself free from delay, and don't just keep looking at well-watered Tibur and the sloping fields of Aefula and the ridge of Telegonus the parricide. Get away from cloying affluence and that pile which almost touches the clouds above; stop being fascinated by the smoke and wealth and noise of prosperous Rome. Often a change is welcome to rich people; and simple meals at the small homes of poor men, without costly hangings and purple coverlets, smooth their anxious brows. Now the father of Andromeda is showing brightly the fire he kept hidden before; now

Procyon is raging and the star of furious Leo, as the sun brings round the days of drought. Now the shepherd with his lethargic flock wearily makes for the shade and the river and shaggy Silvanus' thickets, and the bank is silent without a breath of wind. You are worrying about what system is right for the country; and in your anxiety for Rome you are apprehensive about what China and Bactria (once governed by Cyrus) may be plotting, and the Don with its internal feuds. God in his wisdom envelops in thick night what the future has in store, and laughs if a mortal creature becomes unduly distressed. Make sure that you calmly set the present in order. Everything else flows along like a river, which at one time glides peacefully in mid channel down to the Tuscan sea, at another eats away boulders, tears up tree-trunks, and rolls them past, along with animals and houses, amid the echoing roar of the hills and the surrounding woods, when the wild flood stirs up the quiet water. That man will live happily as master of himself who can say at the end of every day 'I have *lived*'. Tomorrow let the Father fill the sky with black clouds or clear sunshine; he will not, however, undo what is past, nor will he recast or cancel what the hurrying hour has once carried away. Fortune, delighting in her cruel business and remorselessly playing her high-handed game, switches her unpredictable favours; now she is kind to *me,* now to someone else. I praise her while she stays; if she flaps her swift wings, I relinquish what she has given, wrap myself in the cloak of my virtue, and go courting honest Poverty who has no dowry. It is not my way, if the mast creaks in the gales from Africa, to descend to piteous appeals and by prayers to make a bargain that my merchandise from Cyprus and Tyre will not increase the wealth of the greedy sea. In that crisis, with the help of my two-oared dinghy, I will be carried safely through the Aegean's tumult by the breeze and by Pollux and his twin.

****

At a time when there are anxieties about Russia and the Middle East, a major poet, aged about forty, belonging to the foremost imperial power of the day, writes from the country to a slightly older friend, a distinguished public figure who is residing in the capital. He speaks attractively of the countryside, inviting his friend to come and forget his worries amid the joys of good wine and conversation. Horace to Maecenas from the Sabine hills, or Tennyson to F.D. Maurice from the Isle of Wight? For Tennyson,

the historical situation (one assumes) came first. However, once
he had decided to write to his friend, life and literature interacted;
and he thought of Horace. It could, indeed, have been Horace
who persuaded him to send a poem instead of an ordinary letter.
Not that his attitude to Horace was one of simple enthusiasm. We
are told that Tennyson's father made him recite all four books of
the *Odes* before he left school.[1] Later in life, when reminded of
Byron's line 'Then farewell, Horace, whom I hated so', Tennyson
said, 'I too was so overdosed with Horace as a boy that I don't do
him justice now I am old'.[2] Nevertheless, that early acquaintance
survived; and at no time did Tennyson lose his respect for Horace
as a technician. 'The Horatian Alcaic,' he said, 'is perhaps the
stateliest metre except the Virgilian hexameter at its best'.[3] (One
recalls the tribute to Virgil: 'Wielder of the stateliest measure ever
moulded by the lips of man'.)

Tennyson himself wrote a set of four Alcaic stanzas beginning:

> O mighty-mouthed inventor of harmonies,
> O skilled to sing of time and eternity,
> God-gifted organ-voice of England,
> Milton! a name to resound for ages.

These he later called 'a bit of a *tour de force*'.[4] However, in a number
of his lyrics he experimented with *modifications* of the Alcaic.

In *Maurice* he uses a stanza rhyming AABA, in which the first
two lines consist of four iambic feet: 'You'll have no scandal while
you dine, / But honest talk and wholesome wine'.[5] The third, having
its first and fifth syllables unstressed, is a lighter version of the
Alcaic third: 'And only hear the magpie gossip'; while the fourth
is a true Alcaic fourth, but catalectic (i.e. with the final unstressed
syllable missing): 'Garrulous under a roof of pine'. If the metre
of *Maurice* recalls a Horatian Alcaic, albeit in a somewhat lighter
form, the same is true of the structure. The stanzas are arranged in
groups of one, three, six and two – the kind of symmetry beloved
of numerologists. Thus the first stanza, with its opening 'Come',
is linked to the last two ('Come' in line 41 and 'come' in line 47),
while stanzas 2-4 and 5-10 form units – units which, with their
rather mannered syntax, convey a perceptibly Latinate effect.

This effect was a conscious decision; for originally line 5 read 'But you are of that honest few'; line 13 'And here far off from noise of town'; and line 25 'Here, if below the milky steep'.[6] Not all the changes produced satisfactory results. In line 5 'being ... due' is hard to accommodate within the syntax of the sentence; and in line 12, in spite of the brackets, one tends to construe '... come to the Isle of Wight'. However, what we associate with railway advertising would not have troubled anyone in 1855 and the present reading is certainly preferable to the discarded 'Here in the sweet little Isle of Wight'.

In lines 13-16 Tennyson wrote one of the finest stanzas in the poem. 'And here far off from noise of town' gave way to the more compact 'Where, far from noise and *smoke* of *town*', which produced a clear echo of Horace's *fumum ... strepitumque Romae* ('the smoke and noise of Rome'). In line 15 'All round' took the place of 'About'. This gave a more sonorous pair of opening syllables in which 'round' was in assonance with 'brown' and 'down'; and at the same time it produced a more fully Horatian effect by bringing in a spondee. Another, final, point indicates continuity and change. In Horace's ode Maecenas looks out over the plain to the east of Rome and his gaze dwells longingly on Tusculum, described in a grandiose periphrasis as *Telegoni iuga parricidae* (literally 'the ridge of Telegonus the parricide').[7] In Tennyson it is the poet in the Isle of Wight who watches the twilight falling on his garden 'close to the *ridge* of a noble town'.[8]

Stanzas 5-10 are held together by other strands as well as syntax. In line 19 Tennyson substituted 'only' for 'sitting', thus contrasting 'gossip' and 'garruluous' with 'no scandal' and 'honest talk'. In the following stanza the link is obtained by repeating 'pine' from line 20 by way of explanation. The next link is one of colour, for 'milky' in line 25 takes up 'chalk' in 24. In line 26 the 'ship of battle' foreshadows the 'war' discussed in the following stanza. In 35-6 one observes the repetition 'dearer ... dear ... dear', while in 37-9 we have 'how ... how ... how ...' and 'more and more'. Then, in the two closing stanzas, the series is rounded off by 'Come ... come'; also 'pay one ... Nor pay but one'; and 'many, many and many ...' – an incantatory device which adds emphasis as well as coherence.

In this, the longest part of the poem, Tennyson moves away from Horace's ode for reasons which will be discussed presently. Still, it is worth observing that the talk of politics and war in 29-34 is precisely the kind of thing that Maecenas is urged to forget in lines 25-8 of the ode. Moreover, though he moves away, Tennyson does not quite abandon Horace; for the scene at the table in Farringford recalls the scene at Horace's farm in *Sat.* 2.6.[9] There, after speaking of the simple food and wine, Horace says the conversation will not be about frivlous topics but rather questions of moral theory 'which touch us more closely' (72-3). So too Maurice will have no scandal or gossip but 'honest talk and wholesome wine'.[10] Eventually the talk will turn from politics to 'dearer matters' (35). As with Horace, these are matters of morality, but morality of the practical kind that inspired Christian socialism.

To see why Tennyson's poem diverged from the ode, we need to bear in mind the nature and circumstances of the four men, and in particular the relations between poet and guest. F.D. Maurice was the son of a Unitarian minister. He went to Trinity College, Cambridge, in 1823. Two years later he moved to Trinity Hall, where he took a first in the Civil Law exams of 1827. However, as he did not belong to the Church of England, he left Cambridge without actually taking a degree and, after doing literary work in London, entered Exeter College, Oxford, with a view to taking holy orders. He obtained a degree in 1832, having been baptised as a member of the Church of England in the previous year. In 1834 he was ordained; and, while there is no reason to doubt his sincerity, this move certainly assisted his career. He was appointed to the Chair of English History and Literature at King's College London in 1840; the Chair of Divinity was added in 1846. For long he had wished to promote a scheme for women's education and, in 1848, was instrumental in founding Queen's College, Harley Street. Six years later he was a leading figure in the establishment of a working men's college. Maurice was, therefore, a man of tremendous drive and charisma, whose blend of Christian piety and social conscience put him years ahead of his time. Unfortunately for him, he was also an independent thinker; and one important feature of his independence was that he could not accept that a god of love would subject his children to eternal torment. In a letter to his friend F.J.A. Hort in 1849,[11] he started from *John* 17.2: 'And this is life eternal, that they might know thee, the only true God, and Jesus Christ whom thou hast sent'. If therefore (he reasoned) eternal life is the knowledge of God, eternal perdition must be the lack of that knowledge. This led him to reinterpret the so-called Athanasian Creed,[12] which, taken literally, consigned to damnation all unbelievers, including the virtuous heathen: 'Whosoever will be saved: before all things it is necessary that he hold the Catholic faith'. Later Maurice came to believe that, as it was so widely misunderstood, the Athanasian Creed should be omitted from the Church of England service altogether.[13] In the meantime, in 1853, he put forward his view of 'eternal life' (ζωὴν αἰώνιον) in a published essay,[14] whereupon he was dismissed from his Chair at King's by the College Council. Hence Tennyson's reference in stanza two: 'Should eighty-thousand college-councils / Thunder "Anathema", friend, at you'.

The poet had known Maurice from their Cambridge days, when they were both members of 'The Apostles' – a club which then, as in the 1930s, did not shrink from unorthodox opinions. Though he sometimes found his thought hard to understand, Tennyson, like John Stuart Mill,[15] greatly admired Maurice; in 1852 he had asked him to be godfather to the young Hallam. According to Mrs Tennyson, he wanted Hallam to be able to say, 'My father asked Mr Maurice to be my Godfather, because he was the truest Christian he knew in the world'.[16] So now, in January 1854, two months after Maurice's disgrace, Tennyson wrote inviting Maurice to visit Farringford in the spring.[17] The opening words are not unduly insistent: 'Come, when no graver cares employ'; the invitation is conveyed in an easy informal style which adopts the child's position *vis à vis* the visitor: 'Godfather, come and see your boy'; and the stanza closes with a graceful compliment to Maurice's warm personality: 'Your presence will be sun in winter, / Making the little one leap for joy'. J.B. Steane comments: 'The heart is in the right place, but the verse is doggerel'.[18] That seems very wide of the mark. Better to recall Tennyson's own observation about his poem *To E. Fitzgerald*: '*Belle comme la prose,*' he said, 'is the French expression for that kind of poetry, and a very good one. It also applies to my lines of invitation to F.D. Maurice'.[19]

Whereas Horace presents an inland scene in an Italian summer, Tennyson describes a coastal scene in an English winter. In other places (e.g. *Epistles* 1.16) Horace gives details about his farm, but not here: the shepherd by the river could be anywhere in Italy. Tennyson, however, watches the twilight 'falling brown' over his 'careless-ordered garden'. Trunks, bare branches, soil and perhaps some rotting leaves give the light a brownish tinge, so that it scarcely occurs to us that the arresting 'brown' has been sought as a rhyme. Another memorable touch is the dreadnought steaming past the Needles. We may share some of Goldwin Smith's discomfort that, at a time of grave political crisis, a machine of war should be viewed with such detachment.[20] Yet the ship is not imagined *solely* as an aesthetic object; if seen, it may give rise to lively discussion about the impending war. Moreover, one would be sorry to sacrifice that hypothetical picture in which, as though in a forerunner of some impressionist painting, the great vessel would 'on thro' zones of light and shadow / Glimmer away to the lonely deep'. Those two lines, so instinct with the spirit of Tennyson's romanticism, lay far outside the classical poet's sensibility.

As for international events, in 1850 Louis Napoleon asserted his right to place Latin monks in holy places in and around Jerusalem; he was supported in this by Austria and Spain. In retaliation, Tsar Nicolas of Russia claimed not only the holy places for the Orthodox Church but also the right to protect all Christian citizens of Turkey. These claims worried Britain; for they seemed to form part of the Tsar's general policy of encroachment at the eastern end of the Mediterranean. In July 1853 Russia occupied the Turkish principalities to the north of the Black Sea. In October Turkey declared war on Russia and, in November, won a victory at Oltenitza. By way of reprisal, Russia destroyed ships of the Turkish navy in Sinope on 30 November. This caused a storm of anger in Britain and France and, on 4 January, their fleets moved into the Black Sea. This move was followed by a declaration of war on Russia (27 January). These, then, are the events referred to by Tennyson in stanzas seven to nine. The northern sin was the Russian attack on Sinope; the emperor was the Tsar, not Louis Napoleon.

Yet political disputes, even so grave as these, do not lie at the centre of the poem; in fact they figure as little more than topics of conversation. The theological background is more important; and here one recalls the familiar fact that the nineteenth century was increasingly a century of doubt. One thinks of the effect of Malthus at the beginning, then the growing interest in geology and paleontology, the controversies aroused by the higher criticism of the Bible, then (three years after *Maurice*) the uproar caused by *The Origin of Species*. This intellectual ferment is well documented in J.S. Mill's *Autobiography*, in Edmund Gosse's *Father and Son* and in the writings of Matthew Arnold, T.H. Huxley, Leslie Stephen and countless others. Tennyson, a parson's son, was led to question many traditional beliefs. This is what makes his *Lucretius* such a deeply interesting poem – a poem which, unlike his respectful and affectionate tribute to Virgil, betrays disturbing inner conflicts. In the end, after all his struggles, he seems to have managed to retain his faith in God and immortality; but he was clear that such faith, whether firm or precarious, went far beyond anything that could be proved:

> *Strong Son of God, immortal Love,*
> *Whom we, that have not seen thy face,*
> *By Faith and Faith alone embrace,*
> *Believing where we cannot prove*

This hard-won belief was accompanied by a distrust of dogmatic formulas: 'There lives more faith in honest doubt, / Believe me, than in half the creeds'. (Cf. 'For nothing worthy proving can be proven etc.' in *The Ancient Sage*, line 66). Tennyson was therefore happy to support Maurice in his clash with the ecclesiastical establishment; and he looked forward to talking to him about the Christian approach to social problems. Accordingly *Maurice* is a gesture of friendship, a delightful invitation, complete and self-contained. It does not offer any theological assurance; for none was needed and, in any case, Tennyson was not the man to provide it.

The recipient of *Odes* 3.29 was a very different sort of man. Unlike F.D. Maurice, who died with a benediction on his lips,[21] Maecenas was far from serene. A brief character sketch has been

given in ch. 12 above (pp. 143 ff.), where it was pointed out that
he was probably in charge of Rome during Augustus' absence in
Spain (27-24 BC). In any case we infer from 3.29.25-8 that he
had worries about home affairs and about problems in the east.
So it was only natural that Horace should urge his friend to take
a break. The occasion of the invitation and the philosophy that
underlies it, combine to produce a more complex – and in the end
a much weightier – poem than Tennyson's *Maurice*.

'Etruscan scion of royal kings' – a grandiose address; *so*
grandiose, in fact, as to produce a smile. The same kind of hyper-
bole is applied to Maecenas' mansion on the Esquiline: it is a
'cloud-capp'd tower';[22] and the reason suggested at this point for
Maecenas' delay is undisguisedly facetious: he is fascinated by
the luxury of the capital. The deliberately mannered style includes
some cleverly varied triads: wine, roses, perfume; then (sweeping
round from north to south and increasing in length) *udum Tibur,
Aefulae declive arvum* ('well-watered Tibur, the sloping fields of
Aefula') and the historic *Telegoni iuga parricidae* ('the ridge of
the parricide Telegonus'); then (again increasing in length because
of the elided *fumum*) the smoke, wealth, and noise of Rome. In
stanza four (a transitional stanza in the middle of the first group
of seven) all this affluence and grandeur is starkly contrasted with
the simple meals and small premises of the poor. Yet the visitor
to the Sabine farm can hardly have been thought of as slumming;
for the house had eight servants and the estate was large enough
to maintain five families.[23]

Stanzas five to seven reinforce the invitation by recording
what is happening in the sky and in the countryside. The weather
is described in terms of the astronomy bequeathed to Rome by
Alexandria. Again we have a triad: Cepheus (supposedly rising 9
July), Canis Minor (15 July) and the bright star in Leo (29 July).
Into this scene of heat and dryness comes the herdsman with
his animals, making for trees, river and bushes; the riverbank is
still and silent. All this time Maecenas is worrying about what
is best for Rome, in domestic and foreign affairs. This, the real
reason for his remaining in the city, is described with the same
kind of teasing exaggeration. *Seres* is a vague name for orientals;
Bactra, the furthest province of Parthia, is described as it was five

hundred years before; the Scythians, represented by the Don, which flows into the north-eastern corner of the Sea of Azov, are said to be occupied with internal squabbles; what serious plots could be devised by such people?

Beneath this whole opening section lies the idea, which is central to Horace's life and art – that, as the natural world moves through a regular process of change (*sole dies referente siccos* – 'as the sun brings round the days of drought') so in life one should aim to achieve a pattern of controlled alternation (*vices*) between work and rest, city and country, high style and conversation, grave and gay.

In stanza eight, as the gentle teasing dies away, the tone becomes more sombre and impersonal. God deliberately conceals the future; being a somewhat satirical deity, he laughs when mortals become unduly agitated (*trepidat,* though general, glances back at Maecenas and his neuroses). Deal calmly with what is present. All else is unsure. The stream of life changes like a river; the only fixed thing is the past – and even that is carried swiftly away. Although the level of style is higher, there are links with what has gone before. Various words imply alternation – *nunc* ... *nunc* (34 and 36), *vel* ... *vel* (43 and 45). The river flows into the Etruscan sea; which reminds us that the river is the Tuscan Tiber and that Maecenas himself is Tyrrhenian (1).[24] Pattern is again observable – not triads now but sound effects (as in *nube polum pater occupato*) and chiastic arrangements (*atra nube* ... *sole puro*; *quodcumque* etc. before *efficiet*; then *quod fugiens* etc. after *reddet*). Yet these features are overshadowed by that terrific picture of the river in spate, which, like the description of Pindar's verse in *Odes* 4.2, sweeps across the stanza-divisions and even produces a hypermetric line which has to be elided into its successor (*cum pace delabentis Etruscum / in mare*). The description includes the breathless polysyndeton of 37: *stirpesque raptas et pecus et domos (-que* ... *et* ... *et)*, and the rhyming sequence *Etruscum, adesos, domos, montium,* which is most uncommon. However, striking as that passage is, does it not recall lines 17-20, where blazing Cepheus shows his fire, the *canicula* rages and Leo is mad with fury? The violence is analogous; only the element is different – there fire, here water.

In the four closing stanzas Horace slackens the emotional

tension and concludes, as he so often does,[25] on a lighter note. In doing so he applies to *himself* this perception of how things are. As in *Odes* 1.34, the god who produces change merges into the figure of Fortuna, who plays her grim game, favouring now one, now another. With the word *manentem* she becomes a (rather loosely attached) wife. Horace praises her while she stays with him; but, when she flies away, he relinquishes what she brought him (i.e. her dowry), wraps himself in the cloak of virtue and goes in search of honest Poverty, who has no dowry at all. Again we have the motif of change, illustrated by a scene of violence in the natural world – this time a storm at sea. Now, however, the emphasis is not on the disaster itself so much as on Horace's escape. Instead of bemoaning the loss of his rich merchandise (which recalls the wealth of Rome in stanzas three and four), Horace will take to the life-boat and make port with the help of Castor and Pollux. So by prudently adjusting to those changes which are beyond his control, the wise man will make the most of prosperity and lessen the impact of hard times. It is essentially a doctrine of hedonism, but hedonism with an inner core of stoic toughness – a combination which enables a man to live life to the full and, at the end, to proclaim defiantly with Virgil's Dido, *vixi, et quem dederat cursum Fortuna peregi* ('I have lived, and I have completed the course assigned by Fortune'; *Aen.* 4.653).[26]

So Tennyson was right to abandon Horace's ode after the initial invitation. Had he stayed with it he would have been led into areas to which he could never have asked the Rev. F.D. Maurice to accompany him.

Related Material:

'Tennyson and Lucretius' in *The Classical Tradition in Operation* (Toronto, 1994) 91-116.

16 Romantic Love in Classical Times?

[From *Ramus: Critical Studies in Greek and Roman
Literature* 10 (1981) 140-58.]

I start with four quotations: (1) 'That all European poetry has come
out of the Provençal poetry written in the twelfth century by the
troubadours of Languedoc is now accepted on every side.' (The
writer is talking of love poetry.); (2) 'The passion and sorrow of
love were an emotional discovery of the French troubadours
and their successors.'; (3) 'French poets in the eleventh century
discovered or invented, or were the first to express, that romantic
species of passion which English poets were still writing about
in the nineteenth.' ; (4) 'The conception of romantic love which
has dominated the literature, art, music, and to some extent the
morality of modern Europe and America for many centuries is
a medieval creation.' Those words come from a Frenchman, a
German, an Englishman and a Scot – namely Denis de Rougemont,
E.R. Curtius, C.S. Lewis and Gilbert Highet – a distinguished
quartet, not lacking in knowledge or influence.[1] The view they
represent has met with little opposition and is, in fact, so widely
held that it may be regarded as orthodox. The layman finds it all
the easier to accept in that 'romantic love' is readily connected with
the first definition of 'romance' given by the *OED*: 'The vernacular
language of France as opposed to Latin'.

Let us, then, consider the poetry of the troubadours in very
broad terms and inquire what exactly was new and distinctive
about the type of love it conveyed – a love which since Gaston
Paris' famous article in the *Romania* of 1883 has been known as
l'amour courtois or 'courtly love'. In approaching this pheno-
menon we can leave aside the vexed question of origins. Was
such love primarily due to the influence of Muslim Spain, or to
the beliefs of the Cathars, or to neoplatonic philosophy, or to the
theology of St Bernard and Christian attitudes to the Virgin Mary?

191

These and other views were assembled and lucidly discussed by
Roger Boase in a book published in 1977;[2] and anyone entering
that field of inquiry would do well to start from there.

For our purpose we must inspect the poems of the troubadours
themselves, or at least a selection of the better known pieces.[3] When
we do, we encounter an almost bewildering diversity, as one might
expect in a tradition which lasted for almost two hundred years. Not
only do the poets write in different genres and styles, but the themes
they choose and the manners they adopt are wide-ranging and
various: thus Guillaume IX, the earliest representative, sometimes
brags in an earthy style about his conquests, sometimes complains
about rejection;[4] Marcabru denounces the court, with its avarice,
deception and false love;[5] Raimbaut d'Orange debates with Guiraut
de Borneil on the virtues of the plain style;[6] Peire d'Alvernha
makes fun of other troubadours, mentioning no fewer than twelve
by name;[7] while, in a later period, Peire Cardenal inveighs against
the cruelty and corruption of the clergy;[8] and Guiraut Riquier, at
the end of the tradition, ponders sadly on the decline of his world
– a decline reflected in Saracen victories and in the squalor of life
around him.[9] Partly because of this diversity there has been much
disagreement about the nature of the troubadours' love. One writer,
stressing its spiritual element, says it was 'a kind of love entirely
detached from all idea of generation and the production of the
species. Woman became a religion', while another tells us that
'this literature is completely lacking in delicacy and modesty of
any sort'.[10] For these and other reasons D.W. Robertson and John
F. Benton called, some years ago, for the abandonment of the term
'courtly love'.[11] It was, they said, a misleading abstraction made by
Gaston Paris in the nineteenth century and should not be imposed
on medieval texts.

Yet it seems, after all, as if the term is indispensable, though it
must be used with discrimination. In about 1500 Mario Equicola
thought that there was something special about the troubadours'
attitude to women; and a hundred years earlier Gutierre Daez
de Games described how the ladies in royal households used
to be honoured by their poet-lovers. If the troubadours did not
use the term *amour courtois,* they did speak of *fin' amore,* and
their imitators of *fin' amore* and *hohe Minne.* Even the phrase

'courtly love' has been found in an English poem of 1575.[12] So we shall continue to follow Gaston Paris, but we shall arrange the ingredients of the concept rather differently; for he took as his point of departure the story of Lancelot, whereas we are concerned with the troubadours.

The first notable point, then, has to do with the difference in position between lover and beloved. In the poem beginning *Non es meravelha s'eu chan,* Bernart de Ventadorn says, 'Good lady, I ask nothing of you but that you take me for your servant, and that I may serve you as a good lord, whatever wages come my way'. Before that Guillaume, in *Mout jauzens me prenc en amar,* had said 'Every joy must humiliate itself and every might obey Midons, for her sweet welcome and for her sweet pleasing look'. His mistress can even work miracles: 'Through the joy of her, the sick can be made well, and through her anger the healthy man can die and the wise man become childish'. (Midons, of course, is *meus dominus* ['my master'] – a phrase which signifies the exchange of roles presupposed by the courtly convention.) Later on, Arnaut Daniel, in *En cest sonet coind' e leri* stresses the ennobling effect of his service: 'Each day I am a better and a purer man, for I serve and worship the noblest lady in the world'. The quasi-religious element is even more plain in the next stanza: 'I hear a thousand masses and pay to have them said. I burn lights of wax and oil; so may God grant me success with her, where no striving avails me'.

The tradition, therefore, presents us with two figures – the knight and his lady. Even if the troubadour is of humble birth, as Cercamon, Marcabru and Bernart de Ventadorn are said to have been, he still assumes the *persona* of a knight. The lady, for her part, is higher than her lover; and she has an emotional as well as a social ascendancy over him. Even in the very few cases where the emotional roles are reversed, as with the handful of women troubadours, the lady retains her superior status.[13]

The second main feature is that, as a rule, the lady is someone else's wife. How, you may ask, can we express this degree of confidence when so many of the ladies are addressed by 'screen names' or by none at all? Well, no doubt there were exceptions; but girls tended to marry young, and the unmarried would not have had the social opportunities allowed to a lord's wife for carrying on an affair; if a man was courting an unmarried girl he would normally address himself to her parents; finally the terms used by the troubadours, such as *domna, frowe* and *madonna,* are usually taken to imply that the lady was married.[14] Various explanations have been offered for this phenomenon. It as been pointed out that in eleventh and twelfth century Provence men out-numbered women; that the women of the aristocracy were exceptionally cultured and emancipated; that, as most marriages were not based on love, romantic feeling would tend to find expression in other channels. When consulted on the question, Marie de Champagne and her ladies ruled that a married couple could not enjoy love: *amorem non posse suas inter duos iugales extendere vires,* the reason being that love was incompatible with any legal tie.[15] This may strike us as a piece of casuistry (as indeed it is); but one recalls that Héloise was strongly against marrying Abelard for this very reason. It is also worth remembering that even in the verse of Dante and Petrarch, where sexuality has been refined out of existence, the poet's relation to his mistress remains, in principle, adulterous.

No doubt, then, the social factors I have mentioned played their part. Yet I am inclined to think that there was something in the nature of courtly love itself which discouraged marriage. This becomes clear when we reach the third distinguishing feature, namely the importance of frustration. It is true that, in the later phases of the tradition, sensual desire is played down and sometimes disavowed altogether.[16] Even in the first generation of troubadours, one finds occasional stanzas in which the singer protests that his only wish is to serve and exalt his lady.[17] But in the great majority of the troubadours' love-poems, in spite of their elaborate structure of rhetoric and polite manners, the basis remains that of desire. It is desire, however, rather than fulfilment; indeed desire as *opposed* to fulfilment. For if the lady had obliged her lover she would have ceased at once to be unobtainable. By becoming obtainable she would have lost her status as an ideal; enchantment would have disappeared with distance.

Desire without possession was often acknowledged as torment; but it was torment of a peculiar kind. 'This love wounds my heart with a sweet taste,' says Bernart de Ventadorn, 'so gently I die of grief a hundred times a day and a hundred times revive with joy. My pain seems beautiful; this pain is worth more than any pleasure'.[18] In his famous study of Tristan and Iseult, Denis de Rougemont points out that, even when the two lovers are in a position to fulfil their desire, they seem to contrive reasons for abstaining. Why, for instance, do they sleep with Tristan's sword between them? Because, says de Rougemont, they are really in love, not with each other, but with love itself. And since such love cannot be satisfied in this world, he argues, they are ultimately in love with death.

However, if availability is the enemy of desire, might not despair, resulting from endless frustration, be an equally dangerous threat? The troubadours seem to have been well aware of this. Sometimes, if the lady gave no sign of love, the poet would upbraid her for her callousness and direct his attentions elsewhere. More often, after a period of depression, his hopes would revive and he would persevere. For, as Cercamon said, 'A man will hardly belong in court if he despairs of love'.[19]

Courtly love, then, was a delicate thing which might perish from inanition. So various techniques were developed for maintaining excitement. The lady's identity must be kept a mystery; otherwise the slanderers who infested the court would pass the word around and soon the precious intimate affair would become a subject of common gossip. If the flame was still in danger of extinction, oxygen might be supplied by a rival. For, according to Andreas Capellanus, love thrives on jealousy.[20] Even quarrels should not be too sedulously avoided; for they too can provide fuel for love.[21]

In these grey ambiguous conditions words tended to shift their meaning. If a poet sang of 'fine love' as opposed to coarse love or villainy, he was probably talking about manners rather than morals. 'Loyalty' might mean 'discretion' rather than 'fidelity to a single partner'; and 'chaste love' might be contrasted, not with 'carnal love', but with promiscuity. In Andreas' treatise 'pure love' involves every kind of intimacy short of intercourse, which turned it into 'mixed love'. We also learn how precarious 'pure love' is when we hear that, if one partner desires 'mixed love', the other is bound to comply.[22]

Such, then, in very general terms, was the phenomenon of

courtly love. I shall not ask how common it was in real life or to what extent it mitigated the general brutality of medieval manners. Both questions are hotly debated by experts;[23] but, though important, they are not germane to our purpose. Instead, we have to ask whether there was any classical precedent for this attitude to love. I believe the short answer is 'no' and that, when J.P. Sullivan tried, as it were, to meet the medievalists head on, he chose the wrong tactics.[24] Peter Dronke, in his splendid work on the rise of the European love lyric, also opposed the orthodox position; but by substituting 'courtly experience' for 'courtly love', he shifted the argument onto a much broader basis.[25] I should also like to alter the basis of the argument – but in a much simpler and more limited way. To put it briefly, it seems to me that Curtius and the others are right in the claims they make for the new and distinctive status of courtly love; but they are quite wrong in passing directly from courtly love to *romantic* love. No doubt those romantic attitudes which flourished in the nineteenth century and which, amazingly, are still not extinct, derived in a large measure from the troubadours. However, as early as the renaissance, the distinctive features of courtly love were already being modifed. One has only to think of Romeo and Juliet. Juliet is not socially or spiritually exalted above Romeo; she is not someone else's wife; and both she and her partner regard marriage as the natural and proper fulfilment of their love. The same is true of Hermia and Lysander, Orlando and Rosalind, Ferdinand and Miranda, and numberless couples since, in literature and life. Even in the medieval period similar examples may be found.[26] After some strange vicissitudes Aucassin marries Nicolette in Beaucaire; and they live there happily for many years. True, Nicolette turns out to be a princess; but, when they first met, she was a slave-girl bought from the Saracens. So theirs is the very reverse of the courtly situation. Before them we have the real-life romance of Héloise and Abelard. Opinions are divided about Abelard. (Personally I have always regarded him as rather a worm.) However, there can be no doubt about the depth and intensity of Héloise's love: 'You are the sole cause of my sorrow, and you alone can grant me the grace of consolation. You alone have the power to make me sad, to bring me happiness or comfort ... . When I was powerless to oppose you in anything, I found strength at your command to destroy myself.'[27]

If we think of the clearest examples that come to mind, we shall probably conclude that what we call romantic love represents a combination of features, somewhat as follows:

1. An immediate or very early visual impact is made on one or both of the lovers. 'Who ever loved that loved not at first sight?' as Shakespeare said, in a line borrowed from Marlowe.[28]

2. This impact is revealed by a series of familiar symptoms. Here is how Fielding describes the condition of Tom Jones: 'As to Sophia, he was far from being in a state of tranquillity; nay indeed he was under the most violent perturbation ... he loved her with an unbounded passion, and plainly saw the tender sentiments she had for him; yet could not this assurance lessen his despair of obtaining the consent of her father, nor the horrors which attended his pursuit of her by any base or treacherous method ... . At the approach of the young lady he grew pale ... . If his eyes accidentally met hers, the blood rushed into his cheeks, and his countenance became all over scarlet. If common civility even obliged him to speak to her ... his tongue was sure to falter. If he touched her, his hand, nay his whole frame, trembled.'[29] Fielding, of course, portrays these symptoms with the tolerant amusement of a man of the world. But Jones himself is not amused.

3. Not only is the beloved frequently in the lover's mind; the vision he has of her is, from a disinterested viewpoint, considerably idealised. Stendhal describes the habit as follows: 'At the salt mines of Salzburg, they throw a leafless wintry bough into one of the abandoned workings. Two or three months later they haul it out covered with a shiny deposit of crystals. The smallest twig, no bigger than a tom-tit's claw, is studded with a galaxy of scintillating diamonds. The original branch is no longer recognisable. What I have called crystallisation is a mental process which draws from everything that happens new proofs of the perfection of the loved one.'[30]

4. His emotional preoccupation colours the lover's attitude to other things. It may even bring an improvement in his character, making him less selfish and more willing to forgo his own wishes.

5. The lovers have in mind a long-term attachment, in which marriage is usually desired, even if it happens to be impossible. Not only do they pledge themselves to life-long devotion and mean it; they sometimes even affirm that their love will last beyond the grave.

6. Physical fulfilment is postponed – or else is followed by early separation. This postponement or separation functions as a kind of ordeal by which the couple's love is tested. The barrier may take many forms: distance caused by war or abduction, antagonisms of race, class or religion, parental disapproval, marriage to another party. Rejection too must be included; for there is of course no guarantee that romantic devotion is reciprocated. Yet there is never any doubt, as there is in the courtly convention, that fulfilment is the lovers' ultimate aim.

If that brief account seems too amateur and impressionistic, we can seek support from a sociologist who has carried out extensive investigations with questionnaire and card index. In his book entitled *The Colours of Love*, John Allen Lee distinguishes three primary loves, which he terms *eros, ludus,* and *storge*.[31] Placing them on the circumference of a circle he assigns red to *eros*, blue to *ludus*, and yellow to *storge*. (There are, needless to say, many intermediate shades.) *Storge* is closely related to friendship, develops gradually and involves no violent emotions. According to Lee, it is solid, durable, and prosaic – an excellent basis for family life. *Ludus* is the exciting but superficial hedonism found, for example, in Ovid's *Amores* and *Ars Amatoria*. The so-called 'ludic lover' exploits his or her charm and wit – and is not above deception. Once successful, however, he or she becomes bored and switches easily to another partner. For him (or her) love is indeed a game. However, it is not clear, at least to me, that he takes any other aspect of life any more seriously. Errol Flynn was a good modern example of the type. It is in the category of *eros* that we must look for romantic love. According to Lee, lovers of this type have a fairly definite idea of the physical type that attracts them. When they meet it they are immediately impressed; and they experience an intense emotion which becomes the centre of their life. Their love is therefore unlike *storge*; but it is also distinct from *ludus*; because it involves the whole personality, *eros* has far greater reserves of stamina and patience. Its depth is tested by frustration.

Before proceeding to the classical evidence, let us return for a moment to our medievalists. It was not just *courtly* love that they denied to the ancients: they said *romantic* love was unknown before the eleventh or twelfth century. C.S. Lewis, for instance, claimed that the French poets 'erected impassable barriers between us and the classical past'. 'In ancient literature love seldom rises above the levels of merry sensuality, or domestic comfort, except to be treated as a tragic madness, an ἄτη which plunged otherwise sane people (usually women) into crime and disgrace.'[32] We shall return to tragic madness; but first let us think about the magnitude of what is being said. We are being asked to accept not just that romantic love did not *derive* from the Greeks and Romans, but also that the phenomenon was entirely unknown in the ancient world. If Lewis was right, there is indeed a gulf between the two epochs in a vastly important area of experience. But *was* he right?

In handling our classical sources it will not be enough to collect instances of *eros* and *amor,* as if they in themselves were sufficient to refute the medievalists. Often the texts are too fragmentary to be of any use: 'I lie wretched with desire' (δύστηνος ἔγκειμαι πόθῳ). So says Archilochus.[33] He is smitten with desire; that is all we know. Did Euripides, as we are sometimes told,[34] present a romantic treatment of love in his *Andromeda*? I rather doubt it; but the evidence is lacking either way. Again, many poems are too short. Meleager wrote several epigrams about the pretty Zenophila, who was an accomplished lyre-player and inspired him with burning passion (πυρὶ φλέγομαι).[35] Was this romantic love? In view of his other attachments, almost certainly not; but we can't be sure. A further difficulty comes from the fact that a 'ludic lover' often employs the rhetoric of romantic passion. 'She flooded my soul with the rays which issued from her divine face with the same speed as those of the sun shedding his light through the universe.' That is Casanova describing the overpowering effect

of Signora F;[36] but a few chapters earlier he had been equally over-
whelmed by Donna Lucrezia; and soon he will be in love again
with the innocent Cristina. Lee actually classifies Casanova's
love as 'ludic eros'. Perhaps he is right; but it seems more likely
to me that Casanova has become such an expert in deception that
he is now deceiving *himself*. A similar scepticism is prompted by
Anacreon: 'Golden-haired Love hits me yet again with his bright
ball' (σφαίρῃ δηῦτέ με πορφυρῇ / βάλλων χρυσοκόμης ῎Ερως);[37]
or 'Love struck me yet again like a smith with a great hammer'
(μεγάλῳ δηῦτέ μ' ῎Ερως ἔκοψεν ὥστε χαλκεὺς / πέλεκει.[38] δηῦτε
... δηῦτε ('yet again ... yet again') – one thinks of the susceptible
Dietrich, in *The Blue Angel* 'Falling in loveagain'. So too, when
Mimnermus speaks in his famous lines of 'Secret love and gentle
gifts and bed' (κρυπταδίη φιλότης καὶ μείλιχα δῶρα καὶ εὐνή,[39] it
sounds as if he is not thinking of a serious romantic attachment but
is rather generalising from a succession of pleasant experiences.
We must conclude, I think, that the remains of Greek elegy and
lyric do not contain enough evidence to refute the medievalists'
case. A large number of texts in other genres must be ruled out for
the same reason.

One final category which I want to exclude is homosexual
love. There is a view which holds that romantic love *did* exist in
antiquity, but only in homosexual relationships. One scholar, for
example, says 'The emotions and sentiments that are nowadays
assigned to the realm of romance were then associated with attach-
ments between people of the same sex, an ugly consequence of
the segregation of men and women in social life and education'.[40]
Whether or not a certain type of homosexual love – like that
found in the Platonic tradition – may be termed 'romantic' is
indeed a matter for discussion; but I do not intend to discuss it
– partly for reasons of space, but mainly because 'romantic love',
as employed by the medievalists, is a predominantly heterosexual
concept; so we must use the term in the same way if we are to
meet their arguments.

Thanks to scholars like Douglas MacDowell and W.K. Lacey,[41]
we now have a pretty clear picture of the legal position of wives
in Athenian society; and we know how most marriages came into
being: they were arranged by the groom and the bride's father. Often

the girl had no say in the matter and knew little about her future husband. In Xenophon's *Oeconomicus* we meet Ischomachus, who has the reputation of being a perfect gentleman (καλός τε κἀγαθός).[42] He doesn't pass his time indoors, because his wife can look after the house – thanks to *his* training. 'What,' asks Socrates, 'was the first thing you taught her?' 'Well,' says Ischomachus, 'since she was already docile and sufficiently domesticated to take part in a conversation, I said to her "Tell me, my dear, do you realise why I took you, and your parents gave you to me (for obviously we could both have found other partners to sleep with)?"' Before the girl can reply, a preliminary answer is given: it was to maintain an efficient home and to produce children who would look after the parents in their old age. The whole statement is made doubly depressing by the fact that it is kindly meant. Clearly such a relationship did not leave much scope for romance. But why, we may ask, was the girl obliged to marry such a pompous old prig? Could she not have met and married some dashing young fellow closer to her own age? Well, it seems that meetings of that sort were rarely allowed to take place. Sandbach goes further and says that 'social conditions in Athens made it virtually impossible for a young man to meet a marriageable girl in private'.[43] We cannot hope to quantify exceptions to this rule; but it is perhaps reasonable to point out that oriental society was certainly no more liberal than Greek and yet we find numerous examples of romantic love in *The Arabian Nights*.[44] Similarly, while romantic love flourished in the nineteenth century, when women's scope was still restricted, it is now beginning to wither in a period when women have obtained far greater emancipation.

It is, however, time to consider some cases. Here, first, is a young male who is utterly infatuated: everything takes second place to his love. In daytime he mopes and pines; at night his beloved dominates his dreams. He remembers how he first saw her and how he fell hopelessly in love. Now he makes a pitiful appeal: perhaps he is not very good-looking, though he is not to be despised; for he has substantial possessions including a comfortable home; and he is by no means unaccomplished. If only she would join him, she could enjoy the presents that await her and share his way of life. This does not sound like a smooth seducer. In fact he is rather naive, as the author means him to be; for this is the young Polyphemus from Theocritus, *Idyll* 11. The framework, if you like, is one of light burlesque; but Polyphemus' feelings are not so very different from those of the passionate shepherd in Marlowe's 'Come live with me and be my love'.

For a fuller and more weighty treatment of the same emotion, we may turn to *Idyll* 2. On her way to a pageant, Simaetha passed a boy coming away from a wrestling school. On seeing his good looks, she fell violently in love, paid no attention to the pageant and began to pine away at home. In the end she invited the boy to her house. When he entered, she turned hot and cold and could not even speak. Thus began a passionate affair, which has lasted until very recently. Now, however, Delphis (the boy) has not visited Simaetha for a fortnight; there are rumours that he has taken up with someone else. So, in her grief, Simaetha tries to win him back with magic spells. It is the most powerful of all Theocritus' poems, and has, of course, nothing to do with pastoral.

A longer, but equally persuasive study of passion is found in the third book of Apollonius' *Argonautica*, where Aphrodite's rascally son inspires Medea with love for Jason. She at once becomes restless and agitated, seized with 'a sweet pain' (190). She pictures Jason constantly in her mind – how he looked, what he was wearing, what he said, how he moved. Surely there never was such a man (457). She is distraught with fear; and she weeps at the thought of his death. She dreams Jason is taking her away (622); thinks of confiding in her sister; but collapses in tears on her bed (655). At great danger to herself, she resolves to cast a spell on the fire-breathing bulls (739); but she is racked with misgivings and cannot sleep. When Jason begs for help, she agrees, adding a sad little coda (1069 ff.): 'If ever you return home remember the name of Medea and I'll remember you though you are far away'. At this point Jason, too, is overcome by Eros (1077): he tells Medea of his homeland and promises that, if she goes with him, she will be honoured and their love will last until death (1120-30). We shall return to the sequel; but, considering the story so far, I do not see how we can refuse to call Medea's love romantic.

From Greek Alexandrian poetry one passes naturally to Catullus. In the Lesbia cycle we find the lover stunned at the sight of his lady's beauty. The barrier in this case is one of marriage; but, for a while at least, it is surmounted and the partners share a love which, for Catullus at least, is broader and deeper than sexual passion. Then come doubts about Lesbia's commitment; then estrangement and reconciliation; then rejection; and finally disenchantment and disgust. The distinguishing feature of these twenty or so short poems is their intensity – an intensity marvellously embodied in their language, sound and rhythm. One thinks of the insistent repetitions, the incantatory effects of assonance and rhyme, the painful elisions. One might in fact reverse Wilfred Owen's famous phrase and say 'the pity is in the poetry'. This romantic element in Catullus is too familiar to need further comment. But what, you may say, did Lewis make of it (for he had, of course, *read* Catullus)? Here is his answer: 'If Catullus and Propertius vary the strain with cries of rage and misery, that is not so much because they are romantics as because they are exhibitionists'.[45] That, one can only say, is a wretched piece of sophistry. For what are we to say of Shakespeare, Burns and Tennyson? What of Yeats, who in more than one sense belonged to the last romantics? Are they all to be waved aside as mere exhibitionists?

As for Propertius, I have already implied (note 24 above) that his love was not really of the courtly type: it was not adulterous and, though Cynthia may have been his *domina*, he did not worship her with the quasi-religious devotion of a troubadour. Yet one can hardly deny that his love was *romantic*. In the first poem we hear that his infatuation has lasted a whole year; so it is no transitory caprice. The barrier here is Cynthia's refusal, or inability, to love the poet as he loves her. In spite of his pain, he idealises her beauty and talent (though not always her moral character); and he confers dignity on her by comparing her to the heroines of legend.[46] He is convinced she is the only girl he can ever adore and that his love will last beyond the grave.[47]

I am not, of course, maintaining that Propertius, any more than Catullus, was a romantic poet through and through. Even some of the Cynthia poems are wide awake, realistic, even humorous, the best example being 4.8. An interesting balance is achieved in 1.3, where Cynthia asleep is seen through an alcoholic haze as lovely, gentle and vulnerable, while Cynthia awake is full of angry accusations and querulous self-pity. A revealing comparison is supplied by Goethe's imitation *Der Besuch* ('The Visit'), where the lady remains tenderly idealised throughout (she doesn't wake up) and the poet, unlike Propertius, is intoxicated only with love.[48]

When Ovid is mentioned in connection with courtly love, he is thought of primarily, if not solely, as the author of the *Amores* and *Ars Amatoria.* As the discussion widens to embrace romantic love, he is then set aside as being too worldly and cynical to have contributed anything to the tradition, except by accident. (I am thinking of Lewis's famous idea of 'Ovid misunderstood'.) The unfairness of this can be seen if we consider simply the love of Hero and Leander in *Heroides* 18. Up to now Leander has managed to evade his parents and to keep his love a secret. He sits on a rock, thinking of Hero and chafing at the stormy sea, which for seven nights has maintained a barrier between him and his beloved. He recalls the first time he swam across by moonlight; how Hero put her lamp in the tower to guide him; then welcomed him on the shore. He speaks of her as his *domina* (176) and swears she is worthy of heaven (169). These are all the characteristics we need. The love may be conveyed through the conceits of Ovidian rhetoric but it is none the less romantic for that.[49]

Passing over the weaker testimony of Tibullus, I would mention briefly some indirect evidence. The kind of love deprecated by Lucretius (*De Rerum Natura* 4.1058 ff.) is surely love of the romantic kind, with its *cura, ulcus, furor* and *aerumnae* ('worry', 'wound', 'frenzy' and 'woes'). Though described mainly in physical terms, it is not to be confused with simple sex; for sex is explicitly recommended as a means of *avoiding* such emotional disturbance.[50] Horace's testimony, too, is largely negative (as in *Sat.* 2.3.247 ff.). We almost never see him in love.[51] In his teasing, good-humoured way he shows us *other* people in love;[52] and he assures us that in his younger days he knew the condition well enough.[53] On the whole, however, the *Odes* give the impression that, although he could acknowledge the value of *storge* (1.13.17-20), he was now too old and too wise for romantic *eros.*

It is time now to touch on the position of marriage *vis-à-vis* love. Granted, they were not necessarily, not even usually, related. However, we should beware of yet another false dogma, represented this time by the words of Engels: 'Love, in the modern sense of the word, appeared in antiquity only outside the bounds of official society. The point where antiquity stopped in its search for sexual love is just where the middle ages started: adultery'. I take this to mean that, for a Greek or Roman citizen, romantic love could only take place with a foreigner or a freedwoman or with someone else's wife; that marriage was never regarded as its goal. This is actually false, but Engels is frequently quoted with approval by more popular writers, e.g. by Simone de Beauvoir in *The Second Sex*,[54] and so the error is transmitted to many thousands of readers.

We have already cited some evidence bearing on this question; for in the passage of Apollonius, when Medea dreams of Jason taking her away, she sees herself as his wife (623); and when Jason promises her honour and love in his homeland he means, and says, that they will be married (1128). In connection with Catullus we recall the poem (70) beginning *Nulli se dicit mulier mea nubere malle / quam mihi* ('My woman says she would marry no one in preference to me') – words which show that neither Catullus nor his mistress regarded marriage as incompatible with love. It has occasionally been pointed out that some of Catullus' most passionate phrases are also found in Plautus and Terence. This may well surprise; for what has the intensely personal relationship of Catullus and Lesbia to do with Roman comedy's world of silly old men, tricky slaves, parasites, call-girls and pimps? E.P. Morris dealt with the problem by maintaining that Catullus' language in, say, poem 8 (*Miser Catulle*) was not as serious as people had thought;[55] and some distinguished Latinists are inclined to agree. I would much prefer to take the other approach and argue that the lovers in Plautus and Terence (at least in certain cases) are utterly serious.[56] The fact that they have their being within a comedy, where their love is mocked and frustrated, is neither here nor there. We noted earlier how Fielding, too, described the plight of Tom Jones with detached amusement. F.O. Copley, who has written well about comedy, remarks at one point that the ancient love affair 'had nothing whatever to do with marriage'.[57] Surely that is too sweeping. In Plautus' *Cistellaria* Selenium tells her friend Gymnasium about her feelings for Alcesimarchus: *med excrucio, mea Gymnasium; male mihi est, male maceror; / doleo ab animo, doleo ab oculis, doleo ab aegritudine.* ('I am being tortured, my dear Gymnasium; I am in a sad way, sadly suffering; / I ache in my heart, ache in my eyes, ache in my agony'; 59-60)

After an interchange in which the romantic Selenium is played off against the down-to-earth Gymnasium, the latter says, 'This woman's in love!' It then emerges that Selenium has never had dealings with any man except Alcesimarchus – as though Plautus were deliberately separating her from the *meretrix* class (86 ff.). Alcesimarchus, moreover, is very much in love with her (191-3) and has sworn to marry her (98 f.). In Act 2 we hear his feelings from his own lips: he has been away from the girl for six days and is in a very bad way indeed. The lyric certainly gives a comic presentation of his plight but the feelings themselves are serious. There is no need to follow the plot further, except to say that Selenium turns out (of course) to be a free citizen and marries Alcesimarchus in the end. A similar situation occurs in *Curculio* where Planesium marries Phaedromus.

In Terence's *Heauton Timorumenos* Clinia falls desperately in love with Antiphila (*amare coepit perdite*; 98); the love-sick young man (101) almost regards her as his wife (*prope iam ut pro uxore haberet*; 99); but he is compelled by his father to leave the country. Antiphila, we hear, is well-educated, modest and innocent of the courtesan's art (226) – a claim already made for Selenium in *Cistellaria*. She remains faithful to Clinia while he is away; and, when he returns, the lovers enjoy a rapturous reunion (398 ff.) and are finally married. The same happens to Pamphilus and Glycerium in Terence's *Andria*.[58]

In the four plays mentioned here we find all the features of romantic love; and the men are just as prone to it as the women. Since the phenomenon is at least *sometimes* associated with marriage in Plautus and Terence, one assumes that the same was true in Greek new comedy. Unfortunately, because of the scarcity of material we cannot adduce much evidence; but in the *Dyskolos* Sostratus has at least the makings of a romantic hero. In Act 2 he tells how he fell in love with his girl (302); he is keen to marry her, even though she has no dowry; and he promises to love her faithfully (307-9). He even plies a hoe to win her father's approval

(375 ff.), thus entering the tradition which starts with Apollo serving Admetus,[59] then passes through Sceparnio in Plautus' *Rudens* (458 ff.), and on down to Ferdinand who in Shakespeare's *Tempest* hauls logs for Prospero: 'The mistress which I serve quickens what's dead, / And makes my labours pleasures (Act 3, Sc. 1, 6-7).

We can get a little more help from folk-tales, which, if not Greek in origin, were well known in the Greek world. One example is the story told by Chares of Mytilene and reported by Athenaeus about Odatis the beautiful oriental princess who saw a vision of the neighbouring prince Zariadres in her sleep and fell in love with him. He had the same experience of her. After a period of fruitless longing Zariadres came and asked her father Homartes for her hand; but he was refused. Instead Homartes arranged a wedding feast to which he invited friends and chieftains from his own kingdom. When the drinking was at its height he told his daughter to inspect all the men and to present a golden cup to the one she wanted to marry. Meanwhile Zariadres had heard of the celebration; and, coming in disguise, he stealthily made himself known to Odatis. She at once presented him with the cup and he carried her off in his chariot.[60]

No less romantic – and more fully presented – is Ovid's story of Pygmalion.[61] It is too familiar to need recounting; but it is worth recalling that, in Philostephanus' third-century version, the statue had been that of Aphrodite, Pygmalion had been king of Cyprus and his passion had been one of pathological lust. There is no mention of any miracle. Ovid gives us instead a sensitive artist who could love only the ideal and who, by virtue of his love, brought his creation to life. The last Ovidian story I would refer to is that of Pyramus and Thisbe – beautiful young people whose love is mutual and equal; it aims at marriage but is frustrated and forced into concealment – a love which involves all the faculties, overcomes fear, is full of tenderness and concern and is faithful unto death – a sentimental story, if you will, but its popularity is attested by the wall-paintings of Pompei.[62]

From Ovid it is only a short step to the Greek romances. Most of these works are now placed within the period I am discussing – say before AD 250; and, whatever we may think of them as literature, they tell us a good deal about the tastes of the reading public. In

Achilles Tatius' novel, Clitophon, who is nineteen years old, sees
Leucippe coming up from the harbour at Tyre. He is dazzled by
her beauty and at once becomes her slave. Eventually he wins
Leucippe's heart and the two of them elope, as they are obliged
to do, because Clitophon is engaged to someone else. In spite
of Clitophon's urgency, Leucippe will not yield to him, because
Artemis has commanded her in a dream to remain a virgin until her
marriage. Soon the lovers are separated; but, after many improb-
able adventures, the marriage at last takes place in Byzantium. It
is true that we hear very little of the tastes and temperament of
the lovers; nor do their personalities develop to any significant
extent in the course of the story. Yet that is just another way of
saying that Achilles Tatius is not a first-rate novelist. The idealism,
the preoccupation, the barriers, the frustrated yearning and the
unshaken constancy are all there. So, although the work is lacking
in depth and emotional insight, the type of love it portrays can
fairly be called romantic.

Much the same can be said of Heliodorus' novel about Thea-
genes and Chariclea. Longus' *Daphnis and Chloe* is a more
sophisticated work, combining various traditions, including
pastoral, Platonism and new comedy. S.L. Wolff, in his admirable
study *The Greek Romances in Elizabethan Prose Fiction*,[63] denies
that the love portrayed there is anything but sensual; he even finds
it rather salacious. Granted there is a certain piquancy about the
youngsters' experiments; yet over a period of eighteen months we
see them engaged in their daily occupations (an unusual feature in
a work of fiction); they are dutiful in their religious observances
and they remain noble-minded in danger and adversity – and in
good fortune too. Thus, when Daphnis finds a purse of silver, his
only thought is to use it for obtaining Chloe's hand in marriage.
In the last chapter we learn that they grow old together, honouring
their early vow of life-long devotion. If you say that at sixteen
and fourteen they are too young to know what love is, I can only
answer 'so were Romeo and Juliet'.

It is worth noting perhaps that Longus, Heliodorus and Achilles
Tatius had all been translated into English and French before
1600.[64] When these authors are added to Catullus, Virgil and Ovid,
it is clear that, although the main stream of romantic literature may

have come from the troubadours, it was soon joined by a large tributary from the ancient world.

I will not dwell longer on the Greek novels, because their romantic love is mostly of a rather feeble and sentimental kind.[65] This is largely due to the limitations of the writers themselves.[66] Chariton and Xenophon of Ephesus, however, differ from the rest in one small respect, namely that their lovers are already married. The ordeals begin when they are separated soon after their wedding. This will remind us that some of the most famous love-stories have to do with husbands and wives who have been parted by war or death. Laodamia had only one day of married life before her husband's departure for Troy. Orpheus lost his Eurydice shortly after their marriage.[67] We are constantly informed, and rightly, that such myths are the great archetypes of human experience. What nonsense, then, to imagine that the kind of experience in question was unknown to the very people who invented the myths. A non-mythical example of this type of devotion is found in the more famous Xenophon's *Cyropaedia*: Panthea, wife of Abradatas of Susa, is captured by Cyrus; she resists the advances of the officer who is guarding her, appealing successfully to Cyrus for protection; eventually re-united with her husband, she arms him and encourages him as he goes into battle; and, when he is killed, she commits suicide.[68]

Someone may now reply, 'Myths and stories are all very well but can you not find an explicit formulation and defence of romantic love in some ancient thinker?' Well, of course, the Socratic tradition does not help, since it is predominantly homosexual; and Aristotle's treatise Περὶ ἔρωτος is lost; but there is quite a serviceable exposition in Plutarch's Ἐρωτικός.[69] Many views are advanced there, including the idea that respectable women cannot properly bestow or receive passionate love. (No doubt they were supposed to close their eyes and think of Hellas.) Plutarch's own opinion is that *eros* is not only *possible* between men and women but that a romantic relationship is most fully realised in a happy marriage. *Eros* presides over such a union and brings about 'integral amalgamation' (ἡ δι' ὅλων λεγομένη κρᾶσις), whereas those who merely live together are like Epicurus' atoms, colliding and rebounding but never mixing.[70] Plutarch's exposition is followed by the story of a devoted couple who braved incredible hardships under Vespasian. Then the work ends with a marriage in which the bride was ten years older than the groom and was known to have made all the running. So we must not be too rigid in our conception of ancient society.

I have tried to show that 'merry sensuality' and 'domestic comfort' do not exhaust the ancient types of love. I return briefly to Lewis's third category – 'tragic madness'. As experience shows, romantic *eros*, on its own, tends to be short-lived. It may simply wither and die, even when fulfilled; or, in lucky cases, it may develop in conjunction with *storge* into a less heady, more durable partnership. Sometimes, when such feeling encounters an immovable obstacle, the lover's preoccupation, instead of fading away or transferring itself to someone else, develops into a morbid obsession, occasionally leading to desperate acts of murder and suicide. Our sociologist, J.A. Lee, gives this condition a special name – *mania*; and he describes it in psychological terms, maintaining, for instance, that it tends to overtake people who have unhappy memories of childhood, are plagued by self-doubt and are exceptionally demanding, possessive and dependent. In antiquity reports of such love concentrate rather on the *situation* in which the victim is placed. That situation varies. The lover may first be accepted and then later abandoned (like Medea or Dido); he may find that his love is not returned and kill himself or his beloved in despair (like Stryangaeus in Ctesias;[71] or Marius in Horace's *Satires*).[72] In some cases there may, in addition, be some intractable tabu which forbids fulfilment (as with Phaedra). Occasionally the tabu is circumvented by a trick (one thinks of Byblis, Myrrha, Clymenus or of Periander's mother).[73] Acts of desperation follow when the truth is found out.

In the cases of incestuous attraction, the love (even when reci- procated) was doomed to futility and disgrace. The circumstances which blighted it could not have been altered. In other cases, like those of Medea and Dido, the love was 'normal' but only became 'diseased' as the result of events. If, for example, Jupiter's plan for the world had coincided with Juno's, then presumably Aeneas would have stayed in Carthage, Dido's tragedy would never have occurred – and we would all have learnt Punic instead of Latin. Or, to take a modern example, if Lotte's husband had been killed in a hunting accident, she might have consented in the end to marry young Werther and the story would have ended very differently. I suspect that even in the most doomed and unfortunate cases, such as those involving incest, *mania* is not qualitatively different from romantic *eros*. At least it differs only in its direction. Certainly in the other cases *mania* develops *from* romantic *eros* and ought not to be placed in a separate category. If this is true, then the phenomenon of 'tragic madness' proves fatal to Lewis's case.

To sum up, romantic love was not unknown in antiquity; it was not confined to homosexual relationships; nor was it exclusive to couples who would not or could not marry. Granted, it did not represent the prevailing social ethos, as it did in the nineteenth and early twentieth centuries. It was commonly mocked, denigrated and feared. Yet it was undeniably there; and it was always assumed to be there until very recent times. Think of that beautiful and famous scene towards the end of *The Merchant of Venice*:[74] darkness has fallen; Jessica and Lorenzo sit together at Belmont. 'In such a night,' she says in answer to her lover, 'Did Thisbe fearfully o'er trip the dew, / And saw the lion's shadow e'er himself, / And ran dismayed away'. Lorenzo replies, 'In such a night / Stood Dido with a willow in her hand / Upon the wild sea banks, and waft her love / To come again to Carthage'. Then Jessica: 'In such a night / Medea gather'd the enchanted herbs / That did renew old Aeson'. No romantic love in antiquity? Shakespeare would have rejected such a notion with incredulity. And so should we.

17 Classical Humanism and its Critics

[Lecture (to a Canadian audience), published in
Classical Views 15 (1996) 283-303]

By 'Classical Humanism' I understand the rational study of the
Greeks and Romans as fellow human beings. So the concept is de-
fined by a subject, a method and an assumption. As for the criticism,
that began quite early. In the fifteenth century, for example, a row
broke out when the Greek Bessarion, whom Valla called *Latinorum
Graecissimus, Graecorum Latinissimus* ('of Latins the most Greek;
of Greeks the most Latin'), had the effrontery to emend a single
letter of Jerome's Vulgate (at *John* 21.22) on the basis of the Greek
text.[1] He was, of course, strongly criticised, although he was clearly
right. The emendation has long been accepted. Here, however, I
shall be dealing with things that have happened in the last forty
years or so, mostly in the English-speaking countries.

I start with a criticism from an archaeologist. As a Classics under-
graduate at Cambridge in the 1870s, Percy Gardner had chafed at
'the narrow grammatical training' and 'the never-ending exercises
of composition'. In December 1903, as Professor of Archaeology
at Oxford, he welcomed the founding of the Classical Association,
hoping that it would widen and deepen our knowledge of antiquity
by encouraging the study of art and archaeology. Although he
encountered opposition,[2] Gardner was clearly right. Art and arch-
aeology already formed part of the humanists' researches in the
late fifteenth century. (One thinks, for instance, of Flavio Biondo's
Roma Instaurata and *Italia Illustrata*.) And today it would seem
absurd to exclude such studies from a classical curriculum.

Gardner's other point about grammar and composition was also
right. Some readers, no doubt, have heard of the Classics teacher
who looked forward to lecturing on Sophocles' *Oedipus at Colonus*
on the grounds that the text represented 'a veritable storehouse of
grammatical peculiarities'. Eventually, the pendulum swung the

213

other way. When the *Cambridge Latin Course* first appeared in 1972, it placed too little emphasis on grammar, as if Latin could be learned by absorption, like a modern language. As always, the right balance is hard to find. What Gardner apparently *failed* to realise, however, was that the obsession with grammar and composition went along with a severe deficiency in the teaching of literature. Later on I shall discuss various ways of approaching literary texts. First, however, I want to mention some of the broad movements in western thinking which have extended the range of scholarship and enriched the tradition of Classical Humanism.

Most pervasive of all, perhaps, has been the influence of Karl Marx. Whether or not one accepts his political ideology, his analysis of social forces has surely had a profound effect on our subject. One thinks of Moses Finley's work on slavery and the ancient economy, Geoffrey de St. Croix's huge book *The Class Struggle in the Ancient Greek World*, and the work of Frank Walbank and E.A. Thompson on late Roman history.

The same sort of point can be made about Freud. There is, one gathers, considerable scepticism in the medical profession about the value of Freud's theories as therapy. Some of his pronouncements on gender have also been rightly challenged by feminists; yet his work has made it possible for later generations to appraise more fully and more frankly the complexities of sexual behaviour in both ancient and modern times. Moreover, Freud's concept of the unconscious mind has certainly deepened our understanding of the poetic process. It lies behind all twentieth-century investigations of ancient imagery, especially in tragedy and lyric; and, without it, Livingstone Lowes could not have written his classic study of Coleridge, which Eric Havelock, in his turn, used for his articles on 'Virgil's Road to Xanadu' in *Phoenix* 1 (1946-7). Consider also the important role of Anchises in the first half of the *Aeneid*, especially 4.351-3, where he is said to appear every night in Aeneas' dreams urging him to do his duty and leave Carthage; then once more in 5.722 where he summons Aeneas to that all-important meeting in the underworld. Surely that role is illuminated by what the Viennese Freud had to say about the 'father figure'.

Later, in the 1930s, Vienna was also the home of logical positivism – a method soon adopted and modified in England, where it dominated the thinking of the post-war generation; its effects were also felt in Canada and the United States. The analysis of concepts was fruitfully applied to Plato and Aristotle and did much to rebut the criticism that teachers of ancient philosophy were concerned only to expound what those thinkers had said, without inquiring whether they were right or wrong. That criticism was, I suspect, largely valid before the 1950s.

Another investigational tool was developed by ancient historians. Prosopography, or the study of families, careers and factions, was a method employed by Münzer and others in Pauly-Wissowa's encyclopaedia. The most famous British exponent was, of course, Sir Ronald Syme, who in his series of works, beginning with *The Roman Revolution* (1939), showed an astonishing control of a mass of evidence, which he reputedly carried in his head, without the aid of a card index, much less a computer.

I include no more than a mention of the part played by classicists like J.G. Frazer, Andrew Lang, Max Weber and Jane Harrison in the early stages of anthropology, mythology, sociology and the study of religion.[3] Much of what they said, no doubt, has been discarded; but much, too, has entered the bloodstream of Classical Humanism. New insights continue to emerge from those disciplines. One thinks of the work of Bremmer, Burkert, Graf and Vernant; and of the sociological approaches to Roman history taken by Ramsay MacMullen, Keith Hopkins and Thomas Wiedemann. These, our contemporaries, will in their turn face inspection. Some of what they say will be rejected or simply forgotten. In certain points this oblivion will be undeserved (for we must not pretend that Classical Humanism is infallible or invariably just). In forty years' time it may be that some of their insights will be rediscovered, provided we retain a respect for the history of our subject.

In this description I have been trying to bring out the fact that Classical Humanism is not static. It is constantly enriched by admitting new ideas. But this admission is not automatic. New ideas, whatever their source, must be submitted to scrutiny over a period of time. As an illustration, I will mention the kind of sifting which is taking place at present with regard to feminism. After the war, the first important book in the area was Simone de Beauvoir's *Le Deuxième Sexe* (Paris, 1949), of which an English translation appeared in 1953. Yet for various reasons – not all of them clear – the second wave of feminism did not break until the 1960s. Then Betty Friedan, Mary Ellman and Kate Millett began to articulate their dissatisfaction with the lop-sided role assigned to women in contemporary society.[4] This led to complaints about the lop-sided structure of the academic profession, including departments of Classics. As the anomalies began to be corrected, books and articles appeared in increasing numbers on women in the life and literature of Greece and Rome. So once again an important set of new ideas has led to a re-examination of classical culture.

The diversity of feminist writing in the last thirty years has, of course, been immense; and I have read only a small fraction of it. Nevertheless, three categories can, perhaps, be rather crudely distinguished.

1. Radical feminists like Toril Moi, who asserts that 'the aims of feminist criticism are, or should be, revolutionary',[5] and who wants, as her top priority, to oppose 'the exploitative, hierarchical, and authoritarian structures of capitalism'.[6] It would be presumptuous to say that Classical Humanists can learn nothing from such writers; but the larger aims of the latter are very different. Moreover, one cannot help noticing that this zealous radical programme often gives the impression that those women who find satisfaction in running a home and bringing up children are somehow betraying their sex. That implication has already provoked a conservative backlash. Would it not have been better to emphasise the desirability of choice?

2. Those feminists who do focus on the academic world, but who hold that feminist criticism is necessarily opposed to so-called 'masculinist' work. Writers like G.C. Spivak do not see feminist criticism as contributing to a larger enterprise: 'To embrace pluralism is to espouse the politics of the masculinist establishment. Pluralism is the method employed by the central authorities to neutralise opposition by seeming to accept it.'[7] So those outside the movement can expect little co-operation from this quarter. Do such writers hold, I wonder, that no man has imagination enough to envisage a woman's point of view? Certainly one can read quite far into their work without encountering the names of Ibsen and Shaw. Have they never heard of *The Doll's House* or *Candida* and *Mrs. Warren's Profession*? Again, the belief that only women can say anything important about women writers, and hence that only female academics should be allowed to teach Jane Austen, the Brontës and George Eliot, has an obvious corollary – one that is particularly disastrous for female classicists, since the Greek and Roman canon is unalterably male. When we come to female characters in literature, the division of scholarship is equally absurd. When teaching Roman elegy, I used to ask the students to write a letter from Cynthia to a girlfriend on the subject of Propertius: one letter (from a male student) began, 'Dear Fulvia, Here we go again ... Babs called round last night and made the most awful scene'. So women are not the only people qualified to talk about female characters. (Conversely, I have never heard it alleged that only men could write sensibly about male characters.) This is not to deny, of course, that feminists may bring different and valid perceptions to the reading of literature; but that need not rule out co-operation. This brings us to a different kind of feminist.

3. Elaine Showalter says that 'feminist criticism neither must nor should be the exclusive province of women'.[8] She sees the feminist approach, with all the ferment it engenders, as pointing to a renaissance in the humanities. Let us hope she is right. But even if 'renaissance' proves too grand a word, we can already speak of an increased interest in our area of the humanities. Over twenty years ago a special number of *Arethusa* (6.1 [1973]) contained five articles by female scholars and a judicious bibliography by Sarah Pomeroy. Probably fifty percent of the items were by men. Today the percentage would be lower; but we are still talking of a joint humanistic enterprise.

To these three categories of writing, one should add those Classical Humanists who are female without necessarily being feminists. In the middle decades of this century we were familiar with the work of Madge Dale, Lillian Jeffery, Hilda Lorimer, Henrica Malcovati, Jacqueline de Romilly, Lily Ross Taylor, Cornelia de Vogel, and, in Canada, Mary White. Recent and contemporary names are too numerous to mention; but, coming from the UK, I should perhaps note that the Regius Professor of Greek at Cambridge, the Professors of Latin in Dublin and Royal Holloway London, and the Warden of Keble College, Oxford, are all women. And quite properly, of course. But where were all these ladies educated? Many went to schools and colleges which were founded before the first World War, sometimes on the initiative of men and always with their collaboration. Moreover, the female pioneers of women's education in north America and in Britain were determined that women should follow the same syllabus as men; anything less would betray the cause. This has paid off; for the successes we now see at the end of the century, though too long delayed, at least refute the notion of a monolithic establishment of prejudiced men.

So far I have been arguing that Classical Humanism has been characterised by a rather slow-moving, but not inflexible, attitude towards the Graeco-Roman past. Over this century it has assimilated new ideas from many sources. Yet there was always the chance that a nexus of ideas would emerge which could *not* be assimilated, because they involved the negation of Classical Humanism itself. I shall list some of these ideas – ideas which are so widely current that (except in a few cases) I shall not attach them to any specific name or '-ism'. First an anecdote. In Cambridge in the 1930s Bertrand Russell once chided a clever young Austrian who was going through a phase of total scepticism: 'Come, come, Wittgenstein,' he said, 'is there, or is there not, a rhinoceros in this room?' Now it may be that, as some philosophers tell us, the existence of an external world cannot be established by the kind of rigorous reasoning associated with, say, Euclid. From this sensible people now infer, not that the external world is illusory, but that to insist on that kind of demonstration is futile and unnecessary. A recent parallel for this nonsense is the contention that language is a closed system which does not refer to the world outside it. But since man, with his language, is a comparative newcomer to the world, we must believe (contrary to Lacan and others) that things came before language. Again, neither the word 'bread' nor the concept 'bread' can satisfy hunger, though the food to which they refer can.

Recently, at a university high table, I was told that the flamboyant figure on my left did not believe in time. I do not know the reasons for his doubts (he was not an advanced mathematician or a cosmologist, but a mediaeval social historian). I could not help observing that he had managed to arrive in time for his dinner. Again, physicists assure us that sub-atomic entities do not behave like billiard balls. Perhaps not; but, instead of concluding that the world of normal experience has suddenly become unintelligible, we should bear in mind that billiard balls do behave like billiard balls; and that theirs is the world in which billiards are played – and books are written.

According to some contemporary thinkers (I use the word loosely), *no* objective truth exists. So presumably, if one applies the recoil argument, that portentous assertion must itself be rejected. Others tell us that 'History is always already historiography'.[9] Is there not an elementary confusion here? 'History' (*res gestae*) can refer either to events or to an account of events. Events continue to occur, whether recorded or not. In time, the more important become history. Thus it makes perfectly good sense to say that Canada has had a fortunate history and Poland, for example, an unfortunate history, purely in terms of what has happened in those countries. *Accounts* of events are another matter. Although we are now more cautious about accepting Caesar's *Commentaries* and the histories of Livy and Tacitus as true and unbiased narratives, and although we are often faced with two or more different versions of the same event, that does not mean that no assertion by a historian is ever true. There are still survivors to testify that France was invaded in 1940 and Hiroshima was bombed in 1945. Only liars deny the holocaust. If we go back to the late third century BC, although there are no survivors, there is still enough evidence to ensure that anyone who maintained that Hannibal conquered Rome would be regarded as a clown.

Turning now to literary theory, we are told at the start of a much used handbook that, before we can talk sensibly about literature we have to be able to define it.[10] This is simply false. All of us use concepts correctly every day without being able to define them. Some theorists, finding (not surprisingly) that they cannot define literature, have decided that the whole concept is useless. A new

Professor of English across the Atlantic has told his colleagues that
he does not wish the word to be used in the department. ('Discourse,'
it seems, is acceptable.) The fact is, of course, that 'literature', like
many concepts, is inexact; it admits not only positive and negative
cases, but also borderline cases. That does not mean we should give
it up, any more than we should give up using 'red' because it moves
through crimson to blue and through orange to yellow. So, as we
always knew, Tacitus' *Annals* is literature; the consular *fasti* are not;
and Hyginus' fables are debatable.

   That same handbook of theory maintains that no statement of
fact can avoid being a value-judgment, for the speaker always
implies that *this* statement is more worth making than *that,* that *I*
am the sort of person entitled to make it, and *you* are the sort of
person worth making it to.[11] So, if I say, 'Those curtains are red',
that is a value-judgment. Well, well! But there is more to follow;
for, if every statement of fact is an implied value-judgment, and if
(as we are repeatedly assured) every value judgment reflects our
position *vis-à-vis* the prevailing power structure, then, when I say,
'Those curtains are red', I am displaying my position *vis-à-vis*
bourgeois capitalist society. Indeed?

   Let us take the political point a little further. Suppose that some-
one maintains that Juvenal (in his own peculiar fashion) was right
to protest about the condition of the urban poor. What does that
reveal about his or her political stance? Is he a Catholic Christian,
an agnostic liberal, an atheistic communist or just someone with
no political or religious convictions but merely a sense of social
injustice? Surely most people find the inequalities of their society
regrettable.

   Many also find the organisation of universities unsatisfactory.
However, it is noticeable that, in England anyway, the most voci-
ferous complaints come not from scholars seeking tenure in some
marginal institution but from a handful of the privileged elite in
Oxford and Cambridge. Yet the bourgeois liberal authorities do not
seem to have discriminated against *them*. In those departments of
English Literature where the post-modern sceptical relativists have
gained control, advertisements for new staff commonly include
the sentence, 'An interest in modern literary theory would be an
advantage'. That looks like a 'hegemony' in the making, does

it not? Not surprisingly, where that intolerant faction is already entrenched, the students, in their own interests, are obliged to conform.

Yet it is surely obvious that independent thought is best served by having a staff with diverse opinions. In the United States thirty years ago a very accomplished Latinist always travelled about by taxi so that he could distribute the literature of the John Birch Society. I know of no evidence that his right-wing views affected his teaching; for he was a philologist. Even if they did, his influence would have been neutralised by the different beliefs of his colleagues.

I have two more observations to make here: one about linguistics; the other about style. First linguistics: in post-modern writing one sees the name of Saussure invoked again and again. These citations do not prove that the writers have understood Saussure – or have even tried to read him. Let us take just one central point. Saussure distinguishes 'the signifier' from 'the signified'. 'The signifier' is, for example, the succession of sounds d-o-g; 'the signified' is the concept 'dog'. Saussure points out that there is no necessary connection between the one and the other; our four-footed friend could have been represented by a different series of sounds – c-h-i-e-n or H-u-n-d. Saussure therefore calls the connection 'arbitrary'. (An unfortunate choice of word, because there was doubtless some reason, which cannot now be recovered, for adopting the various names.) But note what he says then:

> Le mot arbitraire ... ne doit pas donner l'idée que le signifiant dépend du libre choix du sujet parlant ... il n'est pas au pouvoir de l'individu de rien changer à un signe une fois établi dans un groupe linguistique.[12]

That is, the choice of the signifier is not up to the speaker: it is not in the individual's power to change a sign once it is established in the language of a group. Or again, 'par rapport à la communauté linguistique qui l'emploie [le signifiant] n'est pas libre; il est imposé'[13] – in the community that uses it, the signifier is not free, it is imposed. In other words, you cannot use 'cat' to represent 'dog'. It follows that Saussure gives no warrant for loose talk about 'the free play of the signifier'. If we tried to exercise the licence claimed by Lewis Carroll's Humpty Dumpty (to make words mean whatever we want), civilised communication would soon break down.

Second the matter of style: ancient rhetorical theories maintained that a plain, clear style was the most effective for purposes of exposition and argument;[14] and, on the whole, Classical Humanists have tried to write in a straightforward, logical manner, even if they have often failed to achieve economy and elegance as well. The post-modernists will have none of that: *nous avons changé tout cela.* I first heard of this anti-humanist protest in the 1960s; a Japanese intellectual, we were told, was objecting to the Aristotelian syllogism because it coerced people to a conclusion which they might not wish to grant. It was therefore seen as a tool of the West. About the same time we were being informed from within the West that a clear, logical style was the instrument of capitalist oppression. More recently, the same style has been condemned as a means of perpetuating phallocentric, patriarchal authority. The last contention, it seems, can strike even deeper. In 1991 a feminist sculptor carved the following inscription on a marble tombstone: *Veritas temporas filia* – a noble idea: 'Truth is the daughter of time'. When it was pointed out that the genitive of *tempus* should be, not *temporas*, but *temporis*, she retorted angrily that she 'refused to be confined by male grammar'. Undoubtedly it is difficult to correct howlers on marble; but how much more sensible to do what the vast majority of women scholars (including feminists like Betty Friedan, Kate Millett and Janet Radcliffe Richards),[15] have always done – to resolve that, since a clear, logical style is the most effective vehicle for argument, it should not be monopolised by men.

By taking the other route – that of an oracular and jargon-laden obscurity – post-modern critics (men and women alike) have exposed themselves to damaging attacks. When the American philosopher John Searle demolished the position of Derrida in a famous article in the *New York Review*,[16] Derrida complained that Searle misunderstood him. But if Derrida wanted to avoid being misunderstood, he should have written more plainly. In any case, if (as we are often assured) a writer can claim no control over the interpretation of his work, what right had Derrida to complain? Certainly Searle demolished what most people *thought* Derrida had said.

Clarity of style, conveying clarity of thought, is therefore an aim of Classical Humanism, which we defined as the *rational* study of the Greeks and Romans. Within that tradition, everyone lives in a free republic, the *respublica litterarum*. Opinions are judged persuasive or otherwise according to laws – laws about logic and the use of evidence which are above any individual. If those laws are denied, as some deny them now, that makes it all the easier for a dictator to arise who will proclaim *hoc uolo, sic iubeo, sit pro ratione uoluntas*, ('that's what I want, those are my orders, let my will take the place of a reason').[17] It is not the Humanists who are totalitarian.

Since their intellectual foundations are so defective, one wonders how the post-modernists came to enjoy such a vogue. No doubt it had something to do with the glamour of Paris. (As Raymond Tallis has remarked, 'when the emperor is restocking his wardrobe he usually shops in Paris'.)[18] Yet there was intense opposition in Paris, too;[19] and one hears that there the movement is now regarded as *passé*; nor do the writers in question have any significant reputation as thinkers in the English-speaking countries. (According to one of Searle's less polite colleagues, 'Derrida is the sort of philosopher that gives bullshit a bad name'.) Should we, then, blame the gullibility of people untrained in analytical thought? Or the eagerness of the young – and not so young – to topple the authority of their elders? Or personal vanity? (It is always easier to cut a dash by presenting something novel and exciting.) Whatever the reason, when some would-be sage declares that 'literature is ideology', that 'history ... does not exist', that 'the author is dead', that 'there is nothing outside the text',[20] or (to come nearer home) that 'the medium is the message', Classical Humanists will not feel impelled to bow down and admire the speaker's profundity.

This paper will discuss in its second part some of the ways in which readers concerned with the appreciation of poetry (mainly Latin poetry) may attempt to meet the problems raised in the last forty years. For this purpose, there are three basic points of reference – points which can be represented as the apexes of a triangle, set within a circle: at the top we have the writer and his world; at bottom right the text and its world; and at bottom left the reader and his world. The circle indicates the path of critical interest as it passes from one point to another.

Let us start at the top. In the century before 1914 it was widely assumed that the more one discovered about the writer and his world the better chance one had of understanding his mind and feelings, and hence the nature of his work. In the lifetime of Pound, Yeats and Eliot, a reaction set in: these personal concerns, generally associated with romanticism, began to recede. The issue was still topical in 1939, when Lewis debated 'the personal heresy' with Tillyard;[21] but with the New Critics, the interests of the most influential readers shifted to the second apex, the text and its world (by which I mean other texts, both earlier and contemporary). In the case of the more circumspect, it was mainly a shift of emphasis. As mainstream criticism had neglected imagery, structure and tone (and this, too, was a justified criticism of Classical Humanism), it was now these and other features of a poem's organisation that attracted most scholars' attention. Less prudent critics insisted, as a matter of dogma, that a poet's period and personality were irrelevant to the understanding and appreciation of his work; these voices came mainly from America but, as we have seen, a similar reaction was taking place in France.[22] In many quarters, of course, such voices were ignored. (Margaret Hubbard, editor [with R.G.M. Nisbet] of Horace, *Odes* 1 and 2, described the attitude as 'self-canonised ignorance'.) However, what one rarely got was a discussion of when historical material was relevant and when it was not. For example, no knowledge of history is needed to appreciate Horace's *Diffugere niues* (*Odes* 4.7); whereas some awareness of Augustus' plan for reviving Roman religion and promoting family life *is* desirable in order to understand *Delicta maiorum* (*Odes* 3.6). On the personal, biographical level, inferences from poem to poet and *vice versa* are sometimes valid, sometimes not. Horace's receding hair may be inferred from *Epist.* 1.7.26 ('You must restore the black hair thick on my forehead'). On the other hand Ovid's thinness may *not* be inferred from *Amores* 1.6.5-6 – a conventional joke about emaciated lovers. Reasoning in the other direction, we can use Martial's letter (12.18), which pictures Juvenal attending on the great, to argue that the satirist's remarks on clients are, to some extent at least, based on personal experience; whereas most of Servius' biographical information about Virgil's youth is valueless, being derived from the *Eclogues* themselves. So discrimination is needed. Large sweeping laws, laid down by self-appointed legislators, only discourage thought.

The same applies to intention. Now a writer may indicate his intentions implicitly (as when a poet laureate accepts a commission); or explicitly, by recording them in his diary or letters or revealing them in the work itself. Lucretius, in *De Rerum Natura*, declared his intentions systematically, Horace only in a throwaway phrase – *ridentem dicere verum* ('to tell the truth with a smile'; *Sat.* 1.1.24). It must be stressed, however, that even when a writer's intentions *can* be ascertained, they are no guide to the *value* of his work.

In some kinds of writing, especially drama, intention is a more complex matter. The action of a play and its outcome must be regarded as intentional (i.e. as reflecting the writer's final intention); but the presentation of the characters, their motives and their relations to one another, are bound to vary from one production to the next; and such variations will often depart to a greater or lesser extent from the author's intention (though he may still find them acceptable). These same variations (in the actors' delivery, gesture, facial expression and so on) will also affect the play's meaning.

Here we come to the other sense of 'intention'. It is true even in non-dramatic poetry that the text may be obscure; it may also mean more than its author intended. But that is no excuse for asserting that the basic sense is always undiscoverable. When faced with Catullus' most famous epigram (85):

Odi et amo; quare id faciam fortasse requiris.
⁻Nescio, sed fieri sentio et excrucior.

I hate and love; perhaps you wonder why I do so.
I don't know; but I feel it happening, and I am in agony.

are we to say, 'to know what Catullus intended we would have to get inside his head'? Of course not; yet in recent critical writing one frequently comes across this solipsistic confusion.

As interest moved to that second apex, the study of poems (especially *short* poems) became altogether more thorough and sophisticated. Scholars realised, however, that, although they might not want to say anything about the poet, the text still confronted them with various voices, which could not be ignored. The answer to this problem was the *persona* – a concept with a long history, which regained currency thanks again to Pound and his followers. From them it was taken up by professional critics. (There was an analogous movement in Paris, represented by the phrase *larvatus prodeo,* which Barthes took from Descartes.)[23] Here, too, discrimination was called for. Often the concept of the *persona* was valuable, as it helped the reader to distinguish the different voices and not to assume that any voice was necessarily that of the author. Nevertheless, in 'impersonal' poetry the concept was not needed, in that no one, for example, inquired about the character of 'Homer' or the reciter. In other cases, where the speaker's voice and tone changed in the course of the poem (e.g. *Odes* 2.1), the *persona* was too rigid a notion to be helpful. In still other cases, the presence of the *persona* was hard to establish. In Horace *Sat.* 1.9 (the pest on the Sacred Way) we have an ironical, amusing, self-depreciating character, who is at the same time a member of an elite circle. But how is that figure different from Horace himself as he read the poem to his powerful friends? As we know, people adopt poses in real life too.

Still at this second apex, critics often became impatient with Classical Humanism's treatment of what I have called the world of the text – that is, its relation to other texts. This impatience was justified where an editor simply gave a list of 'imitations'. 'Imitations' – a word used without prejudice in the eighteenth century – took on a pejorative meaning in the romantic period. For if a poem contained imitations it could not be original. Virgil's imitations of Theocritus, for instance, were said to show the 'artificiality' of the *Eclogues.* By the same token, most Latin poetry came to be seen as second-hand and derivative. Yet the answer to this problem was not to ignore the imitations but to investigate their function in their new context. This, of course, is a large and complex subject, now dignified by the term 'inter-textuality'. Is the imitation conscious or unconscious? Is it a parody or a tribute? Or perhaps a parody *and* a tribute? Does it enlist the support of tradition, relying on a shared culture? Or does it claim superiority over tradition? Again, what is the best word to describe a given instance? To speak of 'borrowing', 'influence', 'model' and, most prejudicially, 'plagiarism', implies that the later poet is inferior. 'Reminiscence' and 'allusion' are more neutral. 'Emulation', which is usually the best term, implies the excitement of competition. The currently fashionable 'subversion', 'undermining' and 'appropriation', with their connotations of hostility, even theft, strike me as misconceived and misleading. It is also worth adding, perhaps, that all these last three terms (subversion, undermining and appropriation) imply intention – of which I heartily approve.

Most emulation, of course, takes place within the framework of a given genre. This idea, though highly respectable, had become rather outmoded in Classical Humanism, until it was revived by Francis Cairns. In his *Generic Compositon* (1972) he brought new insights to the tradition by focusing on the sub-genres – 'the send-off poem', 'the birthday poem', 'the serenade' and so on. One's only *caveat* here is that a great poet is always the master of his genre, not its servant.

Moving to the text itself, we come first to the problem of con-stituting it. Here the best question to put to an editor, perhaps, is 'what are you aiming to recover?' In the case of Horace, the aim is simply stated: 'I aim to come as close as possible to what Horace wrote'. With the *Aeneid*, one can hope to recover only the incomplete edition published by Varius. No one, for example, perhaps not even Virgil himself, knew how that portentous line beginning *numina magna deum* (*Aeneid* 2.623) was going to end. Worse is the case of Homer. To answer, 'I aim to recover what Homer wrote,' raises two questions, one about Homer and the other about writing. The Alexandrian vulgate, a rather imprecise entity, is the best one can hope to reach. The situation with Shakespeare is just as bad, though for a different reason; and what are we to do with poets like Yeats, who tinker with their poems over many years? A poet's final version is not always the best.[24]

None of this need induce a critic to throw up his hands in despair, though he does have to admit the limitations of his task, both to himself and to his readers.

Then there is the business of exegesis. Here we start with the simplest, most basic kind of comment: 'this is a purpose-clause', 'that is a spondaic ending', 'here the poet is alluding to the judgment of Paris'. Post-modern critics cannot, on principle, produce editions, though some have the effrontery to review them. Presumably their refusal is due to the fact that editorial comments aim to be, and for the most part are, objectively true. Other equally objective examples are comments on formal features, such as numerical correspondences, chiastic structures, recurrent images – all of them illustrated in Horace, *Odes* 1.4.[25] Such comments lead on to comparisons between, say, *Odes* 1.4 and 4.7 (two spring odes); or between Catullus 45 (Septimius and Acme) and Horace *Odes* 3.9 (*Donec gratus eram*); or in *Aeneid* 6 we may want to put Aeneas' meeting with his father beside Odysseus' meeting with his mother in *Odyssey* 11. We have now come a very long way, and we are still in the business of analytical description. The subjective element, however, may enter when we begin to discuss tone or feeling; and it will certainly enter when we express our preferences.

Often, of two interpretations only one can be true. At *Aeneid* 1.81 Aeolus strikes the hollow mountain *conversa cuspide*. Does this mean 'with the point of his spear' (so Conington, 1863) or 'with the butt of his spear' (R.D. Williams, 1972)? Common sense, plus the examples adduced by Henry,[26] make the latter almost certain. In any case, there is no point in talking about ambiguity. Precision is what we are after. Two (or more) different meanings, however, do not necessarily entail contradiction. In *Aeneid* 2.212 the snakes head for Laocoon *agmine certo*. The *Oxford Latin Dictionary* lists the passage under *agmen* (1b), a sense denoting 'the movement of flowing or gliding objects'. But in other senses (4-8), the word has military associations; and Virgil's snakes prefigure, or form part of, the Greek army; hence sense 1b does not exhaust the meaning. No English word encompasses both ideas.

As we all know, there *are* questions which do not allow definite answers, either because the evidence is too scanty or because the issues are too complex. Some recent critics, however, have decided that all texts are unstable, that no final answer can be given to any question. A couple of years ago in Yale a British scholar gave a paper on *The Rape of the Lock*. In the question period, I asked him whether there could ever be a mistaken interpretation of the poem. After a certain amount of shuffling, he said 'No', though he could imagine that some proposals might be incomplete. So if some fool came up with the idea that the poem was not by Pope, or that it contained no mock-heroic diction, or that it portrayed the squalors of proletarian life, I suppose that scholar would have to say, 'Quite right; though you haven't said the last word'.

Scepticism about texts has led many modem critics on to that third apex, where attention is focused on the reader and his world. Here some of the most confident and insistent voices tell us that every reader is so locked into his own ideology or assumptions that he cannot make an objective judgement about any poem, least of all an ancient one. At this point it may be well to set aside certain types of literature which allow a range of different interpretations without engendering disagreement. I am thinking of instances like Aesop's fables, or a dozen of the most famous Greek myths. Here an unchanging story is continually re-used as a paradigm of some familiar situation. Thus the fall of Icarus can be seen as a penalty for pride or disobedience, *or* as an illustration of the generation gap, *or* as a warning against the dangers of technology, *or* as a symbol of the noble failure of the aspiring intellect. The only criterion, I suppose, is that the application should correspond satisfactorily to the myth.

Where disagreements arise, we may distinguish questions of fact, definition, opinion and taste. New information about a fact of literary history may lead to a general change of judgment. For example, our notion of Aeschylean chronology had to be revised when, in 1952, the discovery of a papyrus showed that the *Suppliants* was not the earliest of his plays. Successive finds of the same kind have reversed Rohde's view of the development of the Greek novel.

Or the crucial fact may be one of linguistic usage. In his sonnet no. 17 Milton urges his young friend, Edward Lawrence, to join him in combating the gloomy weather; there will be a light but appetising meal, wine and some music. The sonnet ends: 'He who of those delights can judge, and spare / To interpose them oft, is not unwise'. Several scholars interpret 'spare to interpose them oft' as 'refrain from interposing them oft'; many others understand it as 'spare the time to interpose them oft'. So the first group thinks it means 'not often', and the second 'often' – two views which are plainly incompatible. The arguments in favour of the first explanation are pursued in ch. 10 above.

Some disagreements can be resolved, or at least reduced, by drawing clearer definitions. Is Euripides a rationalist or an irrationalist? Is Horace a love poet or not? Is the *Metamorphoses* an epic? To take the last question, if the only criteria are that a poem should consist of several thousand hexameters on the subject of gods, heroes and princes (and their female counterparts), then *Metamorphoses* is an epic. However, if, to qualify, the poem must also be about one main hero and tell one over-arching story, then it fails to pass the test. For it is not enough to have a single theme (in this case metamorphosis) or to have episodes arranged in patterned connections. The wide variations in tone might also count against it. So, in the old phrase, 'it depends on what you mean' by epic.

It was stated earlier that actors' interpretations of a character would vary. The same is obviously true of readers' interpretations of a character in a play, novel or epic poem. Yet in the case of a literary character, as distinct from a character in life, the same evidence is available to everyone. Secondly, though the variations may be quite wide, the text still imposes certain limits (no one envisages a shy Agamemnon or an apathetic Dido); and the less complex the character, the less variation there will be. Thirdly, unless they are very naive, readers develop a bifocal vision. That is, they take account, as best they can, of the characters' cultural milieu; they also appraise them in the light of their own moral and social attitudes, of which they are seldom unaware. Often the two procedures lead to the same conclusion; sometimes they do not.

Cultural relativists tell us that the Greeks and Romans are too remote to be treated like this; that, in any case, one society is not in a position to judge the traditions and moral values of another. Once again the generalisation is false. Take the old Chinese habit of binding women's feet, the Indian custom of suttee and the African practice of female circumcision. Provided we recognise the glaring defects of our own society (over-breeding, the pollution of the planet, the manufacture of weapons of mass destruction), surely we are entitled to criticise such evil customs. We are equally entitled to deplore the Roman penalty of crucifixion, the torturing of slaves to extract evidence and, most revolting of all, the murder of human beings in the arena to provide public entertainment.

Usually the problem is less straightforward. Suppose you are a Christian, raised in, and still committed to, a strict moral tradition; you are bound to find Ovid's *Ars Amatoria* frivolous and licentious. Yet many pagan Romans thought the same; and indeed Ovid *relied* on such disapproval to obtain his effect. At the same time, even if you disapprove, you will probably concede that the poem is clever and witty.

Then there is personal taste. Do you prefer Sappho's poem to Catullus' tidier and more mannered version (51)? If you appreciate the objective differences, literary analysis can go no further; *de gustibus non disputandum.* On many issues, however, a long debate has to take place before we decide that we differ from other readers solely on a matter of taste. In discussing such questions we also tend to think of the large shifts in taste which took place between classicism and romanticism – between romanticism and modernism. Yet on any specific issue the historical dimension may be less important than one often assumes. When, for instance, the elder Seneca remarks that Ovid did not know how to leave well alone (*Controversiae* 9.5.17), and when Quintilian adds that 'he was too fond of his own talent' (*Institutio Oratoria* 10.1.88), we know at once what they mean, in spite of the gap of two millennia. On the other hand, we may find ourselves at odds with some of our contemporaries in response to a Senecan tragedy. What they (like Jacobean audiences) admire as powerful rhetoric, we may condemn as vulgar rant.

At the beginning we defined Classical Humanism as the rational study of the Greeks and Romans as fellow human beings. This rests on the assumption that, long before the Mycenaean civilisation was formed, the basic features of human nature had evolved; and that, in spite of the bewildering diversity of beliefs and customs, those features remain the same. In some quarters, of course, this assumption is contested; but its opponents have difficulty in establishing *how* human nature is supposed to have changed – and since when. And think of the implications if their view is accepted. Will it not be all the easier for one nation or one race to decide that those whom it dislikes really are sub-human and may therefore be exterminated without second thoughts?

More positively, when we read that great chorus in Sophocles' *Antigone* which begins πολλὰ τὰ δεινὰ κοὐδὲν ἀνθρώπου δεινότερον πέλει 'there are many wonders, and nothing more wonderful than man' ; 332-3), do we really feel we are listening to the voice of a different species? Are we not flattered to be described in such terms? When we study the first book of Cicero's *Laws,* we may well think he is too optimistic about mankind, that he exaggerates the distinctions between us and the rest of the animal kingdom, that his transcendental account of the origin of justice is a benign fantasy. Nevertheless, it remains true that every society needs laws to protect life, property (public or private) and good faith, and to regulate sexual relations. Without such a structure of minimum natural law, the society will not survive.[27] So we study ancient customs and beliefs to find out our accidental differences (and for many scholars this is the most interesting part of their work); yet by doing so we are enabled to take account of those differences and so to make contact with our fellow human beings. Everything that people have been doing since the flood, 'their wishes, fears, anger, pleasure, joys, their to-ing and fro-ing' – that, says Juvenal (*Sat.* 1.85-6), is the mis-mash of his book. And that, too, is what Classical Humanism is about.

NOTES

CHAPTER 1

1. This paper, first written in 1967, was later revised to take account of the work of Gordon Williams, Ian Du Quesnay and others, and brought up to date on the basis of Wendell Clausen's edn (Oxford, 1994).

2. Cf. the mosaic from Lepcis Magna reproduced in G.Hanfmann, *Roman Art* (Greenwich, Conn., n.d.) plate xxxvii; there, however, the old man (so reminiscent of Hemingway) is baiting a hook.

3. See, e.g., Anton Legner, *Der Gute Hirt* (Düsseldorf, 1959).

4. W. Empson, *Some Versions of Pastoral* (London, 1968) 6.

5. See K. Dover, *Theocritus* (repr. Bristol, 1985) pp. xxviii-xlv.

6. For a fuller analysis, see R.W. Garson *Classical Quarterly* 21 (1971) 188-92; and I. Du Quesnay in D.West and T. Woodman (eds) *Creative Imitation and Latin Literature* (Cambridge, 1979) 35-69.

7. Lions and lionesses do occur in Theocritus but not in a passage like this, which is supposed to reflect the everyday experience of a countryman.

8. Johann Strauss II is said to have handed on his black, silver-topped baton to Léhar, who in turn bequeathed it to Stolz.

9. Virgil supplies an explanatory pun on Micon's name (*parvus* = μικρός Corydon is not identical with Micon; he is simply quoting Micon's epigram.

10. For Alcman, see D.A. Campbell, *Greek Lyric* (Loeb edn) vol. 2, 339; for Sappho, see *Greek Lyric* vol. 1, p. xiii. A fragment of Parthenius reads ῞Ιλαος, ὦ ῾Υμέναιε (Loeb edn, no. 32); cf. Theocritus Idyll 18.58. For Calvus and Ticida, see E. Courtney, *The Fragmentary Latin Poets* (Oxford, 1993) 203-4 and 229.

11. In incorporating elements from other genres Virgil may well have taken a hint from *Idyll* 7, where one speaker recites what is, initially, a *propemptikon* (52-70).

12. See S. Weinstock, *Divus Julius* (Oxford, 1971) 22 and references there.

13. Weinstock (note 12 above) 107.
14. Weinstock (note 12 above) 207.
15. Weinstock (note 12 above) 281 ff.
16. Weinstock (note 12 above) 156.
17. Diodorus 4.84.2-4.
18. Do the lines refer to the forthcoming triumph of Pollio, following his suppression of the Parthini in 39 BC? In that case there is no problem about his tragedies (see Horace *Sat.* 1.10.42-3; *Odes* 2.1.9-12; and Tacitus *Dialogus* 21.7). But why, after campaigning in the hinterland of Dyrrachium, is Pollio supposed to he returning home round the top of the Adriatic? Syme, *Classical Quarterly* 31 (1937) 47-8, suggested that Virgil was poetically assimilating Pollio's route to that of Antenor (*Aen.* 1.242 ff.) – an ingenious, but far from obvious, idea. Bowersock, *Harvard Studies in Classical Philology* 82 (1978) 201-2) argued that Virgil's lines were addressed to Octavian, who in 35 BC *did* campaign in the northern Adriatic. Then, however, the Sophoclean *carmina* have to be seen as the *Ajax*, which Octavian eventually abandoned (Suetonius, *Divus Augustus* 85.2). Yet even the eager anticipation of that work (whose date is unknown) would not have justified Virgil's language; and to say in 35 BC that Octavian's as yet unfinished play would alone be worthy of Sophocles would have been a slight on the tragedies of Pollio. The sentence *a te principium, tibi desinam* ('with you is my beginning, for you I shall end'), as an extravagant compliment, would have suited either man. But those words also imply that a single patron had interested himself in the *Eclogues* from their inception down to the present time. We know from Horace, *Sat.* 1.6.54-5, that in 38 BC Virgil was already a member of Maecenas' circle. So in 35 we would have expected any mention of a patron to refer to him. I am, therefore, in the uncomfortable position of inclining to the traditional view, without being able to meet Bowersock's very reasonable objection. For a lead into the discussion, see J. Farrell, *Classical Philology* 86 (1991) 204-11.
19. E.g. I. Du Quesnay, *Papers of the Liverpool Latin Seminar* (1976) 31-5; R. Nisbet, *Bulletin of the Institute of Classical Studies* (1978) 64; and W. Clausen (ed.), *A Commentary on Virgil Eclogues* (Oxford, 1994) 121-3.

20. I have not included the much discussed Saloninus mentioned by Servius on *Ecl.* 4.1 and 11.

21. No precise reference to Hercules is seen by Conington, Page, Coleman or Nisbet (64-5) in lines 15-16. There *is* a reference to Hercules in the final line: cf. Theocritus, *Idyll* 17.20-33; and Homer, *Odyssey* 11.602-4. But this is usually taken in a general sense: 'Any child who does not smile at his parent(s) will not grow up to be a hero like Hercules'. Granted, since Antony claimed descent from Hercules (Plutarch, *Antony* 4.2), some readers may have been disposed to add 'from whom your father, Antony claims descent'. My argument is that, although Virgil allowed such an interpretation, he did not require it. For the association of Romulus, Scipio Africanus, Pompey, Caesar, Antony and (a few years later) Augustus with Hercules, see A.R. Anderson, *Harvard Studies in Classical Philology* 39 (1928) 422-36.

22. The stones, rushes and mud of 47-8, however, are Italian rather than Theocritean.

23. The legal status of Tityrus has long been a problem. In 1981 Du Quesnay proposed what seemed to me an attractive solution: that Tityrus was informally manumitted – *de facto* free, but *de iure* a slave (*Papers of the Liverpool Latin Seminar* 3 (1981) 115-23). This suggestion, however, is passed over without discussion by Clausen, who thinks that 'Virgil deliberately confuses the private with the public sense of *libertas*' (31) – *libertas* (freedom), in the public sense, being 'the slogan of Octavian and his party' (43).

24. Aelian, *Varia Historia* 3.18; Servius on *Ecl.* 6.13.

25. Lucian, *How to Write History* 57 (Loeb edn, vol. 6, 68); Pollianus, *Anth. Pal.* 11.130.

26. See T.P. Wiseman, *Cinna the Poet* (Leicester, 1974) 47-8.

27. Hesiod, *Melampodia* 1 (Loeb edn, 266).

28. Servius on *Ecl.* 6.72.

29. For Varius and Cinna, see E. Courtney, *The Fragmentary Latin Poets* (Oxford, 1993) 271-5 and 212-24.

30. Gow's edn of Theocritus cites Pindar, *Olympian* 6.100 and *Homeric Hymn* 4.2 and 18.2 as parallels.

31. See P. Levi, *Proceedings of the Virgil Society* 7 (1968) 1-11; R Jenkyns, *Journal of Roman Studies* 79 (1989) 26-39.

32. See G. Williams, *Tradition and Originality in Roman Poetry*

(Oxford, 1968) 234-9.

33. Although Virgil does not say that Arethusa has travelled, not just from Elis, but all the way from Arcadia, that is still probably a safe inference on the basis of Ovid, *Amores* 3.6.30 (*virgo Arcadia*) and *Met.* 5.607; in which case Virgil may well be indicating that this is going to be, in some sense, an Arcadian poem.

34. Half of the *Eclogues* end towards evening (1, 2, 6, 9 and 10), another Virgilian touch.

35. Does he mean (1) 'Instead of writing epyllia in the manner of Euphorion, I will write pastoral poetry as a shepherd lover'? (2) 'Instead of writing elegies in the manner of Euphorion, I will write pastoral poetry in hexameters'? or (3) 'Instead of writing elegies – a form invented by Theocles of Chalcis (see *Suda* under ἐλεγείνειν), I will write pastoral poetry in hexameters'? Against (3) is the fact that Gallus knew certain themes at least of Euphorion (Parthenius, *Tragedies of Love* nos. 13, 26, and 28) and adapted at least one of his poems (on the Grynaean Grove). If 'Chalcidic verse' refers to Theocles, we don't know of anyone who got the point, whereas we do know that Quintilian missed it (*Institutio Oratoria* 10.1.56). Against (2) is the fact that Euphorion is not known to have written any elegies; see B.A. van Groningen, *Euphorion* (Amsterdam, 1977) 251-3. Reading (1) is the least unlikely; but what about Gallus' *Amores,* which were probably alluded to in *Ecl.* 6.64 and seem to lurk behind *Ecl.* 10? Even if there were a satisfactory answer to 'Chalcidic verse', *why* does Gallus resolve to write pastoral – a decision that is cancelled twelve lines later?

36. To bring *Ecl.* 5 into relation with 4, I have treated it after 8. That may well be chronologically wrong. Still, I am inclined to put 8 (except for lines 6-13) and 7 in the first five pieces. Nilsson, cited by Clausen (note 19 above, 238), found the metre of Alphesiboeus' song similar to that of *Eclogues* 2 and 3. Whether Damon's song was added somewhat later must remain a matter for speculation.

37. The phrase comes in Clausen's admirable paper 'Callimachus and Latin Poetry', repr. in K. Quinn (ed.), *Approaches to Catullus* (Cambridge and New York, 1972) 193. I do not know whether he endorses it still.

CHAPTER 2

1. Servius, Thilo-Hagen edn, vol. 1, 2 and 10-11.

2. See Cato, cited by Servius on *Aen*.1.267; Livy 1.2.3; Dionysius 1.64. For further discussion, see R. Heinze, *Virgil's Epic Technique* (tr. Berkeley and Los Angeles, 1993) 143; P.T. Eden (ed.), *A Commentary on Virgil:* Aeneid *VIII* (Leiden, 1975) note on *Aen.* 8.492 ff.

3. See Naevius, *Punic War* in B.H. Warmington (ed.), *Remains of Old Latin* (Loeb edn, repr. London, 1961) nos. 13-17. If Aeneas' speech (1.198 ff.) is taken from Naevius, as Servius says, then presumably Naevius' Aeneas had by then already been told that he was fated to reach Latium. The tempest in *Aen.* 1, Venus' complaint and Jupiter's words of comfort, all come from Naevius (Macrobius, *Sat.* 6.2.31).

4. See Dionysius 1.46-48; R.G. Austin (ed.), *P. Vergili Maronis Aeneidos Liber Secundus* (Oxford, 1964) p. xv; G.K. Galinsky, *Aeneas and Sicily* (Princeton, 1969) 46-9.

5. Tyrtaeus 10.1-2 and 27-8; D.E. Gerber, *Greek Elegiac Poetry*, (Loeb edn 1999); cf. Homer, *Iliad* 22.71-3.

6. See M.C.J. Putnam, *The Poetry of the Aeneid* (London, 1965) 6-7.

7. B.W. Knox, 'The Serpent and the Flame', *American Journal of Philology* 71 (1950) 379-400.

8. W.F. Jackson Knight, *Roman Virgil* (London, 1944) 240.

9. The Bristol Society of Merchant Venturers has as its motto *indocilis pauperiem pati.* In Horace, *Odes* 1.1.18 it is used disapprovingly of the merchant who 'cannot learn to endure poverty'. I understand that the Society, which does much philanthropic work, prefers the translation 'cannot tolerate *other people's* poverty'.

10. R.B. Lloyd, '*Aeneid* 3 and the Aeneas Legend', *American Journal of Philology* 78 (1957) 382-400.

11. The phrase *Romanaque tellus* ('and Roman soil') occurs in Mercury's speech (*Aen.* 4.275). Strictly speaking *Romana* should mean nothing to Aeneas.

12. There was a gap between the fall of Troy (ca. 1180 BC) and the foundation of Rome (ca. 750 BC), which was filled in Virgil's scheme by Alba Longa.

13. Dionysius, *Roman Antiqities* 1.49.4; 50.2, 3 and 4; 51.2.

14. B. Otis, *Virgil: A Study in Civilized Poetry* (Oxford, 1963) 260-1.

15. One might ask how it comes about that, of all the women in the Fields of Mourning, Dido alone has her husband available for comfort (*Aen.* 6.473-4). Could it be that Virgil had become so involved with his own creation that he could not bear to consign her to an eternity of grief?

16. This may sound like a modern comment but it comes from Servius on 3.711: *bene hic subtrahitur ne parum decoro amori intersit* ('he is appropriately removed at this point to save him from being present during an unseemly love affair').

17. *Tityre, tu ... nos ... nos ... tu, Tityre.*

18. K. Gransden, *Virgil's Iliad* (Cambridge, 1984) 217.

19. This is not to say that he has evolved into a specimen of the Stoic 'wise man' (*sapiens*), an unlikely metamorphosis for an epic hero.

20. E.g. R.S. Conway, *Harvard Lectures on the Virgilian Age* (Cambridge, Mass., 1928) 129-49; G. Duckworth, 'The Architecture of the *Aeneid*', *American Journal of Philology* 75 (1954) 1-15 and 'The *Aeneid* as a Trilogy' *Transactions of the American Philological Association* 88 (1957) 1-10; W.A. Camps, *An Introduction to Virgil* (Oxford, 1969) ch. 6.

21. See M.O. Lee, *Fathers and Sons in Virgil's* Aeneid (Albany, NY, 1979).

22. It is not clear whether the three competitors also receive the prizes mentioned in 306-14.

23. P.R. Hardie, *Virgil's* Aeneid: *Cosmos and Imperium* (Oxford, 1986) 85.

24. This idea was proposed by S.G.P. Small, 'The Arms of Turnus' *Transaction of the American Philological Association* 90 (1959) 243-52.

25. The reader will think of his own examples. I mention just a few of the better-known names: T.R. Glover, *Virgil* (London, 1912) 229: 'Heedless of national well-being or divine decree if, at any cost to anybody and everybody, he can gratify his own wishes' – that in spite of *Aen.* 10.280-2. W. Warde Fowler, *The Death of Turnus* (Oxford, 1919) 3: 'Turnus must first be conquered, for he represents the spirit of disunion and strife'. R.Heinze (note 2 above) 167: 'He is even prepared to give up his claim to Lavinia (937). Virgil implies that anyone capable of that has never been worthy either of her or of the throne' – even though the loss of

Lavinia is envisaged in 12.80. B.Otis (note 14 above) 348: 'It is *furor* and *caedis insana cupido* that undo him. His violence is both morally reprehensible and tactically stupid'. R.D.Williams, *The Aeneid* (London, 1987) 19: ' ... brought to disaster by a flaw in his character (violence and lack of respect for the divine will)'. F. Cairns, *Virgil's Augustan Epic* (Cambridge, 1989) 814: 'A monster threatening Italy'. Classicists, however, are seldom unanimous. Having written this note, I am glad to find that W.S. Maguinness (ed.), *Virgil: Aeneid Book XII* (London, 1953) 13, says, 'Book 12 is the culmination of the tragedy. Those who read the book with this realization in mind will not waste their time in attempts to discredit Turnus for his *violentia* or Aeneas for his combination of *pietas* and *saevitia*, but see in them, as Virgil did, two heroic but human figures, opposed by a destiny that needed the one and rejected the other'. There are also some very sensible remarks in W.R. Johnson, *Darkness Visible* (Berkeley and Los Angeles, 1976) 119.

26. See 'Dido's *Culpa*', repr. in S.J. Harrison (ed.), *Oxford Readings in Vergil's* Aeneid (Oxford, 1990) 145-66. My interpretation is opposed by N.M. Horsfall in the same volume (127-44). In ch. 3 in this volume (p. 54) some of Horsfall's assumptions are questioned.

27. *Agitur furiis*: similarly Aeneas is inflamed by *furiae* in 12.956. Some would like to distinguish *furiae* from *furor*. This seems very doubtful but, in any case, it does not affect the issue; for Aeneas 'rages madly' at 10.545, 604 and 802. Something, however, should be added about Allecto. Unlike the Furies in Book 6, Allecto in Book 7 does not punish guilt; she arouses discord; see C.J. Fordyce (ed.), *Virgil: Aeneid VII-VIII* (Oxford, 1977; repr. Bristol, 1990) note on 7.324. As *Amor* was the instrument of Venus in 1.715-22, Allecto is the instrument of Juno and is controlled by her. An earlier instrument was Iris (5.606); but she inflamed only the Trojan women (who again had a good reason for their disaffection). Something much more wide-ranging in power is needed to inflame Amata – Turnus and the whole community. So Juno sets about, literally, raising hell: *flectere si nequeo superos, Acheronta movebo* ('if I cannot divert the gods above, I'll shift Acheron [the underworld]'; 7.312). As a result, Allecto provides some vivid scenes which add a new dimension of horror (7.324-571). But in the end, as we have seen, Turnus' wrath is no more terrible than that of Aeneas. As for Juno, readers may care to look again at the final scene with Jupiter on Olympus (12.319-42) and ask how, if she is simply the divine embodiment of evil and irrational wrath, she can obtain everything she asks for.

28. For all his youth, Pallas, too, was a conventional epic warrior. This is his prayer to Hercules: 'May he (Turnus) when half dead see me tearing off his bloody armour, and may his swooning eyes be forced to look at his conqueror' (10.462-3). For Camilla, see 11.696-8.

29. In his plea Turnus appeals to Aeneas' filial affection. That is what makes Aeneas pause. Neither the appeal for life nor the hesitation is in Homer.

30. 'Towers and Citadels in the *Aeneid*' and 'The Idea of Empire in the *Aeneid*. For references, see Related Material, p. 43.

31. *Iliad* 21.107: 'Patroclus also died, who was a far better man than you'.

32. Hardie (note 23 above) 135.

CHAPTER 3

1. O.M Lee, *Classical Quarterly* 15 (1965) 286-8, refers to Magariños, *Emerita* 15 (1947) 159-60.

2. *American Journal of Philology* 81 (1960) 373-92.

3. R.G.M. Nisbet, *Collected Papers on Latin Literature*, ed. S.J. Harrison (Oxford, 1995) 144-6.

4. Ed. D.R. Shackleton Bailey (Stuttgart, 1985) 68; D.A. West, *Horace: the Complete* Odes *and* Epodes (Oxford, 1977) 77.

5. H.D. Jocelyn, *Classical Philology* 77 (1982) 330-5.

6. For these three items. see D.A. Campbell, *Greek Lyric* (Loeb edn) vol 1, 320-3.

7. see D. Mankin, *Horace's* Epodes (Cambridge, 1995) 97.

8. A.T. von S. Bradshaw, *Hermes* 106 (1978) 165 ff.

9. Nisbet (note 3 above).

10. N. Horsfall, 'Dido in The Light of History' in S.J. Harrison (ed.), *Oxford Readings in Virgil's* Aeneid (Oxford, 1990) 127-44, especially 132 and 134.

11. R. Syme, *The Augustan Aristocracy* (Oxford, 1986) 206.

12. Suetonius, *Life of Horace* (Loeb edn) vol. 2, 488-9.

13. Suetonius (note 12 above) 484-7.

14. See S.J. Harrison (ed.), *Homage to Horace* (Oxford, 1995).

15. See J.P. Sullivan (ed.), *Critical Essays on Roman Literature: Satire* (London, 1963) 95.

16. T.R. Glover, *Virgil* (London, 1912) 203 (cf. 190); T.E. Page in his commentary on *Aeneid* Book 4 (London, from 1894) pp. xvii-xviii and 370.

CHAPTER 4

1. Although Kiessling and Heinze take *hunc* as Achilles and are rightly followed by O.A.W. Dilke (ed.) *Horace:* Epistles *I* (London, 1954), they do not argue the point in detail. The great majority of modern editors take the opposite view. Most recently, however, R. Mayer, in his commentary on *Epistles I* (Cambridge, 1994), agrees with the case set out here.

CHAPTER 5

1. The proposals by G. Jachmann, *Rheinisches Museum* 84 (1935) 193-240, were resisted by E. Reitzenstein, *Philologus*, Supplementband 29 (1936) 71-93 (repr. in W. Eisenhut (ed.) *Properz* [Darmstadt, 1975] 134-59); also by K. Barwick, *Philologus* 99 (1955) 112-32; but they are tentatively supported by P.B. Marzolla, *Maia* 7 (1955) 170-7. Neither of the two foremost experts on Propertius' text – D.R. Shackleton Bailey in *Propertiana* (Cambridge, 1956) or G.P. Goold, 'Noctes Propertianae', *Harvard Studies in Classical Philology* 71 (1966) – urges transposition. There is much to agree with in Barwick's article, which seems to have been unduly neglected.

2. Thus one might distinguish exclamations (1-10), interspersed with narrative (5-8); persuasive general assertion, supported by examples (11-16); threats (17-20); and so on, ending with exhortation (49), corroborative assertion (50) and hypothetical general statement (51-4).

3. At the start Propertius is thinking aloud, recalling his night of joy. He continues to do so at least to the end of line 8. With *quantum* (9) he has begun to address Cynthia, as is plain from *tuis* (10). But what of *quam vario amplexu mutamus bracchia* ('with how many different kinds of embrace did we shift our arms!'). These words could go either with what precedes or with what follows. There is no clear division, nor do we need one; for there is no break in thought. Again, how long does the address to Cynthia continue? In view of *tibi* (27) certainly to the end of 28. In 36 *huius* makes it clear that the direct address is finished: but *quam* (35) brings us back to *prius* (31). So the direct address must be over by the end of 30. Where exactly it finishes is not clear; nor does it matter; for again there is no break in thought. After that Propertius' observations continue to be general down to 48. But this time we encounter the opposite objection; for everyone agrees that a new thought begins in line 41.

4. It is worth recalling Housman's suggestion that the fragment of Ticida should be completed thus: *felix lectule, talibus / sole <conscie> amoribus*. The mistake would have arisen from the confusion of CI with OL. Other examples of this confusion are given by Housman, *Classical Quarterly* 1 (1907) 158.

5. The conjectures are collected by W.R. Smyth, *Thesaurus Criticus* (Leiden, 1970). *Tantum* (Camps) gives greater intensity but lacks the advantage of *secum*; *interdum* (Housman) is flat; *centum* (Smyth) does not give a proper contrast to *multus*; and *si tales iterum* (Baehrens) assumes a further stage of corruption. Surely *tales noctes* by itself may be taken to *imply* 'in the future'. In 39, however, Shackleton Bailey's *et* is an improvement on *haec* (note 1 above, 94).

6. W.A Camps' edn (Cambridge, 1966; repr. Bristol 1985); R. Hanslik edn. (Leipzig, 1979).

7. Housman's objection was this: 'The metaphor of *lucet* is poetical to a modern taste but hardly possible in a Latin writer unless there has preceded something leading up to it' (*Journal of Philology* 22 [1894] 93). One eases this difficulty by pointing to the images of light in the first half of the poem, as L. Richardson rightly does in his commentary (Oklahoma, 1977), note on line 49.

8. Richardson offers a second explanation: 'which you see drifting scattered here and there from their baskets'. But this hardly brings out the force of *natare* and it removes the image of wine, which we have argued to be part of the structure.

9. H.E. Butler and E.A. Barber *The Elegies of Propertius* (Oxford, 1933; repr. London, 2002) 216.

CHAPTER 6

1. Is Persius taking a dig at Ovid's coinage when he uses *reparabilis Echo* in *Sat.* 1.102?

2. With the reciprocal *reportat*, cf. *reddere* (361).

3. *Remittat,* another reciprocal word; cf. *responderat* (380).

4. Cf. *responsura* and *rettulit* (387).

5. For the derivation of *copia* the *Oxford Latin Dictionary* gives *con + ops* ('plenty').

6. Momentarily the *locus* (501) functions for Echo.

7. F. Goldin, *The Mirror of Narcissus in the Courtly Love Lyric* (Ithaca, NY, 1967); L. Vinge, *The Narcissus Theme* (Lund, 1967). For works on the same theme, see D. Bush, *Mythology and the Renaissance Tradition in English Poetry* (2nd edn, New York, 1963) appendixes; and D. Bush, *Mythology and the Romantic Tradition in English Poetry* (New York, 1957).

CHAPTER 7

1. Pittacus of Mitylene (*ca* 650-570 BC), a statesman and lawgiver who ranked as one of the Seven Sages. Cleanthes (331-232 BC), head of the Stoa and an uncompromising moralist.

2. The Scantinian law against sodomy was passed before 50 BC.

3. The Julian law against adultery was introduced by Augustus in 18 BC.

4. See S.F. Bonner, *Education in Ancient Rome* (London. 1977). Corporal punishment was common but the foremost educationist of his day, Quintilian, was against it for all the right reasons (*Institutio Oratoria* 1.3.13-17).

5. According to Martial 7.64, Cinnamus was given the necessary sum of 400,000 sesterces by his lady-friend in order to become a knight.

6. On the whole subject, see J.P.V.D. Balsdon, *Romans and Aliens* (London, 1979) especially 30-58.

7. See S. Treggiari, 'Lower-class Women in the Roman Economy', *Florilegium* 1 (1979) 65-86.

8. See R. Saller, *Personal Patronage Under the Early Empire* (Cambridge, 1982); Peter White, '*Amicitia* and the Profession of Poetry in Early Imperial Rome', *Journal of Roman Studies* 68 (1978) 74-92.

9. See the important paper by H.A. Mason in J.P. Sullivan (ed.), *Critical Essays in Roman Literature: Satire* (London, 1963) 93-167.
10. Cf. the *Digest* 9.3; and 44.7.5.5.
11. *Historia Augusta: Antoninus Pius* 9.1. A long section of the *Digest* (47.9) links fires and collapsing houses. Attempts to limit the height of houses to 70 feet by Augustus (Strabo 5.3.7) and to 60 feet by Trajan (Aurelius Victor, *Ep.* 13.13) were commonly evaded (Vitruvius 2,8.17). Aulus Gellius in the second century AD was one day walking up the Cispian Hill with some friends when they saw 'a tenement block out of control. It was a high building with many storeys, and everything around it was engulfed in a huge conflagration.' One of the friends remarked, 'There's a great income from city property, but the dangers are far greater. If some remedy could be invented to stop houses in Rome from catching fire so constantly (*tam adsidue* – Juvenal's very words), I'd have damned well sold my property in the country and bought in the city' (*Noctes Atticae* 15.1.2-3). As usual there is a mass of material in Mayor's commentary on Juvenal (see his notes and addenda on 3.7 and 197). For a well organised essay on the subject, see Z Yavetz, 'The Living Conditions of the Roman Plebs' repr. in R. Seager (ed.) *The Crisis of the Roman Republic* (Cambridge, 1969) 162-79. Dorothy George writes: 'Two things are conspicuous in the London of the eighteenth century. One, the number of old ruinous houses which frequently collapsed ...' (*London Life in the Eighteenth Century* [London, 1930] 73-4); earlier she speaks of 'the constant fires' (27; cf. 30).
12. A minor result was torn clothes (Juvenal 3.254). Pliny speaks of a young man whose tunic was ripped (*scissis tinicis* – Juvenal's exact words) when he was coming to hear Pliny in court. The significant phrase is *ut in frequentia solet fieri* ('as commonly happens in a crowd'; *Epistles* 4.16.2). It seems remarkable that in all Juvenal's complaints about conditions in Rome he never mentions the smells.
13. See L. Friedländer, *Roman Life and Manners Under the Early Empire*, (English tr. repr. London, 1968) vol. 4, appendix 6, 28-31. One of the exceptions concerned vehicles carrying building materials. This is relevant to Juvenal 3.254-61, lines which describe citizens being crushed to death by a load of marble.

14. The figures are given by Mason Hammond, *Journal of Roman Studies* 57 (1947) 74-81.
15. For this section, see G.W. Bowersock, *Augustus and the Greek World* (Oxford, 1971); and *The Roman World of Dio Chrysostom* (Harvard, 1978).
16. R. Syme, *Tacitus* (Oxford, 1958) vol. 2, 778.
17. For more details about Gallic rhetoricians, see M.L. Clarke, *Rhetoric at Rome* (London, 1953) 145-6. he also says more about Spain and Africa.
18. See Peter White, 'The friends of Martial, Statius and Pliny, and the Dispersal of Patronage', *Harvard Studies in Classical Philology* 79 (1975) 265-300.
19. Mason Hammond (note 14 above) 76.
20. Juvenal says that Statius goes hungry (*esurit*) unless he sells the libretto of his *Agave* to Paris. This rather woolly allegation does not actually say that Statius ever went hungry. He himself says that his family's assets were reduced by expenses (*Silvae* 5.3.117-8); but that is also too vague for critical assessment.
21. *The Vanity of Human Wishes* 349-68.

CHAPTER 8
1. Alan Hughes, in the Introduction to his commentary on the play (Cambridge, 1994) 37, speaks of 'a modern audience's resentment of classical allusions'. Perhaps he's right; but here we are concerned with the young Shakespeare, who was still in his twenties and was doubtless showing off. Greene called him 'an upstart crow'; but the taunt was something of a boomerang, because it was filched from Horace, who had warned Celsus about the danger of stolen plumage (*Epistles* 1.3.15-20). Horace himself had raided the capacious wardrobe of Aesop (Phaedrus 1.3; Babrius 72). I am not qualified to judge how far the allusions, especially in Act 1, indicate the influence of Peele. For the unhistorical history, see T.J.B. Spencer, 'Shakespeare and the Elizabethan Romans', *Shakespeare Survey* 10 (1957) 27-38.
2. The English pronunciation of 'Romulus' tends to disguise the meaning of his name, i.e. 'Roman'. (English also reverses the quantity of the e in 'Remus', which was short.)
3. Cicero, for instance, laid it down that 'the order should be morally

faultless and an example to the rest of the citizens' (*Laws* 3.28). For Rome's moral vocabulary, see D.C.Earl, *The Moral and Political Tradition of Rome* (London, 1967) index.

4. For other observations on the names, see R.A. Law, 'The Roman Background to *Titus Andronicus*', *Studies in Philology* 40 (1943) 145-53; also J. Bate in his admirable commentary on the play (London, 1995) 93-4. In this paper I adopt Bate's lineation.

5. G.K. Hunter in J.C. Gray (ed.), *Mirror up to Shakespeare* (Toronto, 1984) 184-5.

6. See Ovid, *Fasti* 2.533 ff.; and J.G. Frazer's edn, vol. 2, 431 ff.

7. The episode is referred to in Euripides, *Hecuba* 37-41 and 188-90. E. Jones, *The Origins of Shakespeare* (Oxford, 1977) 90-105, maintains that Shakespeare knew Euripides through Erasmus' Latin translation.

8. The usual form of the dictum in modern times is 'Call no man happy until he is dead'.

9. E.g. Cicero, *De Natura Deorum* 3.38 (*iustitia, quae suum cuique distribuit*): Justinian, the *Digest* (Ulpian) 1.1.10.

10. The gentle Virgil shows his unease: see *Aen.* 6.819-23. A less famous case is that of Titus Manlius, who had his son executed for disobeying orders (Livy 8.7).

11. Diana (Phoebe) was also, of course, the Moon goddess.

12. Goddesses could be cruel: Semiramis was a half-legendary Assyrian queen who used to murder her lovers (Diodorus Siculus 2.13.4); nymphs, too, could be dangerous, as Hylas found (Apollonius Rhodius, *Argonautica* 1.1207 ff.); the Sirens need no comment.

13. Virgil, *Aen.* 4.173 ff., the original source, mentions no house.

14. A.B. Taylor, *Shakespeare's Ovid* (Cambridge, 2001) 66.

15. D. Willbern's paper, *English Literary Renaissance* 8 (1978) 159-82 (cited by Bate [note 4 above] 9, note 1) was not available to me; but see H. James, *Themes in Drama* 13 (1991) 128-9.

16. Other examples are the plays on 'hand' in Act 3, Sc. 1. One is reminded of Dryden's complaint that Ovid was 'frequently witty out of season' (W.P. Ker [ed.] *Essays of John Dryden* [Oxford, 1900] vol. 1, 234; cf. vol. 2, 256-7).

17. P. Legouis, *Shakespeare Survey* 28 (1975) 73, cites a Latin translation of Dionysius of Halicarnassus, *The Roman Antiquities*

5.3.2, which had *omnium rerum necessarium indigens* ('lacking all necessities'), though the idea was already in Livy.

18. Maxwell points out that here Shakespeare is drawing on Ovid's description of the bovine Io, who *printed* her name in the *sande with her foote* (Golding, 1.804-5; Ovid, *Met.*1.649 had *in pulvere* – 'in the dust'). A little earlier (1.635-6), Ovid's Io tried to stretch out her arms (*bracchia*) but had no arms to stretch out. Golding, significantly, has 'handes' (1.788-9); cf. *Titus Andronicus*, Act 2. Sc. 3, 6-7.

19. In another work (*Epistles* 107.11), Seneca translates some lines of the Stoic Cleanthes beginning *duc, o parens celsique dominator poli* ('lead me, o Father, ruler of high heaven'). This was not part of a play, and both thought and context were quite different. Yet in view of *dominator poli* one ought not to rule out a possible influence on our passage.

20. The usual reading is *Mauris* ('Moorish javelins'); but the grammar's *Mauri* suited Shakespeare very well.

21. The Giant Enceladus' part in the revolt against Jupiter is mentioned in Horace, *Odes* 3.4.56; he was struck down by a thunderbolt and imprisoned under Sicily (Apollodorus 1.6.2 [J.G. Frazer, Loeb edn]) or under Etna (Virgil, *Aen.* 3.578-80). Typhon, offspring of Tartarus and Earth, also took part in the attack (Apollodorus 1.6.3); he fathered various monsters, e.g, the Chimaera and the Sphinx (see Apollodorus, [Loeb edn] vol. 2, index). He is said to have suffered the same fate as Enceladus.

22. Apollodorus, 1.1.5-7 (J.G. Frazer, Loeb edn).

23. For other representations see J.D. Reid, *The Oxford Guide to Classical Mythology in the Arts, 1300-1900*, (Oxford, 1993) vol. 2, 1068-70.

24. In Act 3, Sc. 1, 16-22 Titus is explicitly referring to the sequence of the seasons, not to the myth of metals; so 'eternal springtime' (21) can be no more than an ironical glance at Ovid's *ver erat aeternum* (*Met.*1.107). In line 48 of this scene the sequence, I take it, is: 'We are not large like cedars or giants, but in our determination we are solid steel, though our sufferings are intolerable. And since there's no justice here, we will approach heaven'. The phrase 'metal, steel to the very back' is a boast (see Lyly, *Euphues*, in R.W. Bond (ed.), *Complete Works* (Oxford, 1902) vol. l, 207; also all the passages noted in Tilley S842; and *OED steel*, senses 1a and 1f). The reference to the power of shrubs *vis-à-vis* cedars is straightforward, as in *The Rape of Lucrece* 664-5 (even though Tilley's references at C208 show that paradoxically the shrub was sometimes judged the stronger). The expression, then, is surely favourable; so it cannot refer to the iron age. Undue emphasis, I think, is given to the myth by R.S. Miola, *Shakespeare's Rome* (Cambridge, 1983) ch. 3 (which is otherwise perceptive).

25. This version, *pace* Maxwell, is not in Florus 1.17.24, which says only that Appius *intended* to debauch the girl (*stupro destinaret*); for further evidence, see H. Nørgaard, *English Studies* 45 (1964) 140.

26. So Bate (note 4 above) 13-15, rightly; but 'unkindly banished, / The gates shut on me, and turned weeping out / To beg relief among Rome's enemies' (103-5) also reminds us, disturbingly, of an earlier exile (Act 3, Sc. 1, 299).

CHAPTER 9

1. Lineation is that of the Quiller-Couch and Dover Wilson edn (Cambridge, 1962).

2. If we are willing to believe that the sonnet is by Shakespeare, it would appear that he was led to use the word 'tarriance' because he found it in Golding. It occurs again only in *Two Gentlemen of Verona* Act 2, Sc. 7, 90.

3. H.J. Oliver, in his commentary (Oxford, 1982), thinks Shakespeare probably 'pictures Jove as humbling himself before Europa after they arrive in Crete'. That is not what happens in Shakespeare's source. Ovid says that in Sidon the bull 'kissed her hands' (*Met.* 2.863). Their arrival in Crete is recorded in *Met.* 3.2 and that is the end of the story. No one kisses the Cretan strand with his knees or anything else. Back in Sidon, Europa's brother Cadmus is sent off to find her; and that is all we hear about Europa. After many wanderings, Cadmus is told by Apollo to follow a heifer and, where she lies down, to found a city (Thebes). In this, quite separate, narrative it is the heifer that, in Golding's words, 'kneelde down' (*Met.* 3.28); Ovid says *procubuit* ('lay down'). And it is Cadmus who 'did kisse the ground' (Golding 3.30; Ovid 3.24-5). It may be that that these references make Shakespeare's confusion or conflation more interesting; but they do nothing to remove it.

4. The greeting goes back to *Odyssey* 6.149-59.

5. William Lily, *A Shorte Introduction of Grammar* (with introduction by Vincent J. Flynn [New York, 1945]). The phrase is quoted under *Ablativus post verbum* some twenty pages from the end (the pages are not numbered).

CHAPTER 10

1. Thomas Warton simply observes that 'the close of the sonnet is perfectly in the style of Horace and the Grecian lyrics' (*Poems Upon Several Occasions* by John Milton [London, 1785] 362).

2. T. Keightley, *Poems of Milton* (London, 1859) vol. 1, 160.

3. D. Masson, *The Poetical Works of John Milton* (London, 1882) vol 3, 294.

4. F. Neiman, 'Milton's *Sonnet* XX [= 17 Carey]', *Proceedings of the Modern Language Association* 64 (1949) 480-83. In agreeing with Keightley, Neiman was supported by E. Jackson, *PMLA* 65 (1950) 328-9.

5. *The Poems of Milton* (New York, 1972) vol. 2, part 2, 474-5. Woodhouse claimed the support of a dozen scholars from Masson on; and D. Bush, in the same volume (475-6) mentioned an equal number in favour of 'spare time'.

6. J. Carey, *The Poems of John Milton* (London and New York, 1968) 410. This position was also taken by G. Campbell, *John Milton, the Complete Poems* (London, 1980) 504.

7. S. Fish, *Is There a Text in This Class?* (Cambridge, Mass. and London, 1980) 151.

8. Does the same reasoning apply to 'walking not unseen / By hedgerow elms' (*L'Allegro*, 57-8); to 'Baited with reasons not unplausible' (*Comus*, 162); and to 'Be not unlike all others' (*Samson Agonistes*, 815)?

9. J.A.W. Bennett, *Times Literary Supplement* (5 April 1963) 233. The distich was well known in the Middle Ages. Prof. John Burrow refers me to Langland, *Piers Plowman,* B-Text, Passus 12.23, where, in answering the charge of writing poetry when he might be saying his prayers, the poet quotes the first line of the distich. Other references are given in G. Olson, *Literature as Recreation in the Late Middle Ages* (Ithaca, NY and London, 1982) 94, note 6.

Cf. 100, note.10 (Roger Bacon); 114, note 36 (John Mason); 122 (Gace de la Buigne); and 140, note16 (a French translation of the distich). The Middle English translation renders the first line thus: 'Sumtyme among thi bysynesse / Melle solace, gamete and ioyowsnesse (94).

10. J.C. Maxwell, *Times Literary Supplement* (26 April 1963) 314.

11. V. Scholderer, *Times Literary Supplement* (10 May 1963) 341.

12. J.C. Maxwell, *Times Literary Supplement* (17 May 1963) 357.

13. D. Bush, *The Complete Poetical Works of John Milton* (Boston, 1965) 199.

14. E.J. Honigmann, *Milton's Sonnets* (London and New York, 1966) 180-1.

15. J.S. Smart, *The Sonnets of Milton* (Glasgow, 1921) 110-15, argued convincingly that the recipient was Edward Lawrence (b. 1633, elected to the House of Commons 1656, d.1657) and not his brother Henry. His seriousness of mind is illustrated by the letters which he received from Oldenburg, quoted in Smart's appendix, 166 ff.

16. Similarly, Milton's Pyrrha is 'Plain in [her] neatness' (5), while Horace's is *simplex munditiis* (*Odes* 1.5.5). According to Masson, Milton printed the reading *munditie* opposite to his translation in the edition of 1673.

17. *Oxford Latin Dictionary*, *aliquando*, sense 4.

18. At the end of an invitation satire Juvenal puts the point thus: *voluptates commendat rarior usus* ('pleasures are the keener for being less frequent'; *Sat.*11.208). However, that goes a step beyond Milton, in that it gives restraint a hedonistic basis.

CHAPTER 11

1. Quotations are from W.P. Ker's edn of the essays (Oxford, 1902) vol. 2,

2. The fourth book of the *Odes*, which contains the attack on Lyce, was published over fifteen years after the *Satires*. The same historical error is repeated on p. 101, where Dryden associates himself with Holyday's view that 'there was never such a fall as from his *Odes* to his *Satires*'. A similar point occurs in connection with Persius. On p. 70 Dryden says that Persius' words are 'not everywhere well chosen, the purity of Latin being more corrupted than in the time of Juvenal'. This implies that Persius came after Juvenal, which is an odd mistake, given that Persius died in AD 62 – a date very close to Juvenal's birth. Presumably this was just a slip; for on p.103 we are told that, in treating only one main subject in each satire, 'Juvenal ... has chosen to follow the same method as Persius'.

3. *Epode* 6 is aimed at a cowardly libeller. Cassius, who fearlessly denounced men and women of high rank (Tacitus, *Annals* 1.72), died about AD 34, over sixty years after the poem was written.

4. Cf. E.J. Kenney, *Proceedings of the Cambridge Philological Association* n.s. 8 (1962) 38.

5. E.g. the article in the first edn of the *Oxford Classical Dictionary*, which says 'Horace's humour ... is directed against ... foibles rather than vices'.

6. Cf. N. Rudd, *Lines of Enquiry* (Cambridge, 1976) 54-83.

7. W.S. Anderson, *Classical Philology* 57 (1962) 145-60, reminds us that not all of Juvenal's satires are prompted by indignation.

8. Cf. D.E. Eichholz, *Greece & Rome* n.s. 3 (1956) 61-9; J. Butt and M. Lascelles in their contributions to *New Light on Dr Johnson,* ed. F.W. Hilles (Yale, 1959); and especially H.A. Mason in J.P Sullivan (ed.), *Critical Essays on Roman Literature: Satire* (London, 1963) 107-23.

9. Zimri is chosen by Dryden himself as an example of fine raillery. The nearest equivalent to Horace is the thumb-nail sketch of Tigellinus in *Sat.* 1.3-19.

10. For Domitian's fly-catching, see Suetonius, *Domitian* 3.1 (Loeb edn) vol. 2, 344.

11. Suetonius, *Divus Augustus* 54-5 (Loeb edn) vol. 1, 208-11; Dio, 55.4.2-4.

12. The shafts directed at Sextus Pompeius and the forces of Antony and Cleopatra in *Epode* 9 and the celebration of Cleopatra's defeat in *Odes* 1.37 fall outside the domain of *satura.*

13. R. Syme, *Tacitus* (Oxford, 1958) vol. 2, 778.

14. The tradition that Juvenal was exiled is no longer regarded as reliable; see E. Courtney's commentary on Juvenal (London, 1980) 5-8.

15. G. Highet, *Juvenal the Satirist* (Oxford, 1954) 51.

CHAPTER 12

1. For patronage, see M. Griffin, '*De Beneficiis* and Roman Society', *Journal of Roman Studies* 93 (2003) 92-113, which includes references to Brunt, White, Saller and earlier studies. When reading of different models, e.g. 'vertical' and 'horizontal' types of patronage, one has to bear in mind that the nature of a relationship could change, as it did in the case of Maecenas and Horace. It is also worth observing that Horace never refers to his patron as *patronus* but usually as *amicus* (sometimes *pater* or *rex*). He himself is never a *cliens*; that term is applied to men of lower status, like Volteius Mena.

2. For what is known about Maecenas, see Pauly-Wissowa, *Real-Encyclopädie* (Stuttgart, 1893-) 27A, 207-29. There is a good short account in K. Reckford, *Transactions and Proceedings of the American Philological Association* 90 (1959) 95 ff. For Maecenas' Greek, see Horace, *Odes* 3.8.5 – *doctus utriusque linguae* ('learned in either language'); and for his intellectual curiosity, Pliny, *Natural History*, Prefaces to Books 9 and 37. His *Symposium* is mentioned by Servius on Virgil, *Aeneid* 8.310; his *Prometheus* by Seneca, *Epistulae Morales* (Loeb edn) vol. 1, 19.9; the work *De Cultu Suo* ('On his Dress'), mentioned by the Loeb editor, is not reliably attested. For his jewelled verse, see E. Courtney, *The Fragmentary Latin Poets* (Oxford, 1993) 276-7 (no. 2); for Augustus' teasing, Macrobius, *Saturnalia* 2.4.12; and for his decadence, Seneca, *Epistulae Morales* (Loeb edn) vol. 3, 114.4-8

3. For the property of men proscribed, see Scholiast on Juvenal, 5.3 (Favonius); and for property in Egypt, Pauly-Wissowa (note 2 above) 216. His presence with Octavian at Mutina etc. is recorded by Propertius, 2.1.27-34; and Lepidus' rebellion by Velleius, 2.88.2-3, by Appian, *Bellum Civile* 4.50, by Dio 54.15.4 and by Suetonius, *Divus Augustus* 19.1.

4. The marriage to Scribonia was at a time when Octavian was seeking to strengthen his ties with Sextus Pompeius; Scribonia was the sister of Sextus' father-in-law (R. Syme, *The Augustan Aristocracy* [Oxford 1986] 248). For the emperor ill and the imperial residence, see Suetonius, *Divus Augustus* 72.2 and 73.1 respectively; and for Maecenas' influence, Dio 55.7.1-3.

5. On his mansion, see Horace, *Odes* 3.29.10; his walk and his eunuchs, Seneca, *Epistulae Morales* (Loeb edn) vol. 3, 114.4 and 6; his litter, Juvenal, *Sat.* 1.65-6; pool, Dio 55.7.6; clothes, Seneca, (as above) 6; baby donkey, Pliny, *Natural History* 8.170; bisexuality (male), Tacitus, *Annals* 1.54 and (female), Plutarch, *Amatorius* (Loeb edn) vol. 9, 370-1.

6. For his insomnia, see Seneca, *Moral Essays* (Loeb edn) 1.1.3.10; for his fever, Pliny, *Natural History* 7.172; and illness, Horace, *Odes* 2.17.22-5 (with Nisbet-Hubbard). The plot against Augustus appears in Dio 54.3.4-5 and Suetonius, *Divus Augustus*, 66.3. On his wife, see Seneca (as above) and *Epistulae Morales* (Loeb edn) vol. 3, 114.7 – *morosa* ('difficult to please'); on his possible disappointment, Dio 54.6.5; on Augustus' defence of him, Dio 54.30.4; and on Augustus' grief, Dio 55.7.1 and 5.

7. Augustus himself intimated (Suetonius, *Horace* [Loeb edn] vol. 2, 486-8 and 484-6); Maecenas had asserted (Courtney [note 2 above] 278 (no. 4).

8. As for hostile readers, an early example is *Sat.* 1.2.25, where Maltinus (formed from *malta*, 'an effeminate type') was said to be a cover name for Maecenas. Aristippus, the hedonistic philosopher, a contemporary of Socrates, is mentioned in *Epistles* 1.1.18-19, 13.7 and 17.23; see the edn by R. Mayer, (Cambridge, 1994), with his introduction, p. 44.

9. Bentley rejected *vulpecula* on the grounds that foxes do not eat grain. His conjecture, *nitedula* ('dormouse'), was silently adopted by Pope in his imitation; but *vulpecula* was restored to the text of 1740. Shackleton Bailey (Teubner text, 1985) printed Giangrande's *cornicula* ('a little crow'). But Horace's fox is that of fable, not of zoology, and that greedy animal would eat grapes (Babrius 19, Phaedrus 4.3) and cheese (Babrius 77, Phaedrus 1.13). Moreover, in Babrius 86, which is virtually the same story as ours, a fox gets stuck after eating meat and *bread*. See also A.S.F. Gow's note on Theocritus 1.51 in vol. 2 of his commentary (Cambridge, 1952) p. 12. For the Homeric precedent, see *Odyssey*, 4.601-8.

10. Notes on Horace's text: **46.** Syme (note 4 above) 490, records three men called Lucius Marcius Philippus. The first two (consuls in 91 and 56 BC respectively) may be too early. The third (consul in 38 BC) was Augustus' step-brother and held a triumph from Spain in 33 (Syme 403-4); there was also a Quintus Marcius Philippus

(Syme 28, note 111). Whatever Horace's intention, Roman readers after 20 BC would probably have identified his Philippus with one of the above. *48.* The *Carinae* ('Keels' or 'Hulls') was a wealthy residential area on the Esquiline. *76.* The Latin holiday occurred in the spring.

11. The dedication of the first book of epistles at 1.1 reads *prima dicte mihi, summa dicende Camena* ('Named in my earliest verse, you must be named in my last'); in line 105 Horace is still *de te pendentis, te respicientis amici* ('The friend who looks to you for support and protection') – by now perhaps a piece of affectionate hyperbole. In his last book of odes (4.11.17-20): Horace celebrates 12 April as the occasion 'which is almost more special than my own birthday, because from this bright day Maecenas counts the course of his years'. For the instruction to the emperor, see Suetonius, *Horace* (Loeb edn) vol. 2, 484-5.

12. My chief sources for this section are I. Ehrenpreis, *Swift*, 3 vols. (London, 1962-83), L.A. Landa, *Swift and the Church of Ireland* (Oxford, 1965) and D. Nokes, *Jonathan Swift* (Oxford, 1985). Fourteen was not wholly exceptional; in 1745 Burke entered at the same age. There is a malicious story that, presenting himself for an M.A. in Oxford, Swift said that *speciali gratia* meant 'with special merit'.

13. On Temple's disenchantment, see Ehrenpreis (note 12 above) 1.99-100; and on Epicurus, 118; on his praise of Horace, Ehrenpreis 121.

14. On his mission to King William, see Ehrenpreis (note 12 above) 1.144. For Kilroot, see Landa (note 12 above) 18-24; and for Milne, Landa 12-15. My quotations come from the local booklet entitled *A Short History of the Parish of Kilroot,* notes for the years 1683 and 1695.

15. For the post at Canterbury or Westminster, see Ehrenpreis (note 12 above) 1.260-61 and Landa 44-64; on the deanship of Derry, Ehrenpreis 2.10-11 and Landa 29-30; on Laracor, Ehrenpreis 2.13-15 and Landa 36-41; and on appointment as prebend of St Patrick's, Landa 44-51.

16. For First Fruits, see Nokes (note 12 above) 53-115 and Landa 44-64. On Harley's effusive reception of Swift, note: 'He knew my Christian name very well' – *Journal*, ed. H. Williams, 1.46; in his tutorial to Ulysses on legacy-hunting (Horace, *Satires* 2.5.32-3)

Tiresias stresses that *gaudent praenomine molles / auriculae* ('sensitive ears like to hear their own first names'). On Harley's promise, Ehrenpreis 2.403 and Landa 65.

17. Addison to Swift – *Correspondence*, ed. H. Williams, 1.161-2. Pythagoras forbade the eating of beans, allegedly on the grounds that they contained souls.

18. Letter to Lord Halifax – *Correspondence*, ed. H. Williams, 1.142-3; later he adds 1.158-9.

19. 'I entirely submit ...' – *Correspondence* 1.288; 'I have many friends ...' – *Journal,* 22 Oct. 1711.

20. On the threat of dissenters: Swift's position was that of Fielding's Mr Thwackum: 'When I mention religion, I mean the Christian religion; and not only the Christian religion, but the Protestant religion; and not only the Protestant religion, but the Church of England' (*Tom Jones*, Book 3, 3). 'The greatest rake in England': *DNB* XX, 1329 For Swift's reporting of the Gloucester Cathedral incident and his declaration against Wharton, see *Prose Works*, ed. H. Davis 3.57 and 179 respectively.

21. 'Look down, St Patrick ...' in Landa p. xiv and Nokes (note 12 above) 187. For Archbishop King, see Ehrenpreis (note 12 above) 2.662 and Landa p. xiv. 'The great fish' – *Correspondence* 3.329; 'sinking into utter oblivion' – *Correspondence* 1.379. In connection with Swift and Juvenal it is worth recalling that J.V. Luce, *Hermathena* 104 (1967) 78-81, showed that the words *Libertatis Vindicatorem* on Swift's epitaph are derived from Dryden's *Discourse Concerning the Original and Progress of Satire* (W.P. Ker [Oxford 1926] vol. 2, 87), not from any classical source.

22. Notes on Swift's text, which follows that of Pat Rogers (Penguin Books,1983): *1. Support:* Horace had called Maecenas 'the support (*columen*) of his fortunes' (*Odes* 2.17.4). *3-4:* In two famous odes Horace had urged Maecenas to forget for a while his **cares** about home and foreign affairs (3.8.17-24 and 3.29.25-8). Philippus, however, was just a busy lawyer. *6. Cheapening:* bargaining. Collecting books was Swift's one extravagance. *7. Pretty well in case:* as we would say 'in pretty good shape'. *10. Spleen:* morose temper or melancholy. An amusing lie. *14. Mischief:* an interestingly ambiguous word. By now it could mean 'playful malice', but the traditional sense of 'harm' allows a more serious charge. *Meat:* pronounced 'mate', as tea was 'tay'. *15. Crack a jest:* the jest turns out to be a lot more than a harmless prank. *16. Lewis;* Erasmus Lewis (1670-1745), once Harley's private secretary, now a kind of confidential agent. He was in a totally different class from Philippus' slave. Pope says he was rather fat. His role here may well have a basis in fact; for it seems to have been Lewis who told Swift that Harley was eager to see him (Ehrenpreis [note 12 above] 2.392, note 2). *17. An arrant shaver:* a cunning rogue. *19-22:* In fact Harley had first met Swift three years earlier. *26-46:* We must imagine that all this information is imparted by the Dean to a perfect stranger. The picture offers a piquant contrast to Horace's part-time auctioneer. *27-30:* a piece of wry self knowledge. *30. Betimes:* perhaps 'at the earliest opportunity'. *36. Wharton;* Thomas Warton (1648-1715); a year earlier, in *Toland's Invitation to Dismal to Dine with the Calves' Head Club*, an Imitation of Horace, *Epistles* 1.5, we are told that Wharton will attend the function 'unless prevented by a whore' (line 35). Other examples of Swift's attacks have been referred to above. After April 1706 he acted with the Junta (see on line 38 below). *37. The faction;* the *Whigs.* *38. The Junta;* a group of leading Whigs including Somers, Halifax, and Sunderland, whom Swift had courted before becoming a Tory. *40:* The admission would have pleased Swift's friends. *43. The paper-stamp:* a duty introduced in 1712 to suppress political attacks. *46:* In 1713 Swift was very far from retiring as a pamphleteer. *56:* Quite close to the epistle (63-4), where Horace's slave puts his own gloss on the information – a gloss designed to flatter and annoy his superior. *60. Painted monsters;* second-rate, incompetent art. Was Swift thinking of the monstrous picture in Horace's *Ars Poetica* 1-5? *64. Came sneaking to the chariot-side:* a vivid combination of guilt and servility. *67-70:* The broken syntax cleverly echoes Swift's stammering excuses. *74. Commons:* meals. *75. Displayed his talent:* amusingly parallels Horace's tactless chatterer – *dicenda tacenda locutus* ('Having said things which should and should not be spoken'; 72). *77:* cf. 'I soon grew **domestic** with Lord Halifax' – *Journal*, 2 Oct. 1710. *80. 'Gudgeon':* more vivid than Horace's *piscis*; but Swift omits Horace's *decurrere* ('hurried'). Honours even. *84. A canon:* Up to a very late point a place in

Windsor seemed to be a possibility ('The dispute is Windsor or St Patrick's' – *Journal*, 15 April). *86. Never to reside:* an amusing touch of candour. *88. You shall be a dean:* as if Harley had simply to say the word. *89-93:* a comically optimistic vision. For Swift's power-struggles, see Landa (note 12 above) ch. 2. *98. Demurely:* From 1687 *OED* quotes 'He look'd so demurely I thought butter would not have melted in his mouth'. Another piece of self-satire. *99. The silver virge:* a rod about three feet long, which was carried in front of the dean by a virger (*sic*). Swift's may be the virge still in use. *101:* The vexations are all financial. The church suffered from the impropriations of Henry VIII (Landa [note 12 above] 165-5). Clergymen complained that their rents and leases were unfairly low in comparison with those of lay landlords (Landa 103). Swift pursued these grievances in a series of tracts between 1723 and 1736 (Landa 97). *Patents*: certificates of (here unspecified) rights. *Abjurations*: oaths making (here unspecified) renunciations. *103. First-fruits:* These taxes have been mentioned above in the introductory remarks. *Chapter-treats*: presumably expenses incurred in entertaining the canons. *109. The farmers:* Swift complains that the poorest cottier and the most substantial farmer alike regularly take advantage of the clergyman, who is lucky if he receives half of his legal tithes (Landa [note 12 above] 153). *111. Parvisol:* Swift's debt-collector. He was clearly inefficient, but Swift had darker suspicions: 'I look upon him as a knave' – *Correspondence*, ed. H. Williams, 2.48; cf. 1.389 and 2.30). Apparently sums due to Swift were cancelled out by bills. *117-18:* The imaginary gallop manages to ignore the Irish Sea. *120. Old Read:* Harley's doorman 'celebrated for his mendacity' (Ehrenpreis [note 12 above] 2.393). He was only carrying out the kind of instruction that Swift sometimes gave to the dreaded Patrick, as in the case of Leach, the printer: 'I have ordered Patrick to deny me to him from henceforth' – *Journal*, 1.179). *125-9:* a very Swiftian type of teasing. *138:* a final piece of fantasy: the idea that Swift would ever have wished to revert to being a vicar. **23.** 'I have been used barbarously ...', quoted by Ehrenpreis (note 12 above) 2.620. For the thousand pounds, see Ehrenpreis 2.662 and Nokes (note 12 above) 189. **24.** 'I take the liberty ...' – *Correspondence* 2.293-4. For the translation of Horace, *Odes* 3.2.14-34, see P. Rogers (Penguin Books, 1983) 170-1. On material hidden in French archives and Oxford's deception, see Ehrenpreis (note 12 above) 3.9-10 and 2.285 (with 3.23-5) respectively.

25. In the Dublin of the 1930s it was still common to hear a lout described as 'a Yahoo'.

CHAPTER 13

1. G. Sherburn (ed.), *The Correspondence of Alexander Pope* (Oxford, 1956) vol. 3, 416-17.

2. Sherburn (note 1 above) 423.

3. This light-hearted exaggeration was prompted, no doubt, by the epigram in which Catullus greeted the appearance on Cinna's *Zmyrna* nine years after its inception (95).

4. This is a witty extension of Horace's statement that Lucilius confided personal details to his book (*Sat.* 2.1.30-1). In Persius 1.120 the original text probably ran *auriculas asini quis non habet?* (Who doesn't have an ass's ears?'), taking up *quis non* form line 7. A commentator, to explain the reference, then added *Mida Rex* above *quis non?* There is a tradition, however, that the process ran the other way and that *quis non?* was substituted for *Mida Rex* to avoid offending Nero.

5. Chaucer, *The Wife of Bath's Tale*, 95-126; Dryden 165-200.

6. I.e. 'Stand close to the animal's head'.

7. M. Mack, *The Garden and the City* (London, 1969) index, 322, under 'George II'.

8. 'Floppy' is a tr. of Horace's *cognomen* Flaccus; it is playfully contrasted with *attentam* ('pricked-up').

9. T.E. Maresca, *Pope's Horatian Poems* (Ohio State University Press, 1966) 95.

10. Ovid may have put Pope in mind of one of the passages cited by Butt.

11. The phrasing of 117 looks like an extension of Horace, *Epistles* 1.19.41-2, where the poet modestly refuses to recite his works in public; he will not 'assign weight to things of no substance' (*nugis addere pondus*). A conceited writer might, therefore, be said to tip the balance in his own favour by assigning weight to his empty compositions.

12. G. Sherburn, *Pope's Early Career* (Oxford, 1934) 30-3.
13. See Butt's note on p.127.
14. Unfortunately at *Sat* 2.1.70 the Twickenham edn prints *atquae* instead of *atque*. There are some twenty errors in the Latin text which it provides with the *Imitations*.

CHAPTER 14
1. See J.G.F. Powell (ed.), *Cicero, Cato Maior De Senectute*, Cambridge, 1988, section 73.

CHAPTER 15
1. According to Edmund Gosse, *Encyclopaedia Britannica* (eleventh edn), Tennyson told him that he had recited all Horace's *Odes* before going to Cambridge at the age of eighteen. Others say he performed the feat before going to Louth at the age of six; see Charles Tennyson, *Alfred Tennyson* (London, 1949) 24; T. Redpath in Hallam Tennyson (ed.), *Studies in Tennyson* (London, 1981) 105.
2. Arthur Coleridge in N. Page (ed.), *Tennyson: Interviews and Recollections* (London, 1983) 174; cf. *Tennyson and his Friends*, ed. Hallam, Lord Tennyson (London, 1911) 265. In 1867 F.T. Palgrave writes of a walking holiday with Tennyson: 'If not *noctes cenaeque deum*, the half-hours of talk or reading Horace together ... were hardly less divine'; see Page (above) 18. The Latin phrase 'nights and dinners of the gods' is from Horace, *Sat.* 2.6.65 – a passage of some relevance to this discussion (see note 8 below).
3. H.G. Dakyns in Hallam (note 2 above) 194.
4. H.M. Butler in Page (note 2 above) 46.
5. In the opening lines the first iambic is replaced by a trochee: 'Come, when no graver cares employ, / Godfather, come and see your boy'. As Tennyson recited poetry in a declamatory semi-chanting style, he probably sounded many of the opening feet as spondees.
6. Information about earlier drafts is drawn from C.B. Ricks's superb edn.
7. The fashionable hill town of Tusculum was reputedly founded by Telegonus, son of Odysseus and Circe. He unwittingly killed his father.
8. 'Falling' was substituted for 'mellowing' – a clear improvement;

but Tennyson may have been sorry to relinquish 'mellowing'; for, according to C.V. Stanford in Page (note 2 above) 129, the poet's favourite line was 'the mellow ouzel fluted in the elm' (*The Gardener's Daughter* 93).

9. The association of ode and satire was natural enough, since both were about leaving the strain of Rome for the peace of the Sabine hills.

10. At the risk of reviving the spirit of Churton Collins, I would mention that Horace has a neighbour who, like Tennyson's 'garrulous magpie', chatters *(garrit*; 77).

11. See F. Maurice, *The Life of Frederick Denison Maurice* (London, 1884) vol. 2, 17-18.

12. Maurice (note 11 above) 148 and 412-14.

13. Maurice (note 11 above) 618.

14. 'On Eternal Life and Eternal Death' in E.F. Carpenter (ed.), *Theological Essays* (London, 1957) 302-25.

15. J.S. Mill, *Autobiography*, ed. J.M. Robson (Harmondsworth, 1989) 124-6.

16. Maurice (note11 above) 162; see also 143.

17. Farringford, near Freshwater Bay at the south-western end of the Isle of Wight, was originally a medium-size late Georgian house of yellow brick. It was modified before – and during – Tennyson's occupancy. It has also been extended in recent times and is now a hotel, though Tennyson's library has been retained and there are a few interesting memorabilia. I have not expanded on trivial resemblances between the two men: both Horace and Tennyson were genial hosts; both became increasingly uneasy in the city; both extended their premises; and both enjoyed writing in a summer-house. There is no evidence that Tennyson thought of Farringford, in the way Pope thought of his house at Twickenham, as a modern counterpart of Horace's estate.

18. J.B. Steane, *Tennyson* (London, 1966) 146.

19. Wilfrid Ward in Page (note 2 above) 102.

20. Goldwin Smith, 'The War Passages in *Maud*' in J.D. Jump (ed..), *Tennyson: The Critical Heritage* (London, 1967) 187.

21. Maurice (note11 above) 643.

22. This was the vantage point from which Nero is supposed to have watched the great fire.

23. Horace, *Sat.* 2.7.118; *Epistles* 1.14.2-3.
24. Maecenas came from Arretium in Etruria. Augustus once addressed him facetiously as (amongst other things) *ebur ex Etruria* ('Etruscan ivory') and *berylle Porsenae* ('Porsena's beryl); see Macrobius, *Sat.* 2.4.12. *Tyrrhenus,* the Greek adjective for 'Etruscan' was often used by Latin poets.
25. Cf. the end of *Odes* 2.1, 3.3, 3.5 and 4.2.
26. Virgil, *Aen.* 4.653.

CHAPTER 16
1. Denis de Rougemont, *Love in the Western World*, tr. M. Belgion (rev. edn, New York, 1965) 75; E.R Curtius, *European Literature and the Latin Middle Ages* (London, 1953) 588; C.S. Lewis, *The Allegory of Love* (Oxford, 1936; repr. 1959) 4; Gilbert Highet, *The Classical Tradition* (repr. Oxford, 1959) 57.
2. Roger Boase, *The Origin and Meaning of Courtly Love* (Manchester, 1977).
3. E.g. Alan R. Press, *Anthology of Troubadour Lyric Poetry* (Edinburgh, 1971); R.T. Hill and T.G. Bergin, *Anthology of the Provençal Troubadours*, (rev. edn, Yale, 1973); Frederick Goldin, *Lyrics of the Troubadours and Trouvères* (New York, 1973). Sometimes one can assess the range of individual writers; see, e.g., R.T. Perkins (ed.), *The Songs of Jaufré Rudel* (Toronto, 1978); J. Linskill (ed.), *The Poems of Raimbaut de Vaqueiras* (The Hague, 1964); W.P. Shepard and F.M. Chambers (eds), *The Poems of Aimeric de Péguilhan* (Illinois, 1950). Having no facility in Provençal, I rely heavily on translations.
4. *Farai un vers, pos mi sonelh*; and *Pus vezem de novel florir.*
5. *Pus mos coratges s'esclarzis.*
6. *Era. m platz, Giraut de Borneilh.*
7. *Cantarai d'aquestz trobadors.*
8. *Clergue si fan pastor.*
9. *Be m degra de chantar tener.* The variety of the troubadours' poetry is brought out in L.T. Topsfield, *Troubadours and Love* (Cambridge, 1975).
10. Louis Gillet, *Dante* 22; K. Weinhold, *Die deutschen Frauen in dem Mittelalter* 181 – as quoted by R. Briffault, *The Troubadours* (Bloomington, 1965) 103.

11. D.W. Robertson Jr. and John F. Benton in F.X. Newman (ed.), *The Meaning of Courtly Love* (New York, 1968).
12. These arguments are taken from Roger Boase (note 2 above). See also J.M. Ferrante and G.D. Economou (eds), *In Pursuit of Perfection* (New York, 1975), introduction, 3.
13. Meg Bogin, *The Women Troubadours* (Scarborough, 1976) 13-14. She points out that all these ladies were aristocrats. They wrote in a plainer, less formal style than the men.
14. These points were made by Vernon Lee (Violet Paget), *Euphorion* (London, 1885) vol. 2, 145. Occasionally a husband is actually referred to; see, for instance, Raimbaut de Vaqueiras (note 3 above), nos. 3.26 and 6.15. Caution, however, is advisable; see P. Dronke (note 25 below) 46 ff.
15. Andreas Capellanus, *De Amore*, S. Battaglia (ed., Rome, 1947) 180; the passage comes at the end of the seventh dialogue.
16. 'I deem myself richly rewarded by the inspiration I owe to the love I bear my lady, and I ask no love in return ... . Had she granted me her supreme favours, both she and I would have been defiled by the act.' – Guiraut Riquier (1230-92), quoted by R. Briffault (note10 above) 151-2: 'He knows little or nothing of the service of women who wishes to possess his lady entirely. That is not the service of women when such becomes a reality, nor does one yield one's heart for the sake of reward.' – Daude de Pradas (1214-82), quoted by A.J. Denomy, *The Heresy of Courtly Love* (Gloucester, Mass., 1965) 24. That poem presents a piquant contrast between courtly love and sensual gratification. For its text and French tr., see A.H. Schutz (ed.), *Poésies de Daude de Pradas* (Paris, 1933) no.14.
17. E.g. Bernart de Ventadorn, *Lancan vei la folha* 49-50; Peire d'Alvernha, *Ab fina joia comenssa* 17-24.
18. *Non es meravelha s' eu chan* 23-30 (tr. Goldin); cf. Reinmar (end of 12th century), *Der lange süeze kumber mîn*, quoted by F. Goldin, *In Pursuit of Perfection* (note 12 above) 78.
19. Cercamon, *Quant l'aura doussa s'amarizis* 57-8 (tr. Goldin).
20. Andreas Capellanus 2.2 (tr. J.J. Parry [New York, 1959] 153).
21. Parry (note 20 above) 158.
22. Parry (note 20 above) 167.

23. The crucial question is not whether the lyrics contained conventional thoughts and expressions (they clearly did); nor how far the noble ladies of Provence were given to adulterous affairs; but in how many cases the troubadour expected an amatory response (within the limits of the courtly convention) from the lady he addressed. Closely connected with this is the question how far Andreas Capellanus' code was a formulation of actual practice and how far it was just an elaborate game. On this, see W.T.H Jackson, *The Romantic Review* 49 (1958) 243-51.

24. J. Sullivan, *Transactions of the American Philological Assoc-iation* 92 (1961) 528-35, sees the troubadours' service as anticipated by the Roman *servitium amoris* ('love's slavery'); their attitude to adultery by such passages as Propertius 2.23.19-20; their courtesy by the elegists' use of the term *domina*; and their religion of love by the two planes on which Roman elegy moves, 'one the actual relationship with a mistress and the other the invocation and description of the deities that guard or torment the lover' – e.g. Propertius 2.29a; Ovid *Amores* 1.2. Although Sullivan's article has a number of valid points which are relevant to this discussion, I am inclined to doubt if these parallels are conclusive. I have similar reservations about the attempt of G. Lieberg, *Puella Divina* (Amsterdam, 1962), to attach a serious spiritual significance to passages where a girl is compared to a goddess. J. Perret's remarks (*Revue des Études Latines* 41 [1963] 435-6) would seem justified: 'Les mots et les formules religieuses ... ne sont, en réalité, que les superlatifs du langage amoureux'.

25. P. Dronke, *Medieval Latin and the Rise of the European Love Lyric* (2nd ed. Oxford, 1968) vol. 1, ch. 1.

26. 'The theme of the eventual marriage of lovers is common in medieval literature, more so, it seems to me, than that of adultery' – John F. Benton (note 11 above) 23.

27. N. Rawlinson (ed.), *Petri et Abelardi ... et Heloissae ... Epistulae* (London, 1718) 49. The tr. is based on the version by Betty Radice (Harmondsworth, 1974) 113.

28. *As You Like It*, Act 3, Sc. 5, 82; Marlowe, *Hero and Leander* 176.

29. *Tom Jones* 4.6.

30. Stendhal, *Love*, tr. G. and S. Sale (London, 1957) 27.

31. J.A. Lee, *The Colours of Love* (Toronto, 1973).

32. C.S. Lewis (note 1 above) 4.

33. J.M. Edmonds (ed.) *Elegy and Iambus* (Cambridge, Mass., 1931) vol. 2, fragment. 84; M.L. West, *Iambi et Elegi Graeci* (Oxford, 1971) vol. 1, fragment 193.

34. See, for instance, S. Trenkner, *The Greek Novella* (Cambridge, 1958) 57. She presents a lot of interesting material, a good deal of which (inevitably) had been cited by E. Rohde, *Der Griechische Roman und Seine Vorläufer* (repr. Hildesheim, 1960). But as both she and Rohde use 'romantic' in a rather wide sense, only a few of their examples can be used in the present discussion.

35. *Anth. Pal.* 5.139 – *Greek Anthology* (Loeb edn).

36. Casanova, *History of my Life*, tr. W.R. Trask (London, 1967-72) vol.2, ch. 5, 157. One recalls that Casanova was a friend of Daponte and Mozart and influenced the figure of Don Giovanni; he was present at the first night of the opera in Prague.

37. D.A. Campbell (ed.) *Greek Lyric* (Loeb edn) vol. 2, 15; D.L. Page, *Poetae Melici Graeci* (Oxford, 1962) no. 358. .

38. Campbell (note 37 above) no. 413.

39. D.E. Gerber, *Greek Elegiac Poetry* (Loeb edn), no.1; M.L. West (note 33 above) vol. 2, frag. 1.

40. Demosthenes, Ἐρωτικός, tr. N.W. and N.J. De Witt (Cambridge, Mass., 1944) 40.

41. D. MacDowell, *The Law in Classical Athens* (London, 1978); W.K. Lacey, *The Family in Classical Greece* (London, 1968).

42. Xenophon, *Oeconomicus* 6.17 and 7.9-13.

43. A.W. Gomme and F.A. Sandbach (eds), *Menander: A Commentary* (Oxford, 1973) 31-2.

44. See e.g. Powys Mathers, *Arabian Love Tales* (London, 1949), especially 'The Tale of Rose-in-the-Bud and World's Delight', 'The Lovers' Tomb' and 'The Tender Tale of Prince Jasmine and Princess Almond'.

45. C.S. Lewis (note 1 above) 5.

46. See P. Boyancé, 'Properce' in *Fondation Hardt: Entretiens* 2 (Geneva, 1953) 169-209.

47. Propertius 1.11.23 ff., 1.12.19-20 and 1.19.11-12.

48. For this poem (and for other remarks about Propertius), see E. Grumach, *Goethe und die Antike* (Berlin, 1949) vol. 1, 371 ff.

49. For other passages bearing on Hero and Leander, see Arthur Palmer (ed.), *Ovid: Heroides* (Oxford, 1898; repr. Bristol, 2004) 454-7.

50. *De Rerum Natura* 4.1070 ff.; E.J. Kenney, *Mnemosyne* 23 (1970) 380-90.

51. E.g. *Epodes* 14 and 15.

52. E.g. *Odes* 1.8, 1.27 and 3.12.

53. E.g. *Epode* 11; *Odes* 1.5.

54. S. de Beauvoir, *The Second Sex* (New York, 1964) 93.

55. E.P. Morris, *Transactions of the Connecticut Academy* 15 (1909) 139-51.

56. See P. Flury, *Liebe und Liebesprache bei Menander, Plautus und Terenz* (Heidelberg, 1968).

57. F.O. Copley, *American Journal of Philology* 70 (1949) 23.

58. For Pamphilus' feelings, see 270 ff. and 694 ff. The alternative ending makes it clear that the other two lovers, Charinus and Philumena, also marry.

59. Callimachus, *Hymn to Apollo* 47 ff.; Tibullus 2.3.11-32; Ovid, *Heroides* 5.151and *Met.* 2.680 ff.

60. Athenaeus 13.575A-F, who then quotes a rather similar story from Aristotle's *Constitution of Massilia*; cf. Justin, 43.3. For love leading to marriage, see also the story of Periander and Melissa in Athenaeus 13.589F.

61. Ovid, *Met.*10.243 ff.

62. See N. Rudd, 'Pyramus and Thisbe in Ovid and Shakespeare' in D. West and A. Woodman (eds), *Creative Imitation and Latin Literature* (Cambridge, 1979) 173-93. Cf., too, the feelings of Iphis and Ianthe (Ovid, *Met.* 9.718 ff.). As regards marriage, it would be hard to show that the feelings of the wife Alcyone (*Met.* 11.416-73) were different from those of, say, the abandoned Ariadne.

63. S.L. Wolff, *The Greek Romances in Elizabethan Prose Fiction* (New York, 1912, repr. 1961) 130; but see his qualifications, 131-2.

64. For the details, see Wolff (note 63 above) 8-10.

65. See, for instance, the early fragment of the Ninus romance, printed and discussed in B.E. Percy, *The Ancient Romances* (California, 1967) 153-66.

66. By this I do not mean to imply that the novelists are uniformly feeble. But if we ask why antiquity produced no masterpiece of

fiction, it seems better to say that no important writer happened to work in that genre, rather than to seek an answer in the nature of the *Zeitgeist*.
67. For a less famous tale of love, marriage and separation, see Parthenius 36 (Loeb edn) *Rhesus and Arganthone.*
68. Xenophon, *Cyropaedia* (Loeb edn), index under 'Panthea'.
69. Plutarch, *Moralia* 9 (Loeb edn); R. Flacelière (ed.), *Dialogue sur l'Amour* (Paris, 1953).
70. Plutarch, Ἐρωτικός 769F.
71. See J. Gilmore, *The Fragments of the* Persika *of Ktesias* (London, 1888) 109 ff.
72. Horace, *Sat.* 2.3.276 ff.
73. Ovid, *Met.* 9.453 ff. (Byblis) and 10.312 ff. (Myrrha); Parthenius 13 (Clymenus) and 17 (Periander's mother).
74. *The Merchant of Venice*, Act 5, Sc. 1, 1 ff.

CHAPTER 17
1. The Greek had ἐάν. The Vulgate mistakenly had *sic,* which Bessarion emended to *si.*
2. See N. Rudd, *T.E. Page* (Bristol, 1981) 56-57.
3. For a brief summary, see Clyde Kluckholn, *Anthropology and the Classics* (Providence, 1961) ch. 1.
4. Betty Friedan, *The Feminine Mystique* (New York, 1963); Mary Ellman, *Thinking About Women* (London, 1968); Kate Millett, *Sexual Politics* (London, 1970).
5. Toril Moi in Mary Eagleton (ed.), *Feminist Literary Theory* (Oxford, 1986) 198.
6. Moi (note 5 above) 9. Similarly, Lilian Robinson is not terribly interested in whether feminist theory becomes 'a respectable part of academic criticism', but is very much concerned that feminist critics should become 'a useful part of the women's movement', quoted in Toril Moi (ed.), *Sexual Textual Politics* (London, 1985) 23.
7. G.C. Spivak, quoted in E. Showalter (ed.), *The New Feminist Criticism* (repr. London, 1989) 13.
8. Showalter (note 7 above) 4. Cf. Sandra Gilbert's statement, in Showalter (n. 7 above) 32, that feminist humanists all feel that 'if feminism and humanism are not to be mutually contradictory

terms, we must return to the history of ... Western culture and reinterpret its central texts'.

9. Ros Ballaster, speaking of Stephen Greenblatt's work, in Isobel Armstrong (ed.), *New Feminist Discourses* (London and New York, 1992) 285.

10. Terry Eagleton, *Literary Theory* (Oxford, 1983) 1.

11. Eagleton (note 10 above) 13.

12. F. de Saussure, *Cours de linguistique générale* (Paris, 1972) 101.

13. de Saussure (note 12 above) 104.

14. Cicero, *Orator* 20, 69 and 79; Quintilian, *Institutio Oratoria* 12.10.59.

15. Friedan and Millett (note 4 above); J. Radcliffe Richards, *The Sceptical Feminist* (repr. Harmondsworth, 1982).

16. J Searle, *New York Review,* 27 October (1983) 74-9. For a fuller refutation, see J.H. Ellis, *Against Deconstruction* (Princeton, 1989).

17. Juvenal, *Sat.* 6.223.

18. R. Tallis, *Not Saussure* (London, 1988) 4.

19. See P. Thody, *Roland Barthes: A Conservative Estimate* (Chicago and London, 1983) 12, 21, 48, 50 and 54-62.

20. J. Derrida, *De la Gramatologie* (Paris, 1967) 227 (tr. G.C. Spivak [Baltimore, 1976] 158).

21. C.S.Lewis and E.M.W. Tillyard, *The Personal Heresy* (Oxford, 1939).

22. See ch. entitled 'The Death of the Author' in Roland Barthes, *Image, Music, Text,* tr. S. Heath (London, 1977) 142-148.

23. In *Le Degré Zéro de l'Écriture* (Paris, 1964) 37, Barthes writes *'Larvatus prodeo,* je m'avance en désignant mon masque du doigt'. Thody (note 19 above) translates this without comment: 'I come forward pointing at my mask' (10); he also tells us that the phrase is a Latin tag (9). Barthes' translators say it was Descartes' motto (Annette Layers and Colin Smith [London, 1967] 46). For the sake of clarity the following points should be made: (1) 'en désignant [mon masque] du doigt' is an irrelevant addition; (2) there is no evidence that the phrase is a Latin tag; (3) to say that it was Descartes' motto is, at best, an exaggeration; my colleague, Andrew Pyle, kindly points out that the phrase is found in Descartes, *Cogitationes Privatae*

(1619), printed in *Oeuvres* (Adam and Tannery) vol. 10, 213. In classical Latin *larvatus* means 'crazy', though the noun *larva* is used of an actor's mask in Horace, *Sat.* 1.5.64. Possibly Descartes invented *larvatus* to mean 'masked' by analogy with *barbatus* ('bearded'); or possibly he found it in a late Latin source.

24. W.B.Yeats, *Variorum Edn* (1957) 778:

> The friends that have it I do wrong
> Whenever I remake a song
> Must know what issue is at stake:
> It is myself that I remake.

Perhaps; but the self that made the original song perhaps had a right *not* to be remade. Second thoughts are not always best. *The Vanity of Human Wishes*, 159-60, once ran: 'There mark what ills the scholar's life assail, / Toil, envy, want, the garret, and the jail'. However, early in 1775, indignant at the treatment he had received from Lord Chesterfield, Johnson substituted 'patron' for 'garret'. Though understandable as an expression of immediate resentment 'patron' disturbed the rhetoric of the line by importing a sudden flash of sardonic wit, whereas 'garret' led smoothly to the climax of 'jail', a word with which it formed a natural pair.

25. See ch. 3 above, 45 ff.

26. J. Henry, *Aeneidea* vol. 1 (1873) 312-317.

27. See H.L.A. Hart, *The Concept of Law* (2nd edn, Oxford, 1994) 193-200. A.P. d' Entrèves, *Natural Law* (2nd edn, London, 1970) 190-203, accepts Hart's minimum core of natural law but feels the need for a wider concept.